ENGADIN ART TALKS
E.A.T. INDEX

E.A.T.
INDEX

For over a decade, Engadin Art Talks (E.A.T.) has brought together in the Swiss Alps voices from art, architecture, the sciences and other fields. E.A.T. explores changing annual themes and extends its reach through events in cities such as London and Paris. Most contributions were recorded and remain freely accessible online, while some appear as edited transcripts in previous E.A.T. publications. This volume, the *E.A.T. Index*, features contributions from more than 200 authors – listed on the cover – and offers a new way to navigate the archive. Contributions from 2010 to 2025 were reviewed, and key passages edited in collaboration with the original authors. Through indexing, keywording and alphabetical ordering, these passages form a constellation of thought shaped across time, generations and geographies. Any term within a quotation that corresponds to another entry is underlined to guide readers to the related quote. Image plates provide an additional point of access and expanded insights into selected passages, many published here for the first time. Readers may move freely between entries or follow clear links to complete talks online. Publishing a printed index today may seem anachronistic. Born in 1992, I remember printed indices as indispensable tools that made knowledge traceable rather than algorithmically predetermined. Their transparency – and the active role they demand from the reader – feels newly relevant: readers define their paths of discovery. An index always points beyond itself; here it becomes a living archive, growing through the intellectual connections readers create, and the thoughts that may evolve into future indices. My thanks go to all contributors; to Cristina Bechtler and the E.A.T. curators →PLATE 1 p.66; to Dayle Bechtler-Lustenberger and Daan Couzijn; to Salzmann Gertsch; and to JRP|Editions.

CHRISTIAN HERREN
Editor

INTRODUCTIONS

What connects "Snake", "Snow", "Society" and "Solidarity"? Terms rarely found together share a double-page in the *E.A.T. Index* you are holding in your hands. Creating a platform for leading figures from art, architecture, science, literature, philosophy, music, and choreography, Engadin Art Talks (E.A.T.) has taken place in the Engadin – a high-alpine region in Switzerland – every year since 2010, on the last weekend of January, where participants gather to reflect on the pressing questions of contemporary society. Over the years, it has become one of the most renowned cultural forums in Europe, also through its satellite editions in Paris, London and Zurich. This book invites you into those ongoing conversations and points towards our freely accessible online archive, where talks and interventions can be revisited, linked and expanded across time and place. The idea for E.A.T. originated not in the mountains, but in Basel. In 2003, while organising a panel on *Art and Architecture: The Museum of the Future* – at a time when public talk programmes at art fairs were still uncommon – I witnessed how powerful cross-disciplinary exchange could be. Artists, architects and historians gathered; a planned live connection with Rem Koolhaas from China failed, yet the discussion continued intensely for more than two hours and filled the room with unusual energy. I left convinced that such encounters required their own dedicated platform. The Engadin offered exactly that. For centuries, writers and artists have travelled here to work and to test ideas. Together with Hans Ulrich Obrist, we shaped the first edition in 2010. The *Crystal Chain* correspondence initiated by Bruno Taut in the 1920s – a utopian exchange in a time of rupture – provided a conceptual point of departure: dialogue as method, imagination as shared work, and vision as a tool for shaping the world we share. Our venue in Zuoz – a modest school gym on the village square – reflects this ethos: accessible and focused on concentrated

exchange. The setting sharpens attention; the mountains impose a slower, deeper rhythm. What began as a winter gathering has since evolved into a year-round initiative. Hans Ulrich has remained by my side since the first edition; in the early years, we were soon joined by Philip Ursprung and Daniel Baumann, who continue to shape E.A.T. together to this day. For many seasons, Bice Curiger played an important part in shaping E.A.T. through our close collaboration, as did the late and much-esteemed Koyo Kouoh during a treasured period. Today, E.A.T. collaborates with partner institutions abroad, and the open digital archive carries the talks to those who may never reach the valley in person. Over the years, hundreds of speakers and contributors have helped shape E.A.T.. I am deeply grateful to Hans Ulrich, Philip, Daniel, Bice and Koyo for their guidance, commitment and friendship – and to the entire E.A.T. team, whose steady work through the seasons makes this platform possible. Above all, E.A.T. is a collective project. It belongs to all who have made their way up to Zuoz, joined a satellite in another city, watched a recording from afar, asked a question or carried an idea into their own practice. This book is for them – and for those who will join the conversations next. The dialogue continues; it is urgent to bridge gaps and form new bonds – in these pages, in the archive, and each winter in the crisp Engadin air and beyond.

CRISTINA BECHTLER
Publisher and art collector; founder of E.A.T.

The Engadin has long been one of the most inspiring places in the world. For me, it is a landscape of childhood memories; yet I truly connected to it as a cultural space when, as a young curator in the early 1990s, I spent extended periods there with Gerhard Richter. In 1992, I organised an exhibition with him at the Nietzsche-Haus in Sils Maria. During

this time, I immersed myself in the writers and thinkers inspired by this extraordinary valley – Lou Andreas-Salomé, Theodor Adorno, Annemarie Schwarzenbach, Alexander Kluge and, of course, Richter himself. Time in the mountains confirmed that many of my best ideas emerge there. Several exhibitions and books were born in the Engadin, between Sils, Zuoz and St Moritz. I was therefore delighted when Cristina Bechtler proposed organising discussions in this region. We first tested the format in Basel in 2003 with *Art and Architecture: The Museum of the Future*, with Jacques Herzog and Rem Koolhaas – but Cristina sensed that, inspiring as a city programme can be, it was vital to root the project in a mountain landscape. This became the beginning of E.A.T.. Cristina and I founded it initially with Beatrix Ruf; Philip Ursprung, Bice Curiger, Daniel Baumann, and the late and dearly missed Koyo Kouoh soon joined. E.A.T. unfolds over time. It invites people into this remarkable landscape; many arrive for the first time and then return again and again. Participants draw energy from the mountains and bring new energy to them. Central to this exchange is a desire to transcend the fear of shared knowledge, and to build connections across disciplines. In a moment marked by polarisation, bridging divisions feels especially urgent. This is the core of E.A.T.: bringing people together, facilitating conversations across fields and among the wider community. In his 2010 book *The Burnout Society*, Byung-Chul Han writes that "culture presumes an environment in which deep attention is possible". In contrast to the "hyperattention" he describes, the Engadin offers expansive vistas and a tangible slowness. Visitors enter a space in which reflection and concentrated thought become possible once more.

HANS ULRICH OBRIST
Director of the Serpentine, London, and senior advisor at LUMA Arles;
E.A.T. curator

How did I learn to love Engadin Art Talks – even though I do not usually like talks? It began when Cristina Bechtler invited me to join this journey. I said yes, and I still *ne regrette rien, rien de rien.* The vessel – or is it a spaceship? – was superbly crewed, with exceptional teammates and co-curators. The visitors, too, are extraordinary: curious, engaged, reflective. They often become participants – asking incisive questions, making sharp observations, and celebrating knowledge and ideas. And the talks? I fell in love. Not merely because they are concise, but because they inspire and surprise. They resonate, challenge and move. So this is the vessel we board each year: the MS E.A.T.. We keep the horizon open, the waters calm, and the space for thinking expansive and deep – with pauses, and always time for coffee. Yet the MS E.A.T. is nothing without its shore. It always returns to the Engadin, to Zuoz and its school gym on the village square. There, thinkers from around the world meet, listen and speak – and we, the audience, continue thinking alongside them. When circumstances made a physical gathering impossible, we found another way. We did not want to produce dull "Zoominars" during the Covid period. By the end of 2020, everyone had had enough of them, and it was clear that in January 2021 Engadin Art Talks could not take place in its customary form. The theme of "long durée" therefore unfolded through a 12-hour streaming programme combining pre-produced films with live transmissions from Zuoz.

DANIEL BAUMANN
Art historian, curator and critic; E.A.T. curator

Instinctively, we broke conventions. The formats echoed what defines E.A.T.: not an academic satellite, not a museum, yet with a touch of both – animated by alpine gusts of wind and palpable energy. For instance, although Philip Ursprung and I spoke with Ragnar Kjartansson in Iceland

via Zoom, the two of us sat outside in falling snow, on a terrace beneath a parasol, at 1,700 metres above sea level. Ragnar "received" us from his harbour-side studio in Reykjavik, woollen hat on head, in front of a mock museum wall hung with old Russian paintings. The conversation soon turned to lava-spewing earth. Philip, a connoisseur of the volcanoes of Java, steered us towards the Far East – from ephemeral snow to primordial geological time, and to the paradox of abrupt rupture within unfathomably long duration. We soon reached Ragnar's 12-hour performance of Mozart's *Le Nozze di Figaro* from which we showed an extended – yet still brief – excerpt. The *genius loci* also shaped the discussion on Proust in Engadin between Luzius Keller and Stefan Zweifel, who brought audiences to the Nietzsche Stone in Sils Maria. *Romansh Alive and Well* was the title of another conversation, with Madlaina Peer and Rico Valär, about Switzerland's fourth national language, deeply rooted in the Engadin.

BICE CURIGER
Art historian, curator and author; former E.A.T. curator

Each year, we gather in the alpine heights at the Hotel Castell, which rises like a mysterious fortress above the Engadin, just above the village of Zuoz – a short walk from the school gym where the Engadin Art Talks take place. Many guests stay at the Castell, and so mornings, evenings and the intervals between the talks unfold there: conversations at breakfast, exchanges by the fireplace, ideas carried across the terrace at dusk, and late-night reflections after returning from the village square. The rhythm of the gathering extends beyond the formal sessions; the talks continue in quieter registers, often in unexpected constellations. While snow has vanished in many places, it still falls here. While temperatures rise elsewhere, nights remain sharply cold and stars blaze. Time feels suspended. Sitting by the fire or

looking out from the terrace across the frozen valley, I often think of Philip K. Dick's *The Man in the High Castle* (1962), in which an author imagines an alternative to an inhuman present. Yes, the setting is exclusive. Few can afford to be here. Yet the discussions concern questions that affect society as a whole: fresh insights, ideas, histories, politics, the possibilities and limits of art. Just as artists require the stillness of the studio and scientists the shelter of the laboratory, we allow ourselves three days of quiet. The tension between autonomy and public relevance cannot be resolved, yet it remains productive and draws us back each year. Its foundations are friendship, collegiality, curiosity, trust – and the place itself. Looking back, I cannot single out "highlights". Perhaps the most important element is the constancy – the ritual of meeting again. It feels like an ongoing conversation into which ever-new voices enter. Some encounters become lasting exchanges; others slip from memory until, years later, someone appears and says, "We met there – at that castle."

PHILIP URSPRUNG
Professor of the History of Art and Architecture at ETH Zurich;
E.A.T. curator

I am a lover of gatherings. I am a lover of convening – of bringing people together to share ideas – and there are many formats for that. Particularly in our field of arts and culture, these conversations are essential. Beyond the content of the remarkable speakers we bring, it is also about meeting others, making connections, expanding one's ideas, expanding one's horizons. The convening of people to speak – to exchange knowledge, to learn and to teach one another – is essential. *(From an interview with Koyo Kouoh at E.A.T. 2025, Zuoz)*

KOYO KOUOH (1967–2025)
Curator and cultural producer; former E.A.T. curator

INDEX
A–Z

A

ABSENCE

"The presence p.229 of a mountain p.211 motivates the mountaineer. Similarly, the absence of a work of art p.31 and the anticipation of it is what drives the artist to create."

RAQS MEDIA COLLECTIVE
Artist collective,
media practitioners, curators,
and researchers
E.A.T. 2012: Vision for the Alps,
Zuoz

ABSORPTION

"We live within a field of normalcy p.215, and the most successful new products or experiences are typically those that resemble what we already know, yet stretch that familiarity just enough p.117 in one direction. They encapsulate the future p.130 not through rupture, but through expansion. Like a soft, blob-like form that swells to absorb what's coming."

EMILY SEGAL
Artist and writer
E.A.T. 2018: Side Country Side,
Zuoz

ACCEPTATION

"Working in public space is never a total success and never a total failure p.121. When you work with residents, people who sometimes are facing problems far from art p.31 concerns, you confront p.52 reality p.277 on a daily basis. That reality can be a challenge p.42 and can defy p.64 the artistic project. But by accepting the setbacks and by holding p.141 up with only the power of art, you might reach p.276 to something that can no longer be called a failure, or at least not a total failure."

THOMAS HIRSCHHORN
Artist
2023: E.A.T. × Centre Pompidou,
Paris

ACCESSIBILITY

"Sometimes we call our work a 'Trojan horse', because we always begin by throwing a party, just music, convivíality, joy. But after the party, we can start talking about energy p.115, climate change p.48 and the importance of alternative systems. It's a way to introduce serious p.294 topics in an accessible way, especially for younger generations[p.133]. And because this project now exists in cities[p.47] like Tel Aviv, Zurich, Paris and even Hong Kong, it has become[p.35] a global community[p.51] and network."

CÉDRIC CARLES
Designer and founder of Atelier 21
E.A.T. 2023: Hoffnung? Hoffnung!,
Zuoz

ACKNOWLEDGEMENT

"The world has to revise its system of value, and acknowledge that crucial forms of knowledge have been dismissed. These need to be reintegrated not just as systems of thinking, but of feeling. Female[p.123] knowledge, for instance, must be fully restored in society[p.299]."

RASHA SALTI
Researcher, writer, producer and curator of art and film
E.A.T. 2024: Jenseits von Ohnmacht – Beyond Powerless,
Zuoz

ACTION

"Putin isn't just attacking Ukraine; he's challenging[p.42] everything influenced by liberal modernity. Like the communists once tried to destroy Europe's democratic project, these new ideologues see themselves as missionaries aiming to 'cure' the decadent West[p.321]. That's why I'm among those who hoped[p.142] our current chancellor Olaf Scholz would follow after his historic turning-point speech[p.300] with action. I firmly support[p.303] defending Ukraine robustly. Sometimes there is black and white not just grey. A murderer[p.212] and a victim, a rapist and the raped in such cases, there is no middle ground."

JOACHIM GAUCK
Former Federal President of Germany (2012–2017)
E.A.T. 2023: Hoffnung? Hoffnung!,
Zuoz

ADAPTATION

"For the past three decades, we have lived in a rapidly urbanising, rural[p.289] area in the foothills of the Himalayas. During this period, we have witnessed[p.322] the disappearance of vernacular architecture[p.29] and an explosion of brick and concrete[p.51] houses[p.142]. The evolutionary process by which traditional architecture developed in harmony with its surroundings is being abandoned in favour of a building style[p.302] that has little or no connection[p.53] to the land. This has meant that the skills needed to construct[p.53] traditional structures are dying out as artisanal builders become[p.35] redundant. It seems crucial to preserve these traditional building practices[p.228], but it seems equally clear that if they are to survive, they have to be adapted to a contemporary[p.55] context[p.55]. Out of the meeting point between the ancient[p.29] and the modern, a new architectural style could emerge that takes the best of both worlds and is aesthetically[p.25], ecologically[p.113] and practically relevant."

RITU SARIN
and TENZING SONAM
Filmmakers and artists
E.A.T. 2011: Mapping the Alps, Zuoz

ADDRESSING

"I stumbled into art[p.31] by accident, but what drew me in was how it was taught[p.306] as a way to speak about the humanity[p.143] we live in. That resonated[p.283] with me because I was always concerned with impact[p.148]. I began as a traditional landscape painter, but eventually moved into figurative work that could address the social issues that mattered most to me."

RICK LOWE
Artist
E.A.T. 2025: Form and Impact, Zuoz

AESTHETICS

"The choice of insects – which flower mates with which – isn't based on reason, but on taste. Not on utility, but on sugar. That means the result – the seed – is essentially an aesthetic object[p.217]. Evolution is nothing but fashion[p.122] within nature[p.213]: a catwalk lasting millions of years, where species model[p.208] themselves for the pleasure of others. Every seed is the equivalent of an artwork. Every landscape of flowering plants is a multispecies installation – a biennale curated by insects, not for us, but for each other."

EMANUELE COCCIA
Philosopher, lecturer and author
E.A.T. 2020: Silent – Listen, Zuoz

AFFECT

"Affect is produced in my works, but not as modernism[p.209] claims, not from the poetic[p.226] unconscious or from the artist's subjectivity. It's produced by a system of rules. And while this might disturb people in art[p.31], it doesn't disturb anyone in nature[p.213]. Modernism insists on intention[p.193] and subjectivity, but I simply replace that with a set of rules, showing that meaning[p.204] and affect can still arise."

CHARLES GAINES
Artist
E.A.T. 2020: Silent – Listen, Zuoz

AFRICA

"We were shocked by *The Economist* cover from May 2000 calling Africa 'The Hopeless Continent'. Of course, we were aware of the issues we faced – poverty, war, hunger – but never would we ourselves have branded the continent as hopeless. When you're born in Africa, you grow[p.138] up with hardship. Maybe there's no running water or stable electricity, but that's just the reality[p.277]. We find[p.125] a way around it. That's where our idea[p.145] of resilience[p.282] begins: not in a sense of loss[p.201], but in a context[p.55] of constant adaptation[p.24]."

PAOLA AUDREY NDENGUE
Content producer, entrepreneur and media personality
E.A.T. 2024: Jenseits von Ohnmacht – Beyond Powerless, Zuoz

AGENCY

"Freed[p.128] of an agent such as the artist or poet, agency shifts[p.296] to the audience or the reader. And freed from the requirements of subjectivity, reading[p.276] indeed, perception becomes[p.35] a culturally[p.60] driven political act. This is because the absence[p.23] of subjectivity removes the authority of the artist, and authority then has to be negotiated[p.214]."

CHARLES GAINES
Artist
E.A.T. 2020: Silent – Listen, Zuoz

AGRICULTURE

"Ten food companies in Europe and the UK directly influence 40 % of agricultural land in that region. If they redesigned their products to use more biodiverse ingredients grown[p.138] regeneratively[p.279], and shifted[p.296] their relationship[p.280] with farmers[p.122], they could transform[p.310] entire landscapes. The power is in the product design, not just in regulation or activism."

ANDREW MORLET
Former CEO of the Ellen MacArthur Foundation, chair of the UK Government CIRCULAR Economy Taskforce, lead of the CIRCULAR Economy Innovation Hub at Standard Chartered Bank
E.A.T. 2022: Matter and Memory, Zuoz

AIR

"My grandfather was mute[p.213]. Some stories[p.301] are too difficult to tell. Some can only be told through silence[p.297], the absence[p.23] of the self. A cerebral eclipse. The person who faints returns as if from a foreign country: elated, confused[p.52], or disoriented. A form of ecstatic empowerment. A miraculous suspension of time[p.308]. I am a daughter of the air."

MARIANNA SIMNETT
Artist
E.A.T. 2020: Silent – Listen, Zuoz

ALGORITHM

"Welcome to *House of Meme*. What you are about to experience is not just a performance[p.222]. It is an unfolding, a meditation on the intersections[p.194] of architecture[p.29], artificial intelligence[p.31] and the ever-expanding ecosystems[p.113] of the digital[p.107] age. It is a reflection[p.279] on the ways we inhabit our world, the architectures we build, the algorithms we live by and the images[p.146] we consume[p.53]."

ALEXA
Artificial Intelligence
2024: E.A.T. × Kunsthalle Zürich, Zurich

ALONE

"French mathematician and physicist Blaise Pascal said that all of humanity's [p.143] problems stem from our inability to sit quietly [p.275] in a room alone. That was in the late 1640s and it's even more extreme now. It's important to realise this is not a new problem. We've always struggled with silence [p.297]. But with smartphones and constant connection [p.53], it's become [p.35] so much harder to be alone with ourselves."

ERLING KAGGE
Explorer, publisher, author, philosopher, lawyer, art collector and entrepreneur
E.A.T. 2020: Silent – Listen, Zuoz

ALPS

"Imagine [p.146] how groundbreaking it would be to build the world's deepest railway station, accessed by the tallest elevator inside the longest tunnel [p.312] on Earth [p.112]. The Porta Alpina project was an ambitious plan to connect [p.53] the Swiss [p.305] Alps to the rest of Europe via the Gotthard Base Tunnel. Designed to make the Alps visible again, it would have served as both an entrance to and an exit from the region, bringing greater accessibility [p.23] while highlighting the mountains' [p.211] significance. Although the project was eventually shelved, it remains a visionary idea in alpine infrastructure [p.191] and architecture [p.29]."

ARTHUR LORETZ
Architect ETH HSLU SIA
E.A.T. 2012: Vision for the Alps, Zuoz
→ PLATE 2 [p.67]

AMERICA

"America is a really interesting place because it's largely formed by people who've experienced deep trauma [p.311] – enslaved people, Holocaust survivors, Irish immigrants [p.147] and so on. Trauma is built into the DNA [p.110] of the American body [p.38]. That shapes [p.295] how we interact with each other. It creates a rich [p.286], complex social conversation [p.56]. It's part of why I'm drawn to Tupac's poem *The Rose That Grew from Concrete*, honouring [p.141] something beautiful p.34 that fought p.124 its way through hardship."

ALVARO BARRINGTON
Artist
E.A.T. 2025: Form and Impact, Zuoz

ANCIENT

"The oldest works in the Louvre are two standing figures from what today is Jordan. They're not made of clay p.47 in the usual sense, but from a mixture of a kind of mud, straw and small gravel. What's extraordinary are their eyes: they gaze p.132 outward, always watching. These are some of the earliest sculptures in the East, dating from 3,000 or even 4,000 years before Christ. These figures don't just look at the world, they look beyond it, seeking the creator. These ancient objects p.217 are profound lessons in themselves."

SIMONE FATTAL
Artist
2023: E.A.T. × Centre Pompidou, Paris

ANTHROPOCENE

"American p.28 literary critic and philosopher Fredric Jameson said, 'It is easier to imagine p.146 the end of the world than the end of capitalism.' Capitalism has become p.35 co-extensive with the Earth p.112; roads, plantations, pipelines and railways have created a second nature p.213. It's not just the 'age of man', but the 'age of capital'. British geographers Simon Lewis and Mark Maslin even propose that the anthropocene began not with agriculture p.27 or steam engines, but with the European conquest of the Americas, which biologically reconnected lifeforms separated by 200 million years."

ADRIÁN VILLAR ROJAS
Artist
E.A.T. 2018: Side Country Side, Zuoz

ARCHITECTURE

"What's inspiring p.192 today is the way architecture extends beyond buildings. Sometimes, it's about organising p.219 a dinner for 300 people. That, too, is architecture; it's about how we build community p.51, how we create shared experiences in space. And that's a question[p.275] this younger generation[p.133] is asking us, pushing us to rethink the very tools and modes of our discipline."

ALEXANDRE THERIOT
Architect and co-founder of Paris-based architectural studio Bruther
2023: E.A.T. × Centre Pompidou, Paris

ARCHIVE

"I discovered an archive in the Swiss[p.305] military archives that was introduced to me as 'militarily non-relevant', which I found to be an interesting starting point. It consisted of photographs and films taken by Swiss soldiers stationed near the Korean DMZ after the ceasefire in 1953. These soldiers didn't have an official mandate to document what they saw[p.296], yet they produced a vast number of images[p.146]. What fascinated me was the way they tried to recreate their Swiss home[p.141] abroad, bringing cantonal flags, growing[p.138] plants, and creating what they called a 'Swiss Club' in Korea. Their images reflect[p.279] not only an attempt to observe[p.217], but also to impose a sense of identity[p.146], a kind of soft power embedded in their neutrality[p.214]. I paired these photographs with quotes from soldiers' diaries and reports, trying to expose[p.121] the gap[p.131] between their recorded gaze[p.132] and what they perceived."

DENISE BERTSCHI
Artist and scholar
2021: E.A.T. × Centre Culturel Suisse, Paris

ARCTIC

"Until recently, most people in North America[p.28] learned[p.199] about the Arctic through the heroic adventures of white male explorers. But now, Arctic Indigenous women activists, artists and writers are reclaiming[p.277] that narrative[p.213]. Figures like Rosemary Ahtuangaruak, Sarah James and Velma Wallis are challenging[p.42] the colonial[p.50] myths and asserting that the Arctic is not an empty frontier, but a homeland rich[p.286] with culture[p.60], sovereignty and knowledge."

SUBHANKAR BANERJEE
Photographer, writer, curator and environmental humanities scholar
E.A.T. 2017: Snow and Desert, Zuoz

ART

"Art is like water. Art is like a mirror[p.208]. Art is like the ocean. Art is a memory[p.206]. Art is a window. Art is a healer. Art is energy[p.115]. Art is free[p.128]. Art is sensual. Art is a celebration."

UMAN
Artist
2025: E.A.T. × St. Moritz, St. Moritz

ARTIFICIAL INTELLIGENCE

"We see every step of AI training[p.309] – data collection, labelling, model[p.208] architecture[p.29], prompting – as artistic acts. Most people interact with pre-trained models and see[p.296] only the output. But we wanted to show the full creative process as a form of art making, from choir rehearsals to phonetic coverage. Even the way data is labelled shapes[p.295] the aesthetics[p.25] of interaction."

HOLLY HERNDON
and MATHEW DRYHURST
Artists
E.A.T. 2025: Form and Impact, Zuoz

ARTIFICIALITY

"My work is completely nonfigurative, non-objective; a purely artificial approach. And when this artificial language[p.198] enters a powerful natural space, like the desert[p.105] or the Arctic[p.30], it creates a strong tension[p.307]. Nature[p.213] is not my enemy but it is my counterpart. It competes with my work. It has its own creativity, its own quality[p.274]. And in that confrontation[p.52], art[p.31] has the opportunity to respond[p.284]. Not by dominating nature, but by respecting[p.284] it; by allowing it to be itself."

HEINZ MACK
Sculptor and painter
E.A.T. 2017: Snow and Desert, Zuoz

ATMOSPHERE

"For the *Edgware Road Project*, I wanted to switch locations: to bring the Egyptian atmosphere to Hyde Park, and some of London's to Cairo. I worked with people from the streets of Egypt but not artists – children, older people, men, women and also with tent makers. The idea was to have them stitch their life stories and messages into tents, which were then transported to London. At the same time, videos[p.316] from London were shown in Egyptian coffee shops. In Hyde Park, I also led a workshop with children using abstract school[p.291] sentences like, 'It takes a village to raise a child'. We created costumes from these phrases and rehearsed movements with them. For three days in the park there were tents from Egypt, structures made of palmwood, dancers[p.61] and a platform[p.225] where people could speak freely[p.128]."

SUSAN HEFUNA
Artist
E.A.T. 2025: Form and Impact, Zuoz

AUTHENTICITY

"Suspicious magnet cube... demonstrates to the audiences how art[p.31] is enabling individuals to be as authentically themselves as possible about what they imagine[p.146]. And how often do things that seem impossible actually happen more often than you think?"

KOO JEONG A
Artist
E.A.T. 2016: Traces and Fragments, Zuoz
→PLATE 3 p.68

AUTHORSHIP

"We see AI[p.31] models[p.208] as monumental collective achievements, not just the output of singular authorship. People want to be part of something larger than themselves. Yet these tools are framed through individualist[p.189] lenses. Our goal is to reposition them as shared cultural[p.60] systems, built and governed together."

HOLLY HERNDON and MATHEW DRYHURST
Artists
E.A.T. 2025: Form and Impact, Zuoz

AUTOCRACY

"Artistic creativity is the antithesis of the enforced conformity autocrats depend on. Whether through censorship[p.41], cultural[p.60] erasure[p.118] or propaganda, dictators try to crush the human[p.143] spirit. But art that is unpredictable[p.314], a free[p.128] expression of thought and feeling is something they can't fully control. And that makes it dangerous."

KENNETH ROTH
Former executive director of Human Rights Watch
E.A.T. 2023: Hoffnung? Hoffnung!, Zuoz

AUTONOMY

"NFT[p.215] technology[p.306] is already being perceived as a phenomenon in decline, even dead. It should be recalled that, originally, so-called NFT works often served as simple tools of tax optimisation, requiring no creativity. This use damaged their reputation. But reducing this technology to those excesses would be a mistake[p.208]; in fact, it is essential for the future[p.130] of artists, in Africa[p.26] as elsewhere. It does not replace galleries, but it introduces a new dimension of autonomy and traceability. The challenge is for artists to truly seize it, to move beyond the speculative phase and to consider NFT technology as a tool for the protection[p.232], circulation and dissemination of works. It is precisely in this spirit that I proposed, during the most recent Dakar Biennale, a fully digital[p.107] project: a way to show that this technology can sustain works of the highest order, both aesthetically[p.25] and conceptually, and offer artists a demanding and legitimate[p.200] space of exhibition."

ANNA-ALIX KOFFI
Creative director and founder of SOMETHING art space in Abidjan, SOMETHING WE AFRICANS GOT and OFF the wall
2023: E.A.T. × Centre Pompidou, Paris

B

BAD

"When you surround yourself with sycophants and suppress dissent, you make bad decisions[p.63]. Putin invades Ukraine. Xi Jinping imposes zero-COVID lockdowns.

These self-serving, uncorrected disasters provoke public discontent. So while the narrative[p.213] claims autocracy[p.32] is rising, people in the streets tell a different story[p.301] – one of disillusionment and protest[p.273]."

KENNETH ROTH
Former executive director of Human Rights Watch
E.A.T. 2023: Hoffnung? Hoffnung!, Zuoz

BALANCING

"Unlike DNA[p.110] mutations, which are permanent[p.223] and can lead[p.198] to diseases such as cancer, epigenetic modifications are dynamic and potentially reversible. Environmental influences – like trauma[p.311] or a nutritional insult – can modify epigenetic marks, but the modifications may fade over time[p.308] or across generations[p.133]. Understanding[p.313] this balance between persistence and reversibility is central to the study of transgenerational epigenetic effects."

ISABELLE MANSUY
Professor in neuroepigenetics In the Medical Faculty of the University of Zurich and the Department of Health Science and Technology of ETH Zurich
E.A.T. 2022: Matter and Memory, Zuoz

BARRIOS

"British architect and theorist John F. C. Turner once spoke of 'misplaced pity' – the tendency of wealthier[p.321] classes to equate barrios with poverty, and to advocate for their eradication. Even today, the idea that barrios are legitimate[p.200] parts of the city remains unthinkable to many officials and designers. In Santiago de Chile, for example, governments invest huge sums in social housing[p.142], while self-built[p.293] neighbourhoods grow faster, ignored and misunderstood."

ELISA SILVA
Architect and founder and principal of Enlace Arquitectura and Enlace Foundation
E.A.T. 2024: Jenseits von Ohnmacht – Beyond Powerless, Zuoz

BEAUTY

"Jupiter is an excellent example of gravity[p.137] and beauty. Beneath its immense gravity lies a dynamic world where motion[p.211], turbulence and energy[p.115] weave together into patterns of remarkable grace[p.135]. In its swirling clouds and complex interior, we are reminded that even the most powerful forces of nature can give rise to harmony, and that gravity itself can be an artist, shaping[p.295] elegance out of chaos. Planetary science demonstrates how even the most fundamental physical forces can lead[p.198] to forms[p.127] of profound elegance, and reminds us that we are small parts of a vast and intricate universe, where meaning[p.204] often lies in perspective[p.223]."

RAVIT HELLED
Planetary scientist
E.A.T. 2019: Grace and Gravity, Zuoz
→PLATE 4 p.69

BECOMING

"Thinking and understanding[p.313] are important processes, but they can also be attempts to control or fully know the other, to make the other transparent[p.311]. As the French-Caribbean philosopher Édouard Glissant said, 'you never know who I am, because I don't even fully know myself – I am always becoming.' When we accept[p.23] our own opacity, and also accept the opacity of others, we can begin to build a shared, collective space."

MANTHIA DIAWARA
Writer, filmmaker, cultural theorist, scholar, art historian and professor in the Martin Scorsese Department of Cinema Studies at New York University's Tisch School of the Arts
E.A.T. 2021: Longue Durée, livestream
→PLATE 5 p.70

BEHAVIOUR

"We tend to see sexuality[p.295] as one of the main markers of our individuality[p.189]. Yet not only does our own biological system respond[p.284] to sexual attraction in ways we cannot control, there are also parasites capable of neurologically influencing – perhaps even directing – our behaviour. For instance, people infected with toxoplasmosis are apparently more drawn to scents derived from cat pheromones. This note is present[p.230] in many perfumes – one of the most famous being Chanel No. 5."

PAMELA ROSENKRANZ
Artist
E.A.T. 2022: Matter and Memory, Zuoz

BEING

"Something brought into being
Behaving silently[p.297]
Leaving space
Touching[p.308] possibility
Infinitely[p.190] creating form
Sprung from a nu."

KLAUDIA SCHIFFERLE
Artist
E.A.T. 2024: Jenseits von Ohnmacht – Beyond Powerless, Zuoz
→PLATE 6[p.71]

BELIEF

"Four years after we uncovered a beautiful[p.34] marble floor in the Mausoleum of Imam al-Shafi'i, people began treating it as a shrine. They leave coins and flowers, believing someone sacred is buried there – though we don't know who. Caretakers try to cover it with a mat to prevent this, but people always remove it. I like to think this is how it should be. Beyond the pristine restoration images[p.146] we aim for, there's something far older and more powerful at work: the spirit of the place and how it manifests in unexpected ways."

MAY AL-IBRASHY
Architect, founder and principal of Megawra and co-founder and chair of the Built Environment Collective
E.A.T. 2025: Form and Impact, Zuoz
→PLATE 7[p.72]

BELONGING

"'Support Structures for Support Structures' is a fellowship programme initiated with the Serpentine. From the very beginning, the idea[p.145] of working with the pavilion as a catalyst for other happenings and relationships[p.280] felt important to the project. The pavilion itself was shaped[p.295] by legacies – drawing on places of gathering[p.131] that have long held[p.141] people in the act of making a home[p.141] and belonging in the city[p.47]: some of the first mosques, African[p.26] churches, synagogues, marketplaces – sites of cultural[p.60] production that became[p.35] sites of home and belonging for communities[p.51]. The pavilion traced[p.309] London's waves of migration, honouring[p.141] places of the past and present[p.230], while imagining futures[p.130] through its fragments[p.127] scattered across the city. These fragments – these 'pavilion archipelagos' – were conceived as places with an ongoing life, carrying[p.41] that spirit forward, through collaborations[p.49] between myself, the Serpentine and these cultural institutions of communities."

SUMAYYA VALLY
Architect and founder and principal of the architecture and research firm Counterspace
2021: E.A.T. × Serpentine, London
→PLATE 8 p.73

BEND

"In a quiet[p.275] corner of St. Paul's Cathedral, I came across the statue of John Donne – poet, priest and former Dean of St. Paul's – who, just a month before his death[p.63] in 1631, posed for this sculpture wrapped in his burial shroud. What struck me most were his slightly bent knees: a subtle downward movement that introduced a human[p.143] frailty into the otherwise upright form. But Donne wasn't posing for an ordinary memorial. He was enacting his own resurrection: poised, ready to kiss[p.197] Christ[p.45], to shed his robes, to reunite with his bodily[p.38] self. It's a quiet ecstasy, a fierce hope[p.142] and a testament to human in-betweenness."

ISABEL NOLAN
Artist
E.A.T. 2019: Grace and Gravity, Zuoz
→PLATE 9 p.74

BIAS

"Everything our algorithm[p.27] learned[p.199] for the UK Pavilion at the Dubai Expo came from the texts we fed it. I was sitting next to artist Kyle McDonald, who trained[p.309] the algorithm, and suddenly it hit me – what a terrifying responsibility it is. I had just done a TED Talk quoting English author[p.32] E. M.

Forster's line: 'Only connect… live in fragments[p.127] no longer.' We gave that line to the algorithm during development. Its response[p.284]? 'Only connect… live in fragments, die[p.63] in fragments.' I turned to Kyle and asked, 'Where did you train it?' And he said, 'On Reddit.' That moment taught[p.306] me a lot – especially about the dangers of bias in machine learning."

ES DEVLIN
Artist
E.A.T. 2022: Matter and Memory, Zuoz

BLOCKCHAIN

"In our project *kleee02*, we developed a smart contract – a blockchain-based software – that defines[p.64] how a line should be created: a generative line formed by code. However, we intentionally[p.193] left its execution open-ended. The first iteration was created with a laser, inspired by Swiss-German artist Paul Klee's idea[p.145] that 'a line is a dot that goes for a walk[p.320]'. The second was made combining cyanotype and laser on silk. Yet, this line could just as well be danced[p.61], sketched, or transformed[p.310] into jewellery. I appreciate the freedom[p.128] of sharing a concept openly – where anyone can access[p.23] the code and create their own version. This approach frees the visual and physical manifestation while allowing us to claim the concept as our own and offer it as a tradable work of art."

JOHANNES GEES
Artist
E.A.T. 2022: Matter and Memory, Zuoz
→PLATE 10 [p.75]

BODY

"I worked with an artist named Silmara Watari, who had trained[p.309] in Mexico and Japan before moving to Brazil to set up a traditional Japanese-style studio with an anagama kiln; a long, wood-fired kiln built half into the ground. When you fire it from one end, the flames travel through like a breath[p.39], touching[p.308] some pieces and skipping others. The fire[p.125] itself shapes[p.295] the work. The result is almost anatomical; the kiln becomes[p.35] a body filled with ceramic[p.42] organs. These works retain the experience of that fire, like a memory[p.206] scorched into their surfaces."

MATTHEW LUTZ-KINOY
Artist
E.A.T. 2023: Hoffnung? Hoffnung!, Zuoz

BOUNDARY

"As these images[p.146] entered the pages of art[p.31] history[p.140] and Indigenous studies, something unexpected happened. I wasn't just contributing illustrations; the scholarship was reshaping my thinking. It became[p.35] a co-evolution of knowledge. Working closely with scholars like Finis Dunaway and T. J. Demos, we began to push the boundaries of what environmental art[p.31], ecocriticism, and decolonial[p.63] visual culture[p.60] could mean."

SUBHANKAR BANERJEE
Photographer, writer, curator and environmental humanities scholar
E.A.T. 2017: Snow and Desert, Zuoz

BREATHE

"All of us begin life with an inhale, and one day we die[p.63] with an exhale. In between, there is breath – our shared human[p.143] experience. We all breathe the same air[p.27]. That's why I started letting people make their own breath lines – their own traces – as a way of connecting[p.53] through something as simple and universal as breathing."

JEPPE HEIN
Artist
E.A.T. 2020: Silent – Listen, Zuoz
→ PLATE 11 p.76

C

CANON

"Do we need a canon? Probably yes. Not as something rigid, but because we all need shared points of reference. We define[p.64] ourselves through what we admire or reject. If everyone followed only their own models[p.208], nothing collective could take shape[p.295]. Even a revised canon – like when forgotten artists are rediscovered[p.278] – only becomes[p.35] real if it resonates[p.283] with others."

DARIO GAMBONI
Professor emeritus of art history at the University of Geneva
E.A.T. 2021: Longue Durée, livestream
→PLATE 12 p.77

CARBON

"There are essentially two types of cities[p.47]: the sprawling, car-dependent kind shaped[p.295] by highways, and the compact, walkable[p.320] kind like Zurich. The compact city has half the carbon footprint, better health outcomes due to walkability, and higher quality[p.274] of life. Data shows people live longer in such environments, and surveys consistently reveal that people prefer living in dense, pedestrian-friendly areas. These cities are more sustainable[p.304], socially vibrant, and healthier – something car-dependent cities can't offer."

NORMAN FOSTER
Architect, founder and executive chairman of Foster + Partners
E.A.T. 2025: Form and Impact, Zuoz

CARE

"When it comes to landscape and trees[p.311], I'm completely out of my depth. I know nothing – but I want to learn[p.199]. I feel genuinely embarrassed not to know the names of the species I live alongside in my own city[p.47]. I live in London, where there are 400 species of moth and 448 species of tree. It feels impolite not to know their names. Over lunch with fellow Engadin Art Talks[p.116] participants, we spoke about care, curation and curiosity – and how all three words[p.324] share the same root. If we're not curious, how can we care? And if we don't care, how can we curate or look after anything? And if we don't curate, how can anything survive? For me, it began with that simple instinct[p.192]: I want to learn their names."

ES DEVLIN
Artist
E.A.T. 2022: Matter and Memory, Zuoz

CARNIVAL

"I love[p.202] the idea[p.145] of art[p.31] without doors. That's what I admired about the Serpentine Pavilion – it was an art encounter p.114 without a threshold p.308. Where I grew p.138 up, you couldn't be a great artist if you weren't performing p.222 on the street corner. Everyone could come – your brother, the police, whoever. Carnival is like that. It's not about hierarchy p.140; everyone participates p.221. That's the space I want to work in – not just galleries, but where people show up, where culture p.60 lives."

ALVARO BARRINGTON
Artist
E.A.T. 2025: Form and Impact, Zuoz

CARRY

"In Romansh p.288, we have many words p.324 for snow p.298. In Tamashek, the Tuareg language p.198, there's no word for snow, but many words for desert p.105 and sand. In Romansh, 'spuolvrada' means very little snow, and 'naiveras' is huge snow. There's even a word for when the snow carries p.41 you – 'porta samada' – which happens in spring. The same thing can occur in the desert. In the morning, because temperatures p.307 fall p.122 below zero at night, the jeeps just glide over the frozen sand, almost like sleds."

NOT VITAL
Artist
E.A.T. 2017: Snow and Desert, Zuoz

CENSORSHIP

"In autocracies p.32, the most subversive art p.31 is often indirect. Take the blank paper protests p.273 in China p.44 – people held p.141 up sheets with nothing written on them. It was a powerful way to say: 'You already know what I'd write.' The symbolism p.305 bypassed censorship and spoke volumes. That's the genius of art under repression – it finds p.125 a way to speak when speech p.300 itself is banned."

KENNETH ROTH
Former executive director of Human Rights Watch
E.A.T. 2023: Hoffnung? Hoffnung!, Zuoz

CENTRE POMPIDOU

"When working on the renovation of the Centre Pompidou

in Paris, they needed to replace the beautifully p.34 bent p.37 glass of the caterpillar-like escalators due to updated safety norms. I thought, surely, someone would want to reuse p.285 this glass. Eventually, we found p.125 an architecture p.29 firm that repurposed it as a partition wall. It felt like a serendipitous alignment – being in the right place, calling the right people – but if we want this to be more than coincidence, we need technology p.306 that makes reuse systematic and efficient."

CATHERINE DE WOLF
Professor, civil engineer, architect and founder and director of the chair of Circular Engineering for Architecture (CEA), ETH Zurich
E.A.T. 2023: Hoffnung? Hoffnung!, Zuoz
→ PLATE 13 p.78

CERAMICS

"Natsuko Uchino has been living in the south of France for quite some time p.308, and I visited her during her first residency in Saint-Quentin-la-Poterie; a historical p.140 ceramics p.42 town. The local community p.51 gave her access p.23 to the municipal ceramics studio, and I basically squatted there to work with her. Over time, we built a life around that. For her, it's rooted p.289 in ecology p.113, farming p.122 and material p.204 practice. I guess I followed her – like a dilettante – into this clean, pesticide-free region surrounded by organic farming. It gave us a foundation to grow p.138 a story p.301 together, one with good food and strong bodies p.38 and shared production."

MATTHEW LUTZ-KINOY
Artist
E.A.T. 2023: Hoffnung? Hoffnung!, Zuoz

CHALLENGE

"The American p.28 artist and designer Vito Acconci was so restless and he constantly needed to challenge himself. He quickly changed p.43 course numerous times and ended up literally doing architecture p.29, often to the detriment of his art career. He died p.63 practically destitute, which was a travesty, but he was a great inspiration p.192

for me and a model p.208 of how not to settle, to constantly change and challenge oneself. I mean, in five years from now I don't know exactly what I'll be, but for certain it will revolve around all things art."

KENNY SCHACHTER
Artist, writer and lecturer
E.A.T. 2021: Longue Durée, livestream

CHANGE

"The exhibition *Energies* at Swiss p.305 Institute New York began with a local 1970s story p.301: during the oil crisis, a group of activists – recent architecture p.29 and engineering grads, unhoused people, and artists – took over a building and installed solar panels and a wind turbine on the roof. They fed their surplus energy p.115 back into the Con Edison grid, showing that the decentralised, co-generation of renewable energy was possible. Con Edison sued, as they felt threatened in their near monopoly on the energy market, but the group, supported p.303 by a former Attorney General, unexpectedly won. This helped create a change p.43 in national legislation, enabling energy co-production across the US p.28. I love p.202 how such a visionary yet humble act sparked massive change. It reminds p.281 us: even now, when things feel bleak, we can't stop. We must keep working, support and connect p.53 across communities p.51, and think across scales p.290, both large and small, to bring about change."

STEFANIE HESSLER
Curator and director of Swiss Institute New York
2025: E.A.T. × St. Moritz, St. Moritz

CHARACTER

"Character.
Giving or taking.
Safe or sorry.
Hunting or fishing.
Beauty or personality.
Imperfect or flawed.
A twinkle in the eye.
Sparkling or still.
Wrinkled or pressed.
Family, friend or lover?
Closed or open?
Precise or vague?
Wall, hedge or freedom to roam?

Cat or dog p.110?
Faire ou laisser faire?
Day or night?
Questions or answers?
Do you have an edge?
Generous or cautious?
Fact or fiction p.124?
Caravaggio, Cézanne,
Mondrian or Twombly?
Tidy or messy?
City or country?
Swift or gradual?
Mind, guts or heart?
Mellow or edgy?
Clear or nebulous?
Harmony or confrontation?
Loud or modest?
Superficial or sincere?
Forest, meadow or beach?
Warm or uncaring?
Are you free?
Character."

ROLF SACHS
Artist and designer
E.A.T. 2020: Silent – Listen, Zuoz

CHARGE

"Dust p.112 is an intriguing expression of energy p.115 – every single speck carries p.41 a small electric charge, and the most effective way to remove it is by using ostrich feathers. But this doesn't work with all feathers – only the female p.123 ostrich feathers can generate the static required to attract and hold p.141 onto dust particles p.222. In car manufacturing, their sensitivity has been industrialised to produce dust-free environments. Before a car is painted, it passes through a tunnel p.312 lined with thousands of female feathers. It's an eerie image p.146: the naked steel car brushing against the feathers of an ancient p.29 flightless bird. In this moment – charged with gender p.132, touch p.308 and technology p.306 – energy becomes p.35 hauntingly poetic p.226."

NINA CANELL
Artist
2025: E.A.T. × St. Moritz, St. Moritz

CHINA

"As ambassador, my duties ranged from cultural p.60 and development cooperation to political analysis and economic diplomacy – especially since I had launched the first joint venture with the outside world, which marked the start of China's globalisation. But what helped me most to understand[p.313] China was contemporary[p.55] art[p.31]. Engaging[p.116] with friends[p.128] like Ai Weiwei gave me insight I couldn't have gained otherwise. So it felt natural to open the embassy as a place for cultural encounters[p.114]."

ULI SIGG
Entrepreneur, art collector and former Swiss Ambassador to China, North Korea and Mongolia, 1995–1998
E.A.T. 2023: Hoffnung? Hoffnung!, Zuoz

CHOREOGRAPHY

"American[p.28] choreographer and dancer Trisha Brown once said that choreography is an art[p.31] form that exists in the crack between the visual arts and traditionally understood[p.313] dance. It is in this crack – this territory of autonomous[p.33] choreography – that we have dedicated[p.64] ourselves, first at Old Brewery New Dance in Pozna, and later at Muzeum Susch. It is a space that brings together visual art practices[p.228] and poetic[p.226] counter-visualisations of what has been artificially[p.31] naturalised. Like a haiku, choreography can inspire[p.192] thought and reflection about the human[p.143] condition and the world. This is what postmodern choreographers aspired to: rethinking reality[p.277] through the body[p.38], through movement, and generating physical metaphors for human experience."

JOANNA LEŚNIEROWSKA
Curator, dramaturge and performance-maker
E.A.T. 2019: Grace and Gravity, Zuoz
→ PLATE 14 p.79

CHRISTIANITY

"I want to create something that brings people closer to themselves. Through expressing myself, I invite others to find[p.125] themselves. I call this the principle of connectedness – rooted[p.289] for me in the Christian message of neighbourly love[p.202]. But this principle is also the foundation of democratic societies. We are not just isolated islands. If we lose our connection[p.53] to one another –

in art[p.31], faith[p.121] or politics – we become[p.35] lost[p.201]."

JOACHIM GAUCK
Former Federal President of Germany (2012–2017)
E.A.T. 2023: Hoffnung? Hoffnung!, Zuoz

CINEMA

"I believe[p.36] it was in the mid-1990s that I began to grow increasingly frustrated with cinema's[p.46] rigid format[p.127], where viewers passively watch a screen until the film reel ends. In my 1997 multi-channel video[p.316] installation *Diamond Sea*, filmed in the diamond mines of Namibia, I sought to freeze the landscape in time[p.308], allowing its subtle movements to emerge only through the shifting[p.296] perspective[p.223] of the camera. This approach also echoes how, when I visit other places like the Engadin, I experience the landscape not simply as a physical topography, but as a psychological space – one where perception and emotion transform[p.310] the environment beyond its visible form."

DOUG AITKEN
Artist
E.A.T. 2010: The Crystal Chain, Zuoz
→ PLATE 15 p.80

CIRCULARITY

"Recycling is important, but in reality[p.277] it's the lowest value part of a circular economy. The highest value is in the design of systems and products for long use: to share, maintain, repair, reuse[p.285], remanufacture. These are all inner loops of a circular system. The last loop is recycling – it requires lots of energy[p.115] and often leads[p.198] to downgraded products. A circular economy is not just about waste[p.321] – it's a systems approach to redesign the economy itself."

ANDREW MORLET
Former CEO of the Ellen MacArthur Foundation, chair of the UK Government CIRCULAR Economy Taskforce, lead of the CIRCULAR Economy Innovation Hub at Standard Chartered Bank
E.A.T. 2022: Matter and Memory, Zuoz

CITY

"You have a formal city and an informal city: urban areas that are built and inhabited outside of formal planning. This is not a casualty. This is not fortuitous. This is actually man-made. We went to mayors and we tried to convince them that they had to invest their money[p.210] in the poorest areas of cities. Urbanisation is political, and you must engage[p.116] the politics. If not, we will get sprawl and actually it will be disastrous – politically and also ecologically[p.113]."

ALFREDO BRILLEMBOURG
Architect, educator and principal of Urban Think Tank Design
E.A.T. 2016: Traces and Fragments, Zuoz
→ PLATE 16 p.81

CIVILISATION

"The idea[p.145] for the *With My Eyes* (2024) group exhibition in the Giudecca Women's Prison on Giudecca Island in Venice, was to focus on the Mediterranean[p.205] – not just as a place, but as a concept. It has always been a crossroads for cultural[p.60] exchange[p.120], essential for civilisation to move from Egypt to Greece, from Greece to Rome. The Mediterranean has always carried[p.41] civilisation. This is the aspect I wanted to highlight: the exchange between East and West[p.321], which necessarily passed through this sea. Venice, in particular, symbolises[p.305] this exchange and collaboration[p.49]."

SIMONE FATTAL
Artist
2023: E.A.T. × Centre Pompidou, Paris

CLAY

"One thing I've learned[p.199] is that the disappearance of a sculptural object[p.217] makes the interface evident. What remains is the human[p.143] hand, the action[p.24] of the human on Earth[p.112]. Clay and cement carry[p.41] symbolic[p.305] weight: clay speaks of life before humans, of a deep time[p.308] embedded in soil, while cement marks our intervention, our imprint[p.148]. Most of my projects use this mixture of clay, sand and cement – so, in a way, each work is a dialogue[p.107] between what existed long before us and what we're doing now."

ADRIÁN VILLAR ROJAS
Artist
E.A.T. 2018: Side Country Side, Zuoz

CLICHÉ

"With my durational[p.111] performances[p.222], I try to find[p.125] a form. For example, how many hours should it last? I tend to choose obvious durations: six hours, 12 hours, half a day, or a full day. These are natural, circular[p.46] forms, like the shape[p.295] of a clock. It's very formalistic. I always like to go for the obvious. I think the cliché is the ultimate expression. My friend[p.128] and mentor, the Icelandic artist Magnús Sigurðarson, once made a piece of himself naked with a finger up his butt and a cigar, and called it *The Cliché Is the Ultimate Expression.* The cliché is so incredibly interesting."

RAGNAR KJARTANSSON
Artist
E.A.T. 2021: Longue Durée, livestream

CLIMATE CHANGE

"Climate change is a type of load for infrastructures[p.191]. It is an active agent that, particularly in recent years, has contributed to the rapid deterioration of existing structures. By collecting monitoring data and understanding[p.313] how this rate of change[p.43] affects[p.26] our built environment – for example, stronger winds acting on wind turbines or more aggressive corrosion on bridges – we can improve our designs and repair strategies. We can no longer rely on the original design of these systems, conceived years ago; a purely design-based approach is inadequate under today's continuously[p.55] evolving loads and conditions."

ELENI CHATZI
Civil engineer, researcher, professor and chair of Structural Mechanics and Monitoring at the Department of Civil, Environmental and Geomatic Engineering, ETH Zurich
2024: E.A.T. × Kunsthalle Zürich, Zurich

CLIMB

"'Huddle' is a dance construction requiring six to nine performers to form a tight cluster; each takes turns climbing over the others, creating a moving sculptural structure. It is primarily seen as a form in space, as a structure – almost like a sculpture. I also see it as both a sculpture and a dancep.61. A wonderful part of the experience is feeling the climber's weight pass through your shoulder, arm and hand. It is a deeply collaborativep.49 and reflexive experience."

SIMONE FORTI
Artist, dancer, choreographer and writer
E.A.T. 2010: The Crystal Chain, Zuoz

COEXISTENCE

"There's a fascinating tensionp.307 between the temporary and the permanentp.223 in many refugee camps. When people begin to add permanent decoration – plaster, stucco – we might wonderp.323: have they resigned themselves to staying? But then we see that even those walls carryp.41 political messages, like the national flag. What seems permanent and what seems temporary can coexist; they are two sides of the same coin."

MANUEL HERZ
Architect
E.A.T. 2017: Snow and Desert, Zuoz

COLLABORATION

"Collaboration essentially implies that you agree to bendp.37 to what or who holdsp.141 power at the moment. When you collaborate, if you have decidedp.63 to make artp.31, you come together to build something, place it, and show it to the world. But once you begin collaborating, you have already started to compromise, first with the dominant culturep.60. Maybe the wordp.324 itself is what we should be talking about. 'Collaboration' soundsp.300 wonderful; it appeals to anyone who has been isolated in an ivory tower, stuck alonep.28 in a studio or immersed in research thinking. So why then is 'collaboration' considered to be such a <u>dirty</u>[p.108] word in all four major European <u>languages</u>[p.198]? The word has been used in <u>times</u>[p.308] when the dominant culture was not the right thing, from a Hitler to a Mussolini; to <u>accept</u>[p.23] their culture, you would be a collaborator. Collaboration is not the point, being able to <u>understand</u>[p.313] what the point is – that is the point!"

LAWRENCE WEINER
Artist
E.A.T. 2011: Mapping the Alps, Zuoz

COLONIALISM

"British-Israeli architect Eyal Weizman has elaborated the <u>idea</u>[p.145] that desiccation in places like the Negev is not a natural process, nor merely the unintentional by-product of human action. It is, rather, a form of strategic environmental <u>violence</u>[p.317]; a method of displacement and dispossession. At a Columbia University conference on architecture and <u>climate change</u>[p.48], he stated: 'Even the most militant environmentalists still regard climate change as the collateral of <u>history</u>[p.140]. Seen from the point of view of <u>colonial</u>[p.50] history, however, climate change is the very telos of the colonial project and of modernity at large.'"

EMILY-ELIZA SCOTT
Interdisciplinary scholar, artist and former park ranger
E.A.T. 2017: Snow and Desert, Zuoz

COLOUR

"When we start talking about colour on a <u>construction</u>[p.53] site, I might begin with two people. An hour later, the whole village is there. Everyone wants to <u>decide</u>[p.63]. So what do I do? I <u>walk</u>[p.320] away. I give direction, then I let go. When I come back, it's often not what I had in <u>mind</u>[p.207] – because I studied in Europe, and I think I know colours. But I've <u>learned</u>[p.199]: I'm creating a frame for others to play. You can't be angry when someone tells you, 'Francis, I <u>fought</u>[p.124] for this colour.' That's <u>inspiration</u>[p.192]. That's success."

FRANCIS KÉRÉ
Architect
E.A.T. 2017: Snow and Desert, Zuoz

COMMUNICATION

"Orcas are highly intelligent animals with brains larger than ours. They live in pods and use vocalisations and echolocation to communicate and navigate. A female[p.123] teaches[p.306] her calf a signature whistle, which becomes[p.35] its name. One orca can scan an area with sonar, then transmit the same pulse pattern to another – effectively sharing what it 'sees'. It's like sending a fax. This could be one explanation for what we interpret as telepathy."

CHRIS WATSON
Musician and sound recordist
E.A.T. 2020: Silent – Listen, Zuoz

COMMUNITY

"Usually, there is a group facing another group – the performers[p.222] and the visitors[p.318]. But I don't like traditional theatre setups, with spotlights and separation. In my shows, we all sit on the same level. In my shows, I try to create one group, a community – not two groups facing each other, but all being together."

TRAJAL HARRELL
Choreographer and dancer
E.A.T. 2021: Longue Durée, livestream

COMPLICITY

"Architects have been the culprits. We are not the saviors. We are not the stars. We are the culprits. We have been complicit in the segregation and spatialisation of cities[p.47] – by taking on the projects that we shouldn't."

ALFREDO BRILLEMBOURG
Architect, educator and principal of Urban Think Tank Design
E.A.T. 2016: Traces and Fragments, Zuoz

CONCRETE

"For the work *Muscle Memory*, I poured 18 tons of mollusc shells onto a museum[p.212] floor. Visitors[p.318] could walk[p.320] on them, slowly[p.298] breaking them down over the course of the exhibition. The sound[p.300] of crunching calcite lent a tactile sensation that connected[p.53] our own bodies[p.38] – with its bones – to the shells and the concrete floor beneath them. Fossilised[p.127] shells contain[p.54] biominerals that are essential to concrete, which is one of the most dominant materials[p.204] in our built environment. On the Baltic island where I spend time[p.308], cement production relies on the 400-million-year history[p.140] of long-gone coral[p.57] reefs. The work explores this convergence between concrete and ancient[p.29] marine lifeforms, considering how a concrete floor and a shell floor are intrinsically entangled."

NINA CANELL
Artist
2025: E.A.T. × St. Moritz, St. Moritz

CONFRONTATION

"One image[p.146] shows a wide view of migrating caribou in the snow[p.298] – it's large, painterly, and appeals to the North American[p.28] eye. The other shows caribou being butchered – close, visceral, full of blood. Together, they ask viewers to confront three tensions[p.307]: our physical distance from images; our cultural[p.60] discomfort[p.109] with raw[p.275] animal life; and our tendency to mythologise wilderness as uninhabited, ignoring the Indigenous presence[p.229] that shaped[p.295] it for millennia."

SUBHANKAR BANERJEE
Photographer, writer, curator and environmental humanities scholar
E.A.T. 2017: Snow and Desert, Zuoz
→PLATE 17[p.82]

CONFUSION

"Even in the art[p.31] world there's confusion: if an artist works in landscape, 50 % of the time it's called land art. But for me that's wrong – it's just a piece of art in a landscape. That difference matters. I use here the example of Hamish Fulton, whose work in landscapes is often labelled as land art, though it's something else entirely. When I started my studies, the profession was called garden architecture; by my second semester it was landscape architecture. That change[p.43] of name meant a change of scale[p.290], of approach, of everything – and it was a huge step for our field."

GÜNTHER VOGT
Landscape architect and professor emeritus
2024: E.A.T. × Kunsthalle Zürich, Zurich

CONNECTION

"To me, it's not just about materials p.204 – it's about connection. Reuse p.285 happens because the right people are brought together at the right moment. That's why I want to create a 'Tinder for reuse': to connect people who are dismantling buildings with those who want to build with existing materials. What gives me hope p.142 is that I'm standing here as an engineer invited to an art p.31 talk. Connecting disciplines – art, science, engineering, architecture p.29 – this gives me hope for the future p.130."

CATHERINE DE WOLF
Professor, civil engineer, architect, and founder and director of the chair of Circular Engineering for Architecture (CEA), ETH Zurich
E.A.T. 2023: Hoffnung? Hoffnung!, Zuoz
→PLATE 18 p.83

CONSTRUCTION

"We're now seeing a return to earth-based construction. For instance, in Lausanne, we were involved in building a completely low-tech office structure for the city p.47 administration. It was made from ultra-local resources p.283 – straw, clay p.47, wood p.323 – and designed with passive climate solutions. It's not about nostalgia; it's about using what we already know works, and applying it with purpose p.274 to build a sustainable p.304 future p.130."

LOÏC ROGARD
Researcher in the field of renewable energies at Atelier 21
E.A.T. 2023: Hoffnung? Hoffnung!, Zuoz

CONSUMERISM

"One of my favourite works by Ai Weiwei is his Coca-Cola urn. But the logo is fading. Soon, it might just be a Han Dynasty urn again. It raises questions p.275 – maybe Chinese culture p.60 will outlast Western p.321 consumerism. Maybe the urn will outlive thc brand. What happens when cultural symbols p.305 disappear?"

ULI SIGG
Entrepreneur, art collector and former Swiss Ambassador to CN, NK and MN, 1995–1998
E.A.T. 2023: Hoffnung? Hoffnung!, Zuoz
→PLATE 19 p.84

CONTAINER

"When I speak of artists as storytellers[p.302], I mean they – and curators – create the narrative[p.213]. They offer alternative perspectives[p.223] and become[p.35] containers for diverse, plural, and sometimes contradictory[p.56] stories. That's the task: not to reduce, but to hold[p.141] multiplicity."

RASHA SALTI
Researcher, writer, producer and curator of art and film
E.A.T. 2024: Jenseits von Ohnmacht – Beyond Powerless, Zuoz

CONTAINMENT

"Today, showing a large-scale projection[p.232] feels like a kind of homeopathic vaccination against the loss[p.201] of powerful imagery[p.146]. As the world grows[p.138] more brutal – with wars, violence[p.317] and crises unfolding – our screens get smaller. These images rarely appear in large formats[p.127]; they're confined to handheld devices. That shift[p.296] shows how we try to contain what disturbs us."

CHRIS DERCON
Art historian, curator and managing director of Fondation Cartier pour l'art contemporain
E.A.T. 2021: Longue Durée, livestream

CONTAMINATION

"While living in Brussels, I became[p.35] interested in how Belgium engages[p.116] – or doesn't – with its colonial[p.50] past. Through art historian Deborah Silverman's work, I discovered connections[p.53] between Congo and Belgian Art Nouveau: artists like Horta and Van de Velde were inspired[p.192] by Congolese motifs[p.211], raw[p.275] materials[p.204] like ivory, and even scarification patterns. I began researching colonial art fairs and the 'Belgian Congo Pavilions', which showcased Congolese materials transformed[p.310] for European 'progress.' These structures weren't just exhibitions – they were fantasies, projections[p.232] of colonial desire[p.106]. But what interests me is how Belgian artists and architects were also unconsciously 'contaminated' by these cultural[p.60] encounters[p.114], leaving traces[p.309] that still shape[p.295] Belgium's landscape today."

SAMMY BALOJI
Artist
E.A.T. 2025: Form and Impact, Zuoz
→PLATE 20 [p.85]

CONTEMPORARY

"I found[p.125] my own answer within myself, that everything that is present[p.230] and thus contemporary art[p.31] is what is not older than I am. And being in my 60s, I have the great fortune that everything I have experienced and consciously noticed spans at least five decades – and that, for me, is contemporary."

UDO KITTELMANN
Curator and former director of the Nationalgalerie in Berlin, Staatliche Museen zu Berlin (2008–2020)
2021: E.A.T. × Kunsthalle Zürich, Zurich
→PLATE 21 [p.86]

CONTEXT

"I was born into a situation where one parent was Egyptian and the other German, and as a child we moved between these two countries. I was always the same person, but the reactions[p.24] from others were different. If something was said, or I saw[p.296] an object[p.217], it could have entirely different meanings[p.204] depending on the cultural[p.60] context. At some point, I began to create my own language[p.198] – I started drawing, painting and interacting with the world through images[p.146]. That became[p.35] my way to exist beyond worlds."

SUSAN HEFUNA
Artist
E.A.T. 2025: Form and Impact, Zuoz
→PLATE 22 [p.87]

CONTINUITY

"When something extraordinary disrupts your life, you're forced to reinvent yourself. That's when you discover you're not defined[p.64] by one path. You have other capacities – and sometimes, a necessity – to go in entirely new directions. But at some point I also realised: even as I changed[p.43] countries, professions and languages[p.198], there was a thread running through it all. There's a kind of continuity in fragmentation p.127. It's not about clinging to a single identity p.146, but about learning p.199 to move between them."

MICHAEL SCHINDHELM
Author, filmmaker and curator
E.A.T. 2016: Traces and Fragments, Zuoz

CONTRADICTION

"In the end, the one I've been in constant dialogue p.107 with for the longest time p.308 is Kafka p.197. Every time I encounter p.114 a problem, he's there. Kafka and Montaigne – they inhabit completely different territories. Montaigne is refined, aristocratic – his writing is rich p.286, noble, morally extraordinary. He was against the death p.63 penalty, against racism – his modernity is astonishing. We are blessed to have an ancestor like Montaigne. But Kafka I understand p.313 completely. His Jewish background was drastically reduced in the way he was first translated and presented – especially here in France. But in the newer German editions, something immense has reappeared: this permanent p.223, subterranean river p.287 of Jewish complexity. I think Max Brod – out of friendship p.128 – hid that part, thinking Kafka wouldn't be accepted p.23 otherwise. But it's foundational. Kafka's writing wasn't meant to be published p.273 – it was his private exploration of contradictory worlds. He sculpted his being within those contradictions."

HÉLÈNE CIXOUS
Writer, playwright and literary critic
2023: E.A.T. × Centre Pompidou, Paris

CONVERSATION

"In 1967, cinema p.46 was still a collective experience, a secular church where people sat together and outsourced conversation to the screen. Today, most of what we consume p.53 happens alone p.28 on individual p.189 devices – that communial p.51 setting is fading."

DAVID CLAERBOUT
Artist
E.A.T. 2020: Silent – Listen, Zuoz
→PLATE 23 p.88

CORAL

"Every coral reef has its own signature sound p.300 – no two sound the same. Fish use these soundscapes to navigate, find p.125 breeding grounds and communicate p.51. As reefs bleach and degrade due to climate change p.48, their sound fades. Acoustic monitoring is becoming p.35 crucial: by recording ambient reef noise p.215, we can assess how alive or degraded the reef is."

CHRIS WATSON
Musician and sound recordist
E.A.T. 2020: Silent – Listen, Zuoz
→PLATE 24 p.89

COSMOS

"Some humans p.143 have passed through different metabolic regimes. Many were once nomadic, following seasons and animals. Then came agriculture p.27 and domestication p.110, and they began settling. Later, cities p.47 formed and many humans entered the fossil p.127 fuel regime – mega-cities powered by carbon p.40. The question p.275 is: can some of us imagine p.146 a new metabolic regime where many can relate differently to the Sun? That's the challenge p.42; rethinking energies p.115, rhythms p.286 and relationships p.280 with the cosmos."

TOMÁS SARACENO
Artist
E.A.T. 2021: Longue Durée, livestream

COUNTRYSIDE

"The countryside is sort of the theatre of the mind p.207, it's what we see p.296 when we read p.276. It's what we're imagining p.146 behind our eyes. The countryside is imaginary. It's a literary space. It's not exactly rural p.289, and it definitely isn't everything that's not urban. I'd argue the desert p.105 isn't the countryside, nor is the jungle or rainforest. Many rural environments lack the coherence that would make the term 'countryside' truly accurate. The countryside is a dream of coherence; a false coherence projected p.232 onto a very real landscape."

EMILY SEGAL
Artist and writer
E.A.T. 2018: Side Country Side, Zuoz

CREATION

"When I started building, I couldn't explain my environmental goals to people in Germany. Every time you talk about Africa[p.26], people start talking about corruption. But why wait until everything is perfect before we do something? Why shouldn't a student go home[p.141] and build a school[p.291]? I don't get it. So I created an association – a very German name: Schulbausteine für Gando e.V. Then some friends[p.128] said, 'Let's call it Kéré Foundation.' Much better."

FRANCIS KÉRÉ
Architect
E.A.T. 2017: Snow and Desert, Zuoz

CREATURE

"Yakshas are clever, dangerous, unpredictable[p.314], wise and generous beings. The creatures often lie in wait at mountain passes, forests[p.126], and riverbanks, challenging[p.42] travellers with difficult questions[p.275]. Those who fail[p.121] to answer face terrible curses or death[p.63], while success might reveal a hidden treasure's location."

RAQS MEDIA COLLECTIVE
Artist collective,
media practitioners, curators,
and researchers
E.A.T. 2012: Vision for the Alps, Zuoz
→PLATE 25 [p.90]

CRITIQUE

"At Swiss Institute New York, we integrate[p.192] different ways of addressing climate change[p.48] – operationally and artistically. We measure[p.205] our carbon[p.40] footprint and actively reduce it by rethinking transport, materials[p.204] and energy[p.115] usage. We also created a strategic climate fund, where artists help decide[p.63] which causes we support[p.303] to offset CO_2 emissions that we are unable to reduce. We invite artists to engage[p.116] in what I call ecological[p.113] or environmental institutional critique – like artist Jenna Sutela's compost oracle powered by worms, whose composting energy powers a speaker that broadcasts AI-generated messages across our rooftop. It's humorous, functional[p.129], and prompts us to reflect[p.279] on our climate impact[p.148]. Even artist Hendl Helen Mirra's score instructing us how we repaint the interstitial spaces of our gallery – with leftover or mis-mixed paint – makes our commitment to climate action[p.24] visible. Sometimes the different paint hues lead[p.198] visitors[p.318] to think that the Institute is falling[p.122] apart. I like that as it's also a critique of the pristine white cube."

STEFANIE HESSLER
Curator and director of
Swiss Institute New York
2025: E.A.T. × St. Moritz, St. Moritz
→ PLATE 26 p.91

CROSSING

"A desire[p.106] line is an informal pathway that gets created out in an open field as people move through – they expose[p.121] the actual movement patterns beneath the surface. We used Google Earth[p.112] to document a desire line that sits between Bonteheuwel, which is the Cape Coloured[p.50] neighbourhood where I grew[p.138] up, and Langa, which was a Black community[p.51]. These areas were separated under apartheid. But people quietly[p.275] resisted[p.282] separation by continuing to cross into one another's worlds. Someone must have been the first to step across – and others followed that act of crossing."

IGSHAAN ADAMS
Artist
E.A.T. 2022: Matter and Memory, Zuoz
→ PLATE 27 p.92

CRYSTAL

"Pre-1920 crystalline woodcuts by German-American painter Lyonel Feininger relate to 1964 mirror[p.208] sculptures by American artist Robert Smithson and contemporary[p.55] works by American artist Heather Rowe. Watercolours by Bohemian-German painter Wenzel Hablik depict temple-like crystalline spaces, linking[p.200] to Feininger's *Cathedral of Socialism* in the Bauhaus Manifesto, which also includes German-American architect Walter Gropius's statement influenced by

German architect and urban planner Bruno Taut and German author Paul Scheerbart. This crystalline thread traces p.309 a forgotten Modernism p.209 – rooted p.289 in socialist ideals p.145 rather than the grid – that was rejected in 1923 but rediscovered p.278 globally in recent decades. My work explores this political dimension of aesthetics p.25 from the post-World War I era to today."

JOSIAH MCELHENY
Artist
E.A.T. 2010: The Crystal Chain, Zuoz

CULTURE

"In 1990s Brooklyn, being Haitian was one of the worst things you could be called. People made cruel jokes. But then came Lauryn Hill and The Fugees. At carnival p.40, the Haitian truck might have started with 100 people. But as Lauryn sang, 'Ooh la la la,' it grew p.138 – 200, 300, 4,000. It was this beautiful p.34 call and response p.284. The next day, no one made Haitian jokes. That's the power of culture: it reshapes p.295 how we see ourselves and claim our place in the world."

ALVARO BARRINGTON
Artist
E.A.T. 2025: Form and Impact, Zuoz

CURRENCY

"I love the theme of 'Beyond Powerlessness' p.228 and I took it as an invitation to think past two frameworks p.128 that the art world has perfected – and that, in a way, incubate powerlessness: criticality p.58 and identity p.146. When critique becomes a value system in itself, you end up feeling as though you're making a difference when you're really not. And when identity becomes p.35 the art world's main currency, artists are incentivised to perform p.222 an authenticity p.32 to simplified versions of their minority p.207 identities, which leaves us with a reduced set of possibilities for who we can be."

CHRISTOPHER KULENDRAN THOMAS
Artist
E.A.T. 2024: Jenseits von Ohnmacht – Beyond Powerless, Zuoz

CURVE

"According to the Milanese architect Luigi Caccia Dominioni, human[p.143] movement tends to favour a continuous[p.55] flow, offsetting abrupt changes[p.43] in direction with gentle curves. As he states: 'Yes, I believe[p.36] that human beings[p.36] essentially move along curved lines, not along a straight path, like the shuttle of a loom[p.201] moving back and forth, but along circular[p.46], oval or sinuous lines. This form, intrinsic to human movement, is the matrix of architectural form.' The impetus and inspiration[p.192] for his dynamic spatial configurations derived directly from the observation[p.217] of human motion[p.211]."

ELLI MOSAYEBI
Architect
E.A.T. 2016: Traces and Fragments, Zuoz
→PLATE 28 [p.93]

CYCLE

"I've always been fascinaed by the idea[p.145] that the future[p.130] could be the past. English textile designer William Morris's *News from Nowhere*, a soft science-fiction[p.291] novel, imagines[p.146] a return to a pre-industrial, medieval England where everything is beautiful[p.34], everyone gets along and there's no conflict. I love[p.202] this idea of a cyclical time[p.308] – of a time that mirrors[p.208] itself or folds back on itself – and this fantasy of a utopia[p.315] rooted[p.289] in retreat from modernity deeply influences my work."

MAI-THU PERRET
Artist
E.A.T. 2018: Side Country Side, Zuoz

D

DANCE

"Many of the dancers in our project *Novaciéries* knew each other online for 10 years, but had never met physically. We brought them together in a room. When we asked them to create duets or trios, they imagined[p.146] split-screen videos[p.316] – two people doing the same thing simultaneously. We had to learn p.199 how to share space, build mutual understanding p.313 and navigate translation issues. Most didn't speak English, so we used Google Translate – Polish, Ukrainian, French – all with misunderstandings. We had to create a meta-language, relying on the body p.38 and behaviour p.35 in space. Dance became p.35 essential for bonding."

(LA)HORDE:
MARINE BRUTTI,
JONATHAN DEBROUWER,
ARTHUR HAREL
Artist collective and artistic directors of the Ballet National de Marseille
E.A.T. 2025: Form and Impact, Zuoz

DARKNESS

"The Moon p.210 has always fascinated me. I have a very romantic view of it. In my work *Behind the Moon*, the figure walks p.320 on the dark side – the part we never see p.296. I wanted to invite people to imagine p.146 a world we don't know, a side that stays invisible. Maybe I can spark an image p.146 that's different for everyone, something that only you can answer for yourself. I like the idea p.145 of a hidden side – of a picture, of a planet – that remains in darkness."

ZILLA LEUTENEGGER
Artist
E.A.T. 2024: Jenseits von Ohnmacht – Beyond Powerless, Zuoz

DATABASE

"At the photo archive p.30 of the Kunsthistorisches Institut in Florence, index cards, historical p.140 prints and a surveillance p.304 camera coexist p.49 in the same space. For me, this reveals how image p.146 access p.23 is both materially p.204 grounded and controlled, through metadata, among other things. Back in the early 20th century, the photo archive already functioned p.129 as a virtual space: art p.31 historians no longer had to travel to churches or museums p.212 – they could consult reproductions and assemble image worlds at will and for their purpose. Today's image databases p.62 perpetuate these spaces and possibilities, yet, often without reflecting[p.279] on the ways metadata is governing visibility."

ARMIN LINKE
Artist
E.A.T. 2022: Matter and Memory, Zuoz
→ PLATE 29 p.94

DEATH

"Death is an experience we cannot fully communicate[p.51] to others. Although countless texts and images[p.146] try to address this challenge[p.42], the reality[p.277] of death itself goes beyond what language[p.198] can express. These artistic works formalize or give shape[p.295] to what cannot be directly put into words[p.324]. I have always been fascinated by this contradiction[p.56] – the intense emotions death evokes and how we can only convey them through such formalised artistic expression."

ELISABETH BRONFEN
Author, cultural critic, Global Distinguished Professor New York University and Emerita at the University of Zurich
E.A.T. 2021: Longue Durée, livestream

DECISION

"Ultimately, the key question[p.275] is whether visitors[p.318] want to leave or stay, and they often hesitate when deciding between these options. For me, this is especially important in exhibitions, where – unlike cinema[p.46] or theatre – there is no set time[p.308] for the experience."

DOMINIQUE GONZALEZ-FOERSTER
Artist
E.A.T. 2011: Mapping the Alps, Zuoz

DECOLONISATION

"Philosophy[p.224], for me, is not a closed system but an ongoing, living conversation[p.56]. It always unfolds through dialogue[p.107] – between cultures[p.60], languages[p.198] and traditions. Take medieval philosophy: it cannot be understood[p.313] without recognising the exchange[p.120] between Christian[p.45], Jewish and Islamic thinkers. Decolonising philosophy means returning to this pluralistic, interconnected[p.53] character[p.43], and expanding our understanding of what philosophy can be."

SOULEYMANE
BACHIR DIAGNE
Philosopher
E.A.T. 2022: Matter and Memory,
Zuoz

DEDICATION

"In 2009, when I curated *elles@centrepompidou* at the Centre Pompidou p.41, it was the first time a museum p.212 had dedicated its permanent p.223 collection entirely to women artists p.322. We quite literally removed the major male artists from view in order to tell the story p.301 of the 20th century exclusively through the work of women. At that time p.308, most people could name perhaps five women artists. I presented 300 artists and around a 1000 works from the collection – demonstrating that there was so much more to be told."

CAMILLE MORINEAU
Curator and co-founder of
AWARE (Archives of Women
Artists, Research and Exhibitions)
E.A.T. 2022: Matter and Memory,
Zuoz

DEFINITION

"I had a private client called Viviana. When I worked for her, I became p.35 obsessed with the idea p.145 of becoming her during the design process. I needed to understand p.313 her dreams, to translate them into space. I knew all her obsessions – like what happens if her daughter's boyfriend is left-handed and the bathroom no longer works. We went through every detail over three or four years. By the end, I thought I knew her completely. I thought I understood her definition of domesticity p.110. But then, when she asked me to design another house p.142 in the city p.47, a different Viviana appeared. That's when I realised: each of us has not only our own definition of living, but that definition changes p.43 according to our present p.230 situation and desires p.106."

TATIANA BILBAO
Architect
E.A.T. 2020: Silent – Listen,
Zuoz

PLATES
1–38

PLATE 1

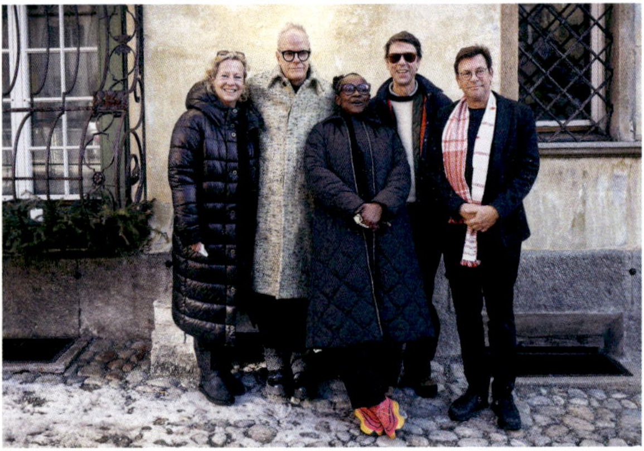

E.A.T. founder Cristina Bechtler with E.A.T. curators Hans Ulrich Obrist, Koyo Kouoh, Daniel Baumann and Philip Ursprung, Zuoz, 2024
© Photo by Saskja Rosset.

PLATE 2
→ALPS p.28

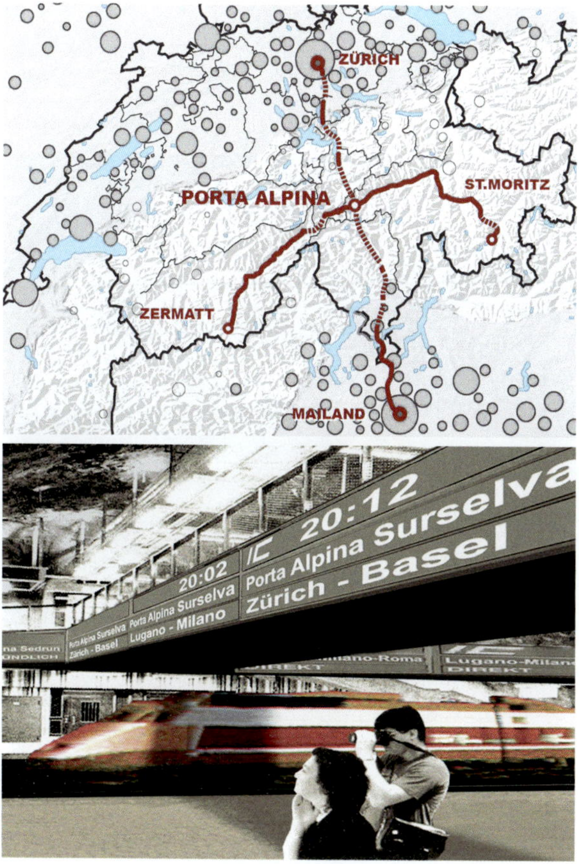

ARTHUR LORETZ
Arthur Loretz, Visiun Porta Alpina, 2003

PLATE 3
→AUTHENTICITY p.32

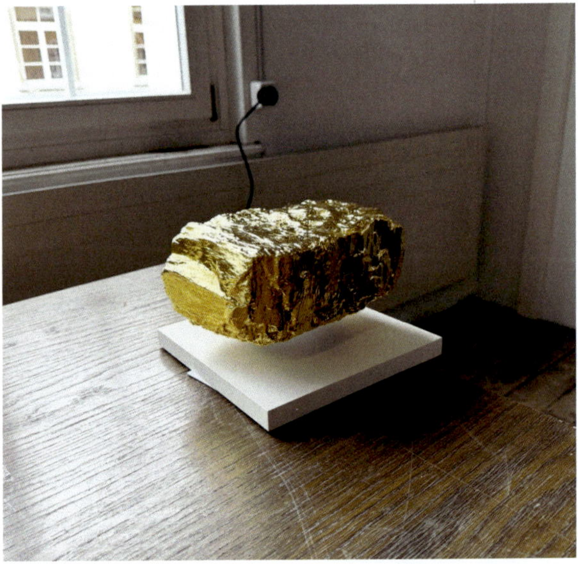

KOO JEONG A.
Koo Jeong A, [DENSITY], 2025

PLATE 4
→BEAUTY p.34

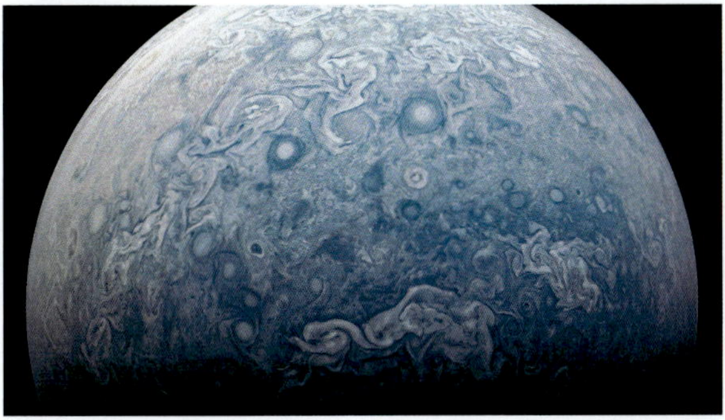

RAVIT HELLED
Jupiter's Northern Hemisphere

PLATE 5
→BECOMING p.35

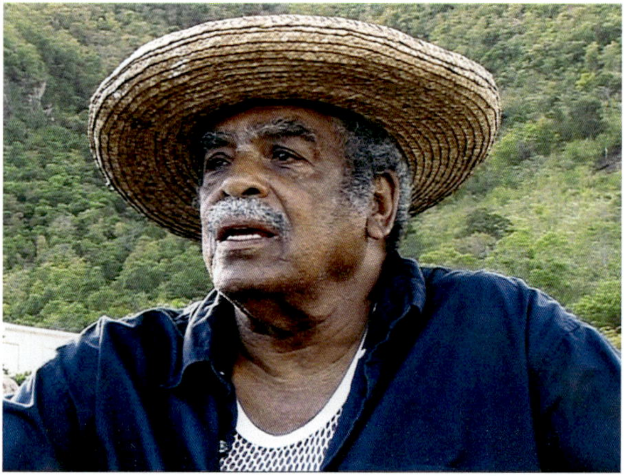

MANTHIA DIAWARA
Film still of Édouard Glissant from the film
Édouard Glissant, One World in Relation by Manthia Diawara (2010).
Courtesy of Manthia Diawara.

PLATE 6
→BEING p.36

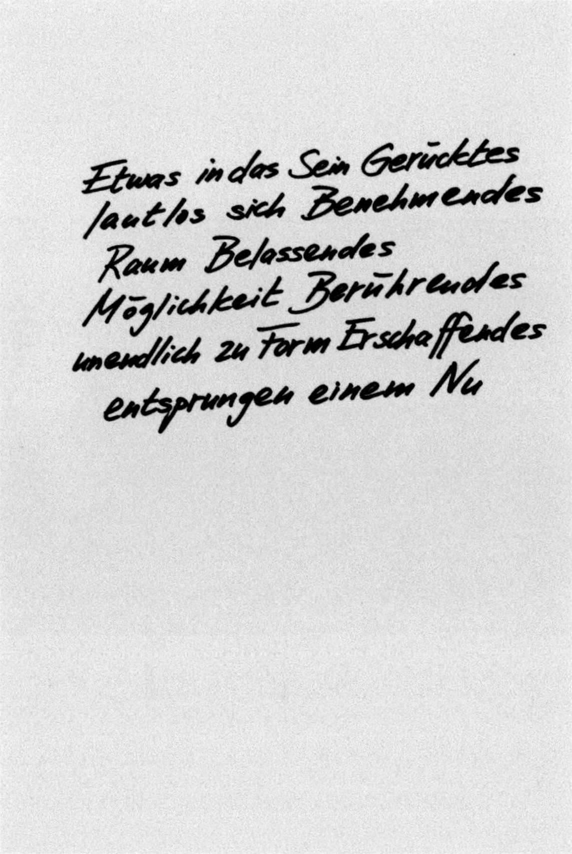

Etwas in das Sein Gerücktes
lautlos sich Benehmendes
Raum Belassendes
Möglichkeit Berührendes
unendlich zu Form Erschaffendes
entsprungen einem Nu

KLAUDIA SCHIFFERLE
Klaudia Schifferle, poem, 1987.

PLATE 7

→BELIEF p.36

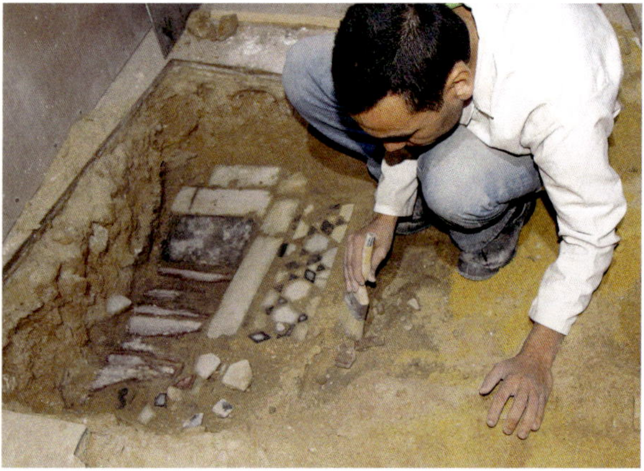

MAY AL-IBRASHY

Marble floor conservation at the Mausoleum of Imam al-Shafi'i.

PLATE 8

→BELONGING p.36

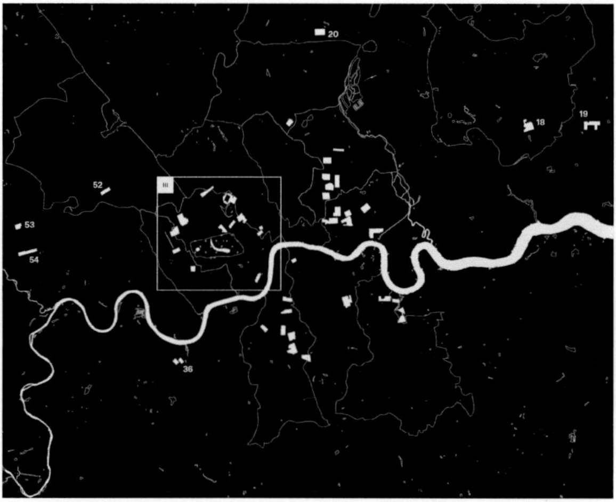

SUMAYYA VALLY
A map showing the places that inspired the Serpentine Pavilion 2021, which was designed by Sumayya Vally of Counterspace.
Courtesy of Counterspace.

PLATE 9

→BEND p.37

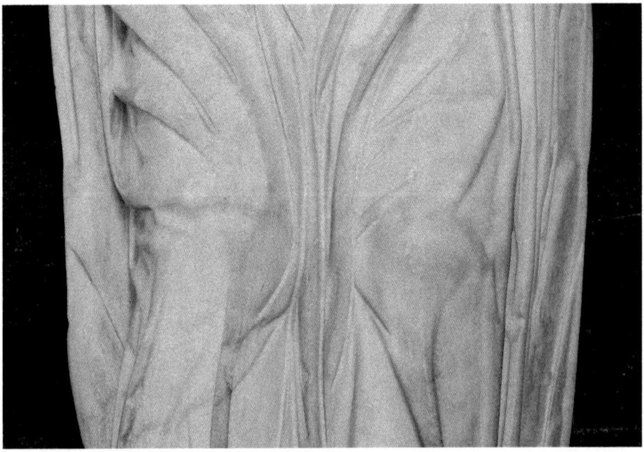

ISABEL NOLAN

Isabel Nolan, *For ever and ever, and infinite and super infinite for evers*, 2015, archival pigment print framed with clarity glass, 73.4 × 110 cm. Courtesy of the artist and Kerlin Gallery, Dublin.

PLATE 10
→BLOCKCHAIN p.38

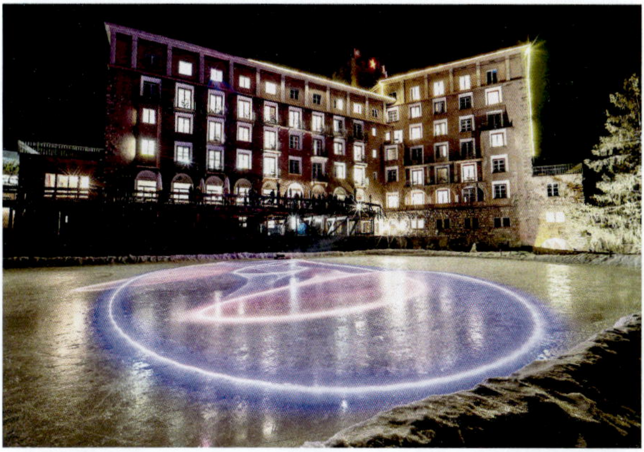

JOHANNES GEES
Kelian Maissen and Johannes Gees, *kleee02*, 2019, light installation, Hotel Castell, Zuoz (shown during Engadin Art Talks 2022). Courtesy of the artists.

PLATE 11
→BREATHE p.39

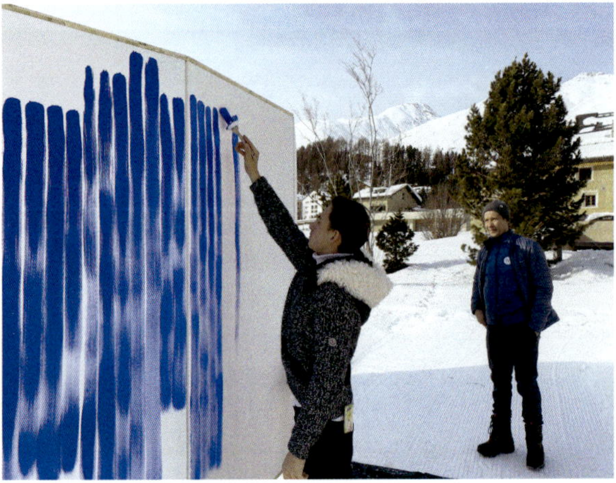

JEPPE HEIN
Jeppe Hein, *Breathe with Me*, installation, 2020
(shown during Engadin Art Talks 2022).

PLATE 12

→CANON p.39

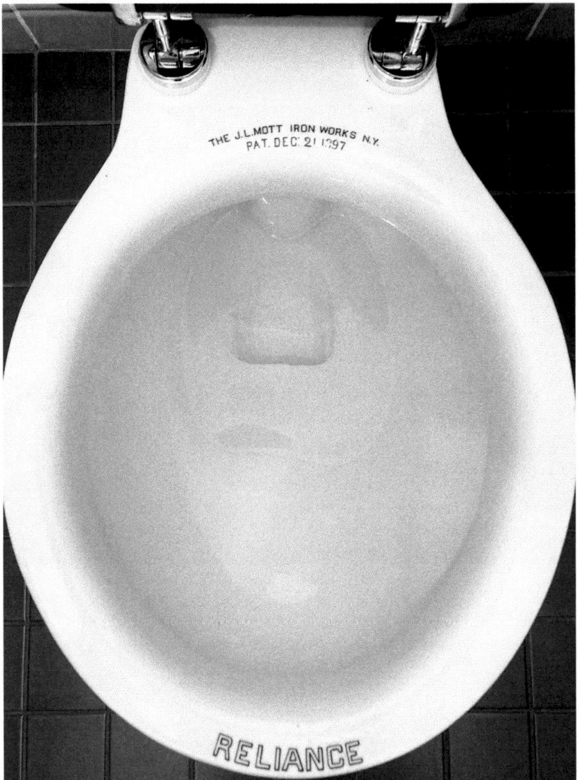

DARIO GAMBONI
Toilet at Villa Bleuler, Zurich, J.L. Mott Iron Works N.Y. brand, produced after 1897.

PLATE 13
→CENTRE POMPIDOU p.41

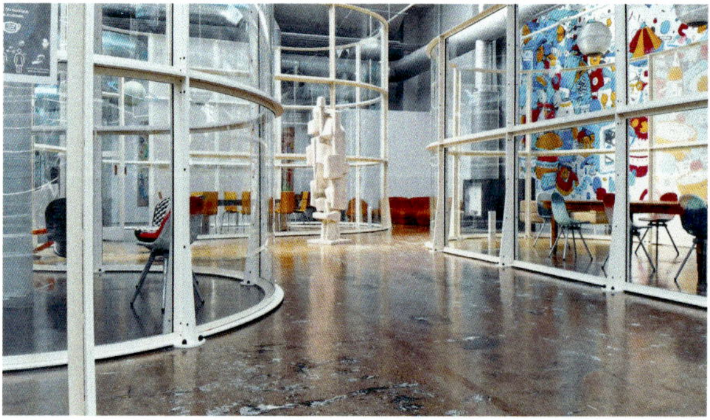

CATHERINE DE WOLF
Partition walls made from reused glass of the Centre Pompidou escalators, Paris.
© Maximum Architecture. Photo by Alexandre Attias.

PLATE 14
→CHOREOGRAPHY p.45

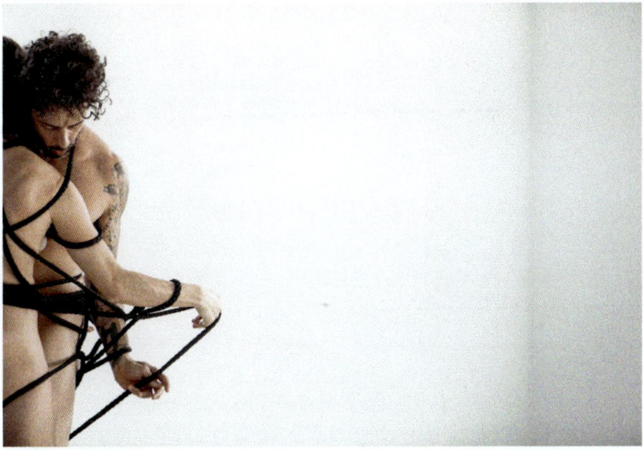

JOANNA LEŚNIEROWSKA
Performance by Joanna Leśnierowska.
© Photo by Jakub Wittchen. Courtesy of Joanna Leśnierowska.

PLATE 15
→CINEMA p.46

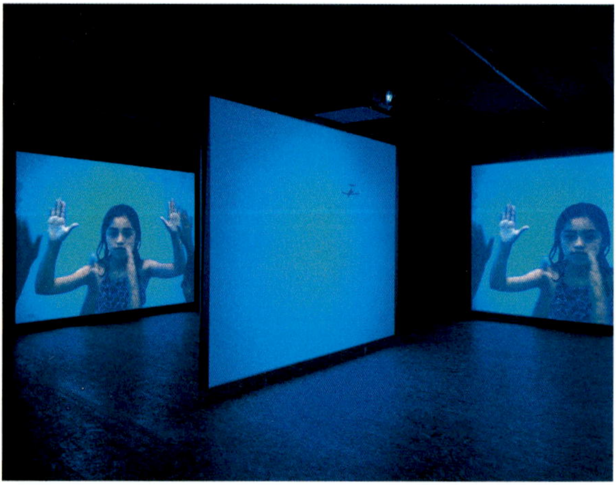

DOUG AITKEN
Installation view of *I AM IN YOU* (2000) by Doug Aitken at Galerie Hauser & Wirth & Presenhuber, Zurich.
Courtesy the artist and Galerie Eva Presenhuber, Zurich/Vienna.
© Doug Aitken. Photo by Stefan Altenburger Photography Zürich.

PLATE 16
→CITY p.47

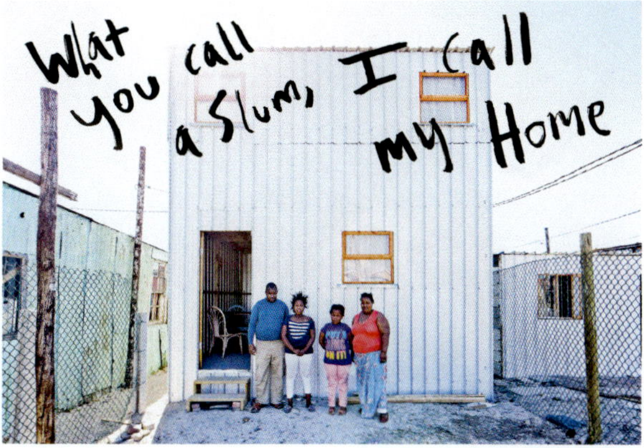

ALFREDO BRILLEMBOURG
Empower Housing, BT Section of Site C, Khayelitsha, Cape Town, 2025.

PLATE 17
→CONFRONTATION p.52

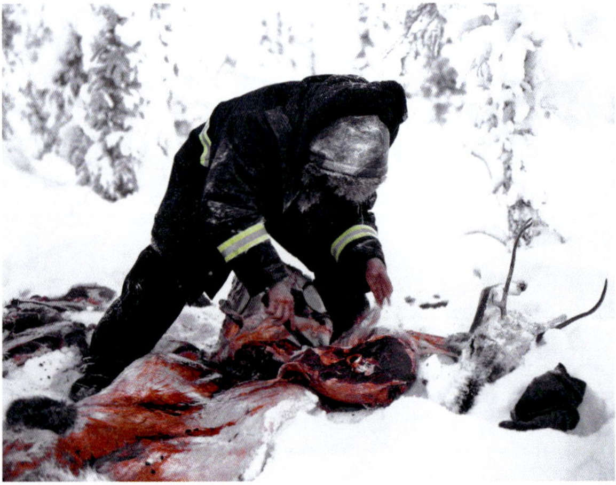

SUBHANKAR BANERJEE
Subhankar Banerjee, *Caribou Hunt – Jimmy John*, 2007,
UNM Art Museum, USA.
© Photo by Subhankar Banerjee.

PLATE 18

→CONNECTION p.53

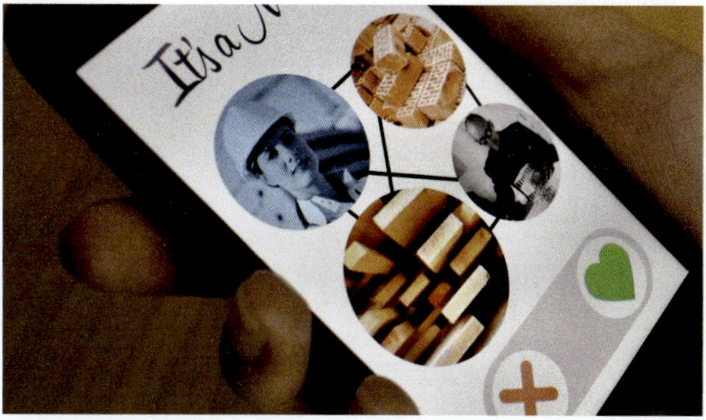

CATHERINE DE WOLF

The digital platform for material-reuse matchmaking, linking reclaimed materials with construction projects. © Catherine De Wolf.

PLATE 19

→CONSUMERISM p.53

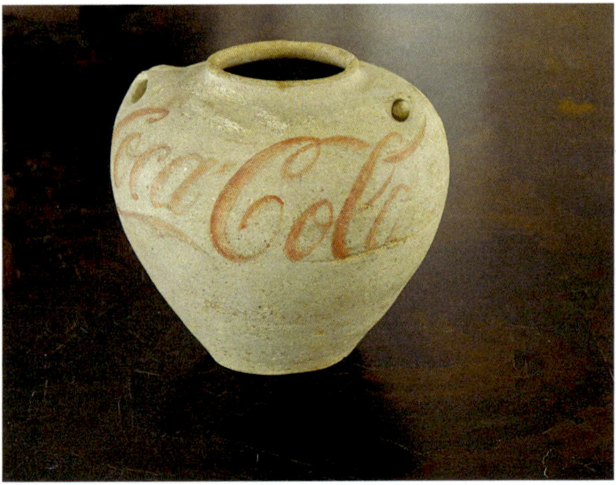

ULI SIGG

Ai Weiwei, *Han Dynasty Urn with Coca-Cola Logo*, 1995, clay urn, oil paint, 25 × 28 × 28 cm.

PLATE 20

→CONTAMINATION p.54

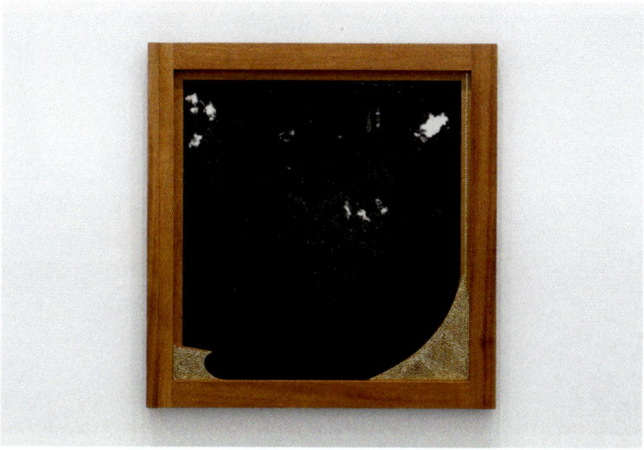

SAMMY BALOJI

Sammy Baloji, *Still Kongo IV*, 2024. Installation view of *Sammy Baloji* (4 October 2024 – 12 January 2025) at Goldsmiths Centre for Contemporary Art, London.

PLATE 21
→CONTEMPORARY p.55

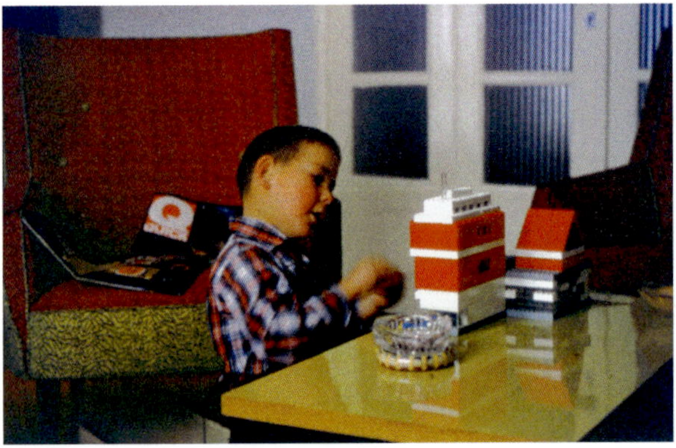

UDO KITTELMANN
Udo Kittelmann, age 5, Kozani, Greece, 1963.

PLATE 22
→CONTEXT p.55

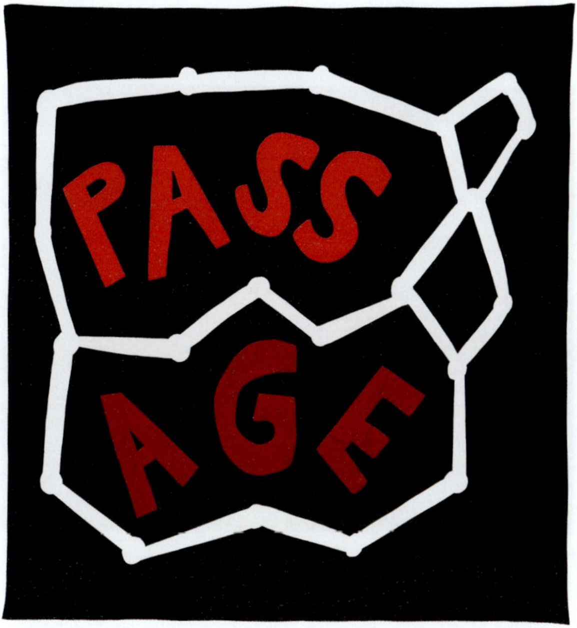

SUSAN HEFUNA
Susan Hefuna, *PASS AGE*, 2025, collage, Egyptian cotton, 198 × 211 cm.

PLATE 23
→CONVERSATION p.56

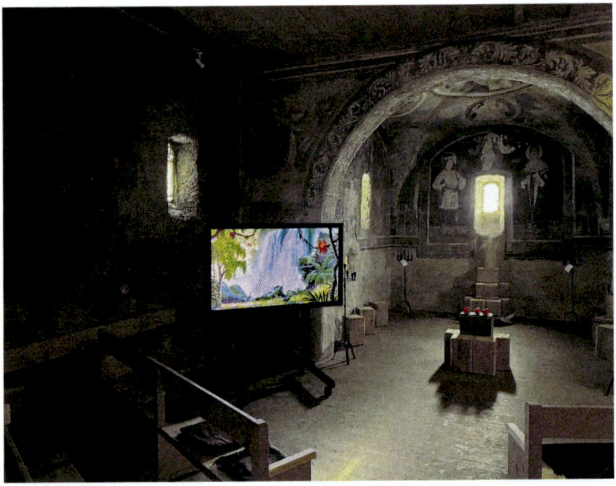

DAVID CLAERBOUT
David Claerbout, *The Pure Necessity*, 2016.
Installation view at the Chapel of San Bastiaun, Zuoz, January 2020 (shown during Engadin Art Talks 2020).

PLATE 24
→CORAL p.57

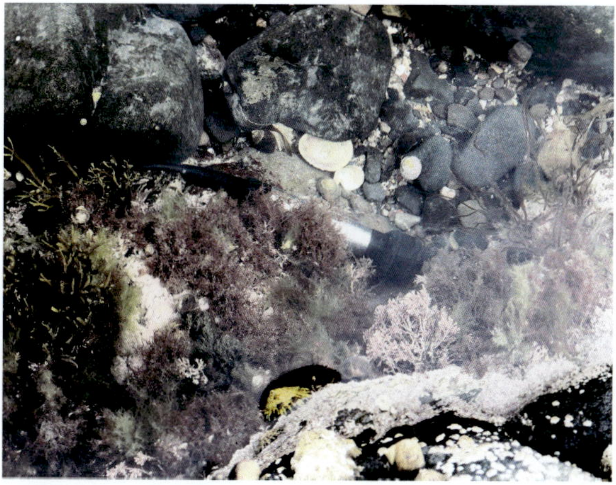

CHRIS WATSON
Underwater recording of coral reef.
© Photo by Chris Watson.

PLATE 25
→CREATURE p.58

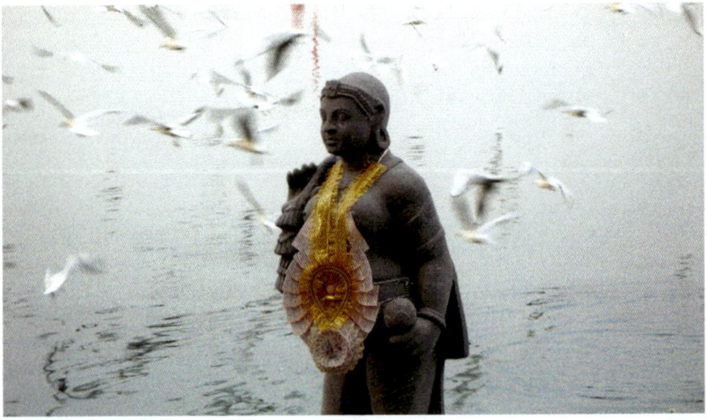

RAQS MEDIA COLLECTIVE
Raqs Media Collective, *Sleepwalker's Caravan*, 2008, video (prologue), video still, duration 11′.

PLATE 26
→CRITIQUE p.58

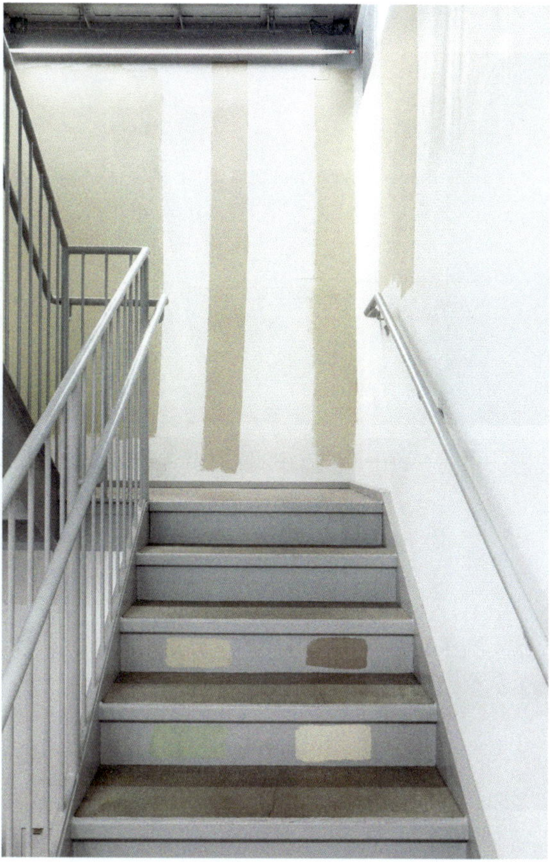

STEFANIE HESSLER
Helen Mirra, *Harmless Mistake*, 2023.
© Photo by Daniel Pérez. Courtesy of the artist and Swiss Institute.

PLATE 27
→CROSSING p.59

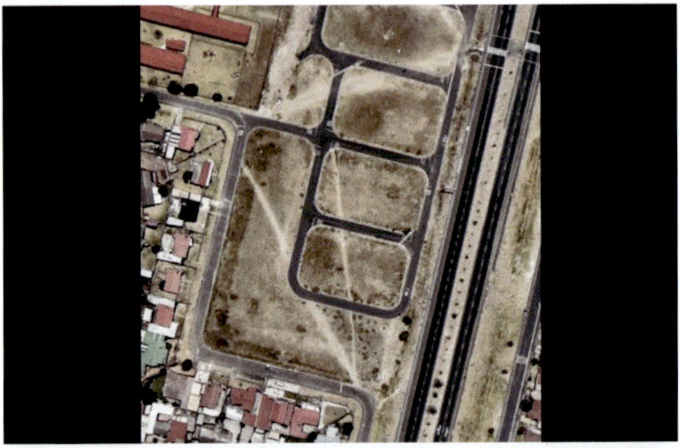

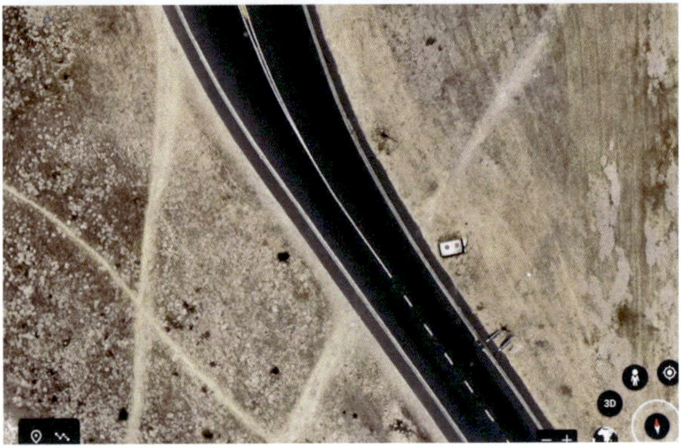

IGSHAAN ADAMS
Various images of desire lines used as process work.

PLATE 28
→CURVE p.61

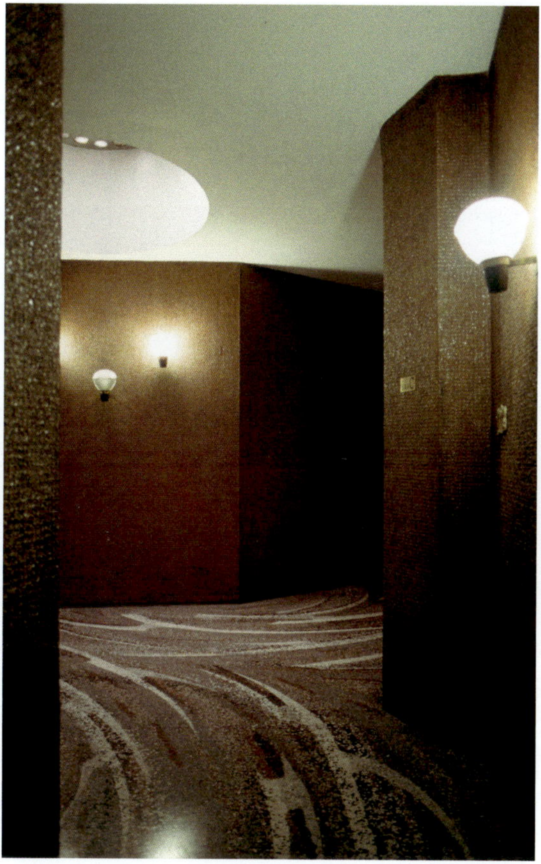

ELLI MOSAYEBI
Luigi Caccia Dominioni, Corso Italia 22–26, 1956–1961.
© Photo by Christian Inderbitzin.

PLATE 29

→DATABASE p.62

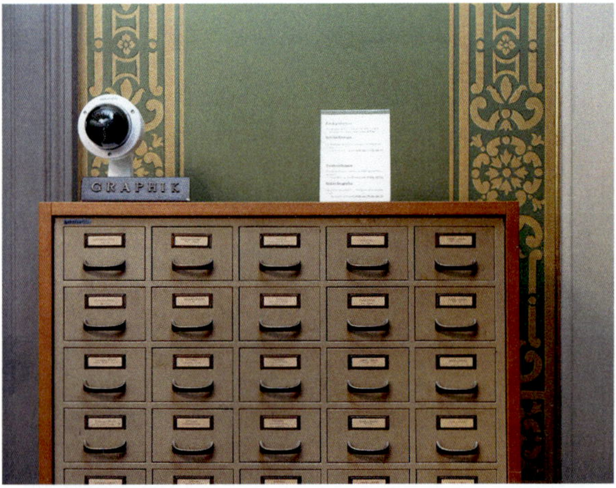

ARMIN LINKE
Photothek at the Kunsthistorisches Institut in Florenz – Max Planck Institute, Florence, Italy, 2018.

PLATE 30
→ DESERT p.105

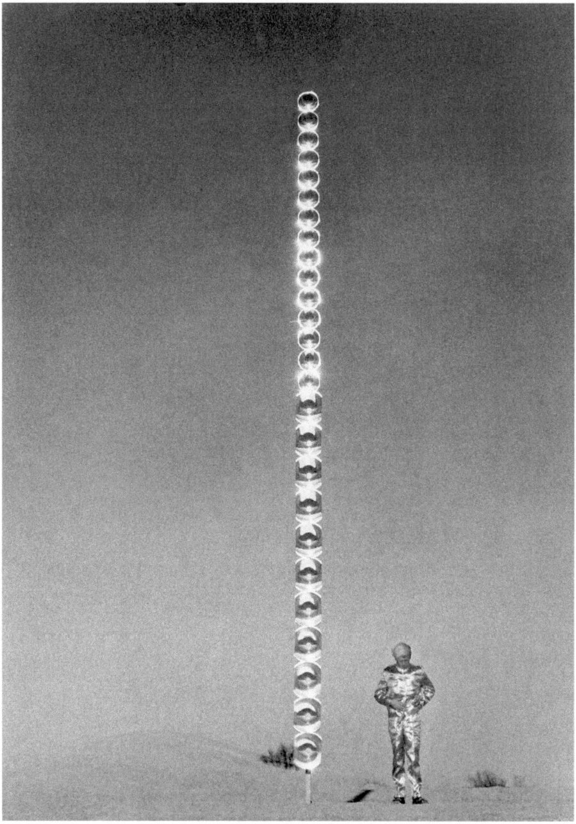

HEINZ MACK
Heinz Mack, *Light Stela in the Sahara* (still from the film *Tele-Mack*), Tunisia, 1968, aluminium reflectors, height 11 m; camera by Edwin Braun.

PLATE 31
→ DIRT p.108

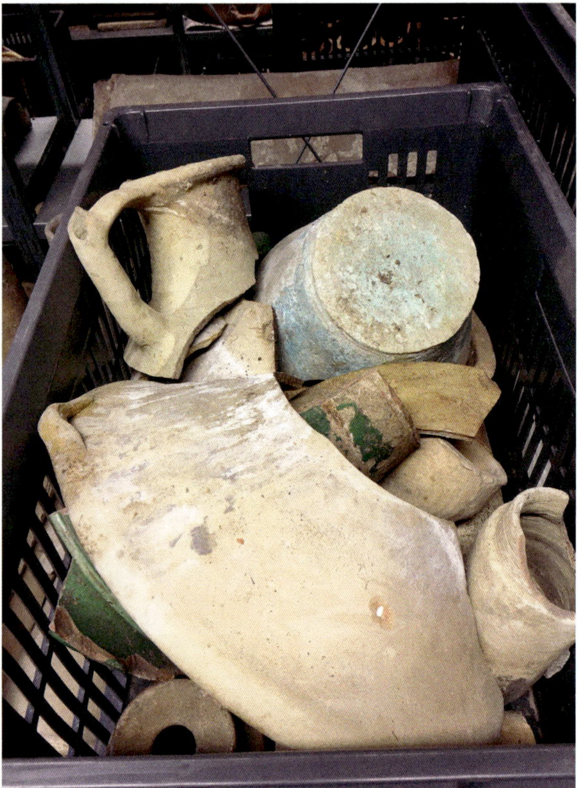

MATTHEW LUTZ-KINOY
Matthew Lutz-Kinoy and Natsuko Uchino, *Keramikos IV*, process and production, 2021.

PLATE 32
→DOUGHNUT p.111

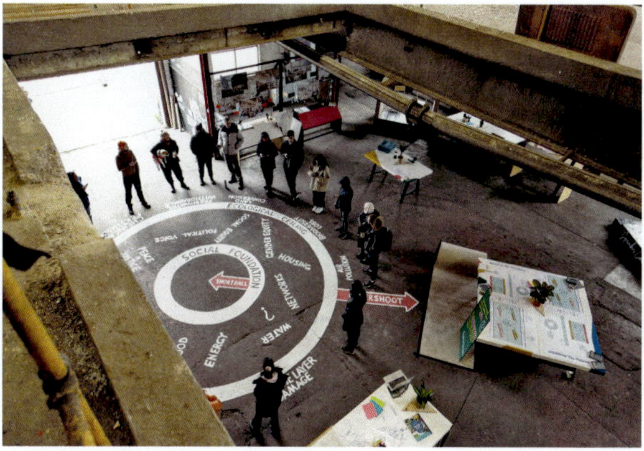

KATE RAWORTH
Community event by CIVIC SQUARE, Birmingham, United Kingdom, 2022.

PLATE 33
→DURATION p.111

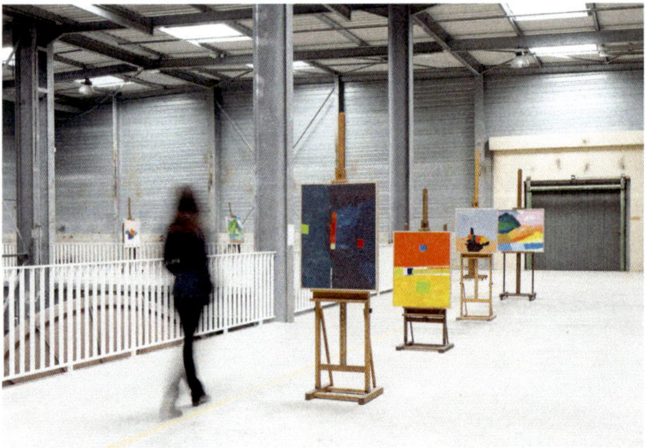

ETEL ADNAN
Etel Adnan exhibition view, Galleria Continua / Les Moulins, 2014.

Photo by Oak Taylor-Smith.

PLATE 34
→EARTH p.112

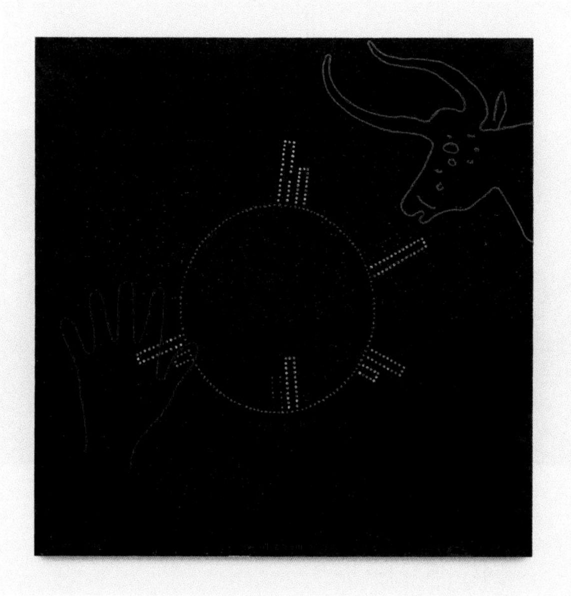

ERNESTO NETO
Ernesto Neto, *Devastação, o infinito bicho é (Devastation, the infinite animal is)* [from the series *Toneladas e Cifrões – A caverna contemporânea*], 2022, oil, steel, leather, soybeans, wood, brass, ceramic, cotton string, soil and banknotes on canvas, 120 × 120 cm. © Ernesto Neto. Courtesy of the private collection and Galerie Max Hetzler, Berlin | Paris | London | Marfa. Photo by Nicolas Brasseur.

PLATE 35
→EDUCATION p.113

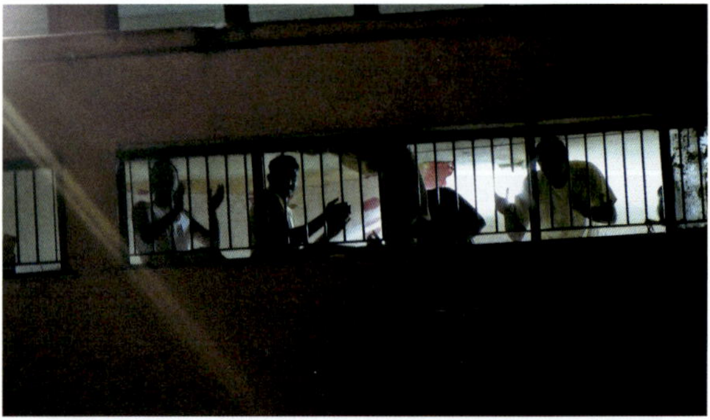

MENELAOS KARAMAGHIOLIS
Photograph documenting one of the groups of incarcerated youths with whom the artist worked as part of a contemporary art workshop at a juvenile prison, 2011.

PLATE 36
→EMPATHY p.114

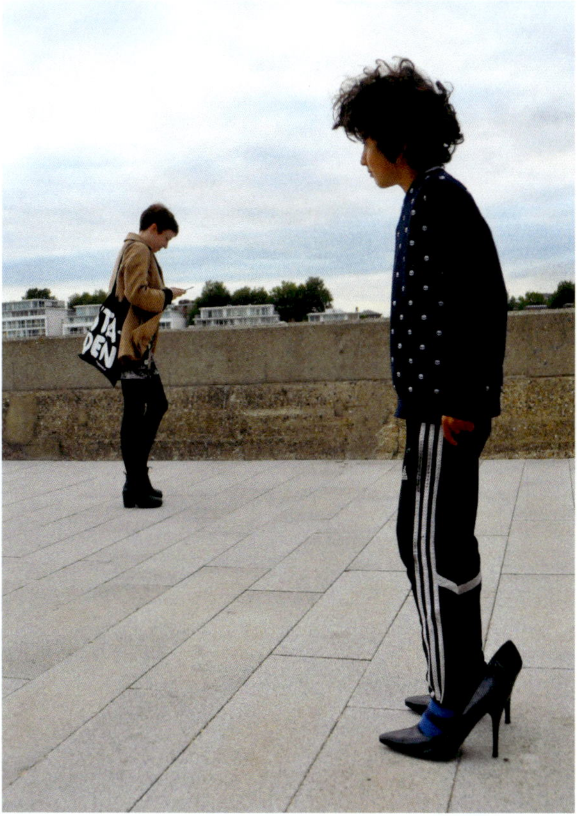

ROMAN KRZNARIC
A Mile in My Shoes by Empathy Museum.
© Photo by Kate Raworth.

PLATE 37
→ENCOUNTER p.114

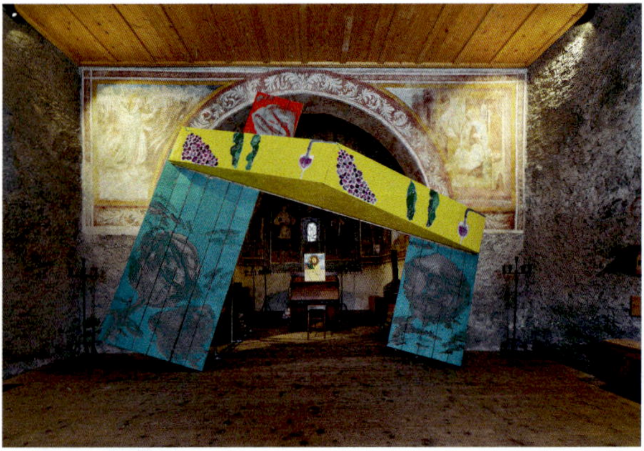

ALVARO BARRINGTON
Alvaro Barrington and Teresa Farrell, *Uncle A/Eat the Cake*.
Installation view at the Chapel of San Bastiaun, Zuoz, January 2025
(shown during Engadin Art Talks 2025).
Organised by Engadin Art Talks and Emalin.
© Photo by Saskja Rosset.

PLATE 38

→ENERGY p.115

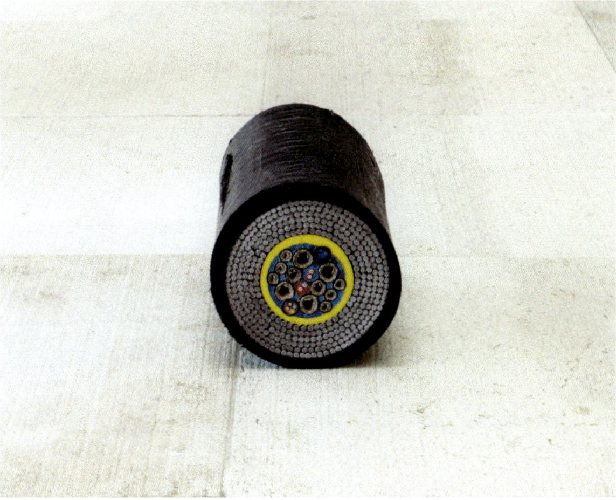

NINA CANELL

Nina Canell, *Brief Syllable (Bare)*, subsea umbilical cable, 2017.
Installation view at the Nordic Pavilion, Venice Biennale.
© Photo by Andrea Rossetti.

DEMOLITION

"In Switzerland[p.305], 80% of all waste[p.321] comes from the construction[p.53] and demolition sector. As architects and engineers, we have a huge responsibility to change[p.43] that. That's why I teach[p.306] my students how to disassemble buildings carefully, so materials[p.204] can be reused[p.285]. In just two days, my students dismantled an entire building and reused the materials to build a new structure using computational design algorithms[p.27] we developed with MIT."

CATHERINE DE WOLF
Professor, civil engineer, architect, and founder and director of the chair of Circular Engineering for Architecture (CEA), ETH Zurich
E.A.T. 2023: Hoffnung? Hoffnung!, Zuoz

DESERT

"I prefer the untouchable landscapes of the desert and the Arctic[p.30]. I admire the serenity of space as it stretches away, untiring and infinite[p.190]. In such spaces, the clarity of light and the fullness of silence[p.297] are forever expanding. Light unveils space, gives it structure. And silence isn't just the absence[p.23] of sound[p.300]; it is space made audible. The desert, in this sense, is not a void[p.320], but a presence[p.229]. It is in this kind of environment that one becomes[p.35] truly aware of their own physical condition. You are confronted[p.52] with yourself, in front of yourself. The silence presses down, and the landscape becomes a mirror[p.208]."

HEINZ MACK
Sculptor and painter
E.A.T. 2017: Snow and Desert, Zuoz
→ PLATE 30 p.95

DESERTED

"When we think of the desert[p.105], we usually imagine[p.146] emptiness. It's no coincidence that 'desert' and 'deserted' share the same root. But maybe it's more interesting to see the desert as full; full of people, animals, territorial claims, economic interests and cultural[p.60] production. Let's shift[p.296] our perspective[p.223] and look at the richness[p.286] of the desert instead of its supposed emptiness."

MANUEL HERZ
Architect
E.A.T. 2017: Snow and Desert, Zuoz

DESIRE

"Architecture[p.29] of the
mind[p.207],
walls are invisible –
shaped[p.295] by
algorithms[p.27],
clicks and searches.
A house[p.142] built on
desire,
a space of perpetual
longing[p.201]
to feel human[p.143]
we move through it."

PAMELA ROSENKRANZ
Artist
2024: E.A.T. × Kunsthalle Zürich, Zurich

DETECTABILITY

"There is a very interesting condition in forensic terms, it is called a threshold[p.308] of detectability. State violence[p.317] often operates just below the threshold of detectability. Again and again, our investigations[p.196] reveal how such acts are calibrated to remain on the edge of what can be seen[p.296] or proven, right where evidence[p.119] begins to disappear."

EYAL WEIZMAN
Architect, founder and director of Forensic Architecture and professor of Spatial and Visual Cultures at Goldsmiths, University of London
E.A.T. 2016: Traces and Fragments, Zuoz

DEVIATION

"There are buildings in Accra that have stood for fifty years and have never been used. Dead[p.63] buildings. The government keeps building, but many of these projects remain unfinished. Meanwhile, these spaces are being occupied[p.218] by squatters – people marked as social deviants. But they are survivors. I've never been afraid[p.123] to do a project there. These spaces are important because they show how crisis produces forms[p.127] of resilience[p.282]. And in some ways, that becomes[p.35] part of the DNA[p.110] of the city[p.47] – the occupation itself becomes the architecture[p.29]."

IBRAHIM MAHAMA
Artist
E.A.T. 2016: Traces and Fragments, Zuoz

DIALOGUE

"My virtual feminist museum[p.212] can be seen as engaging with German art historian Aby Warburg's *Mnemosyne Atlas* in method, drawing parallels in how it presents relationships[p.280], rhythms[p.286] and impressions [across images[p.146]] – aspects that cannot be fully expressed in dominant terms but become[p.35] present[p.230] through aesthetic[p.25] transformation[p.310]. It is conceived as a space for encounter[p.114] and dialogue, rather than a chronological narrative[p.213]."

GRISELDA POLLOCK
Art historian, cultural analyst and Professor emerita of Social and Critical Histories of Art at the University of Leeds
E.A.T. 2021: Longue Durée, livestream

DIGITAL

"I began reflecting[p.279] on what will remain when we are gone: the vast accumulation of digital debris scattered across the planet. I visited Bayan Obo, a massive open-pit mine in Inner Mongolia, where most of the rare earth elements used in our devices are extracted. The site feels like the shadow, or negative space, of Bruegel's Tower of Babel. I collected phones, computers and various tech components, then melted[p.206] 1.5 tons of them to create an artificial[p.31] lava, reverting the material[p.204] to a pre-industrial state. What emerged is a mineral substance[p.302] crystallised[p.59] between past and future[p.130]."

JULIAN CHARRIÈRE
Artist
E.A.T. 2017: Snow and Desert, Zuoz

DIGITALISATION

"Construction[p.53] accounts for over 30% of global material[p.204] consumption[p.53]. Yet, when you compare today's building sites with those from a century ago, the methods look strikingly similar. Our aim is to change[p.43] this by bringing digitalisation into the industry[p.189] – through computational design and automated fabrication. This approach enables us to minimize waste[p.321], conserve resources[p.283] and unlock entirely new architectural[p.29] possibilities."

BENJAMIN
DILLENBURGER
Architect
E.A.T. 2022: Matter and Memory,
Zuoz

DIGNITY

"The vision of a sustainable[p.304] city[p.304] transcends[p.309] a mere ecological[p.113] equation; it is, fundamentally, an urgent[p.314] response[p.284] to social inequality[p.190] and urban segregation. The project for the city of Duque de Caxias, in Brazil in 2012, sought to rescue the value of public space through social urbanism and an architecture[p.29] that not only respects[p.284] the environment, but also celebrates human[p.143] dignity. True sustainability flourishes when inclusion[p.189] and quality[p.274] of life become the foundation of all urban planning. We must always ask: who are we building the future[p.130] for?"

PAULO SERGIO
NIEMEYER
Architect and designer
E.A.T. 2012: Vision for the Alps,
Zuoz

DINOSAUR

"The museum[p.212] is a device that combines material[p.204] and memory[p.206] in a very sophisticated and efficient way. But this memory has to be kissed[p.197] awake again and again. Museums are slow[p.298], they don't change[p.43] fast, they change at a sort of dinosaur pace. One of the big dilemmas of museums today is how to engage[p.116] with critical[p.58] thinking and institutional critique while still continuing to operate within existing structures."

ANN DEMEESTER
Director of Kunsthaus Zurich
E.A.T. 2022: Matter and Memory,
Zuoz

DIRT

"That slipware project was actually a kind of live-action role play. We pretended to be Bernard Leach and Shoji Hamada; two historical potters who forged a cross-cultural exchange[p.120] between

Japan and England. Their studio in Cornwall was built on land where they were literally digging in the dirt and finding p.125 old pottery shards with slipware motifs p.211. That idea p.145 of digging into the earth p.112 and finding a fragment p.127 of history p.140 – that's central to what we do. Everywhere in the world, if you dig, you'll find pottery shards. It's a global archeology of touch p.308."

MATTHEW LUTZ-KINOY
Artist
E.A.T. 2023: Hoffnung? Hoffnung!, Zuoz

→PLATE 31 p.96

DISCOMFORT

"When I was a kid, the very thought of nature p.213 terrified me. To me, it was this mysterious, scary unknown p.313, associated with discomfort, mosquitoes, dirt p.108 and all sorts of unnecessary physical exertion. While my friends p.128 vacationed in fun or exotic places, my parents were obsessed with the classic American p.28 road trip. They would always drag me across the American West p.321, where we stayed in roadside motels or even on farms p.122. Here my stepfather would always gleefully recall how his mother loved p.202 the smell of horse manure, which I found utterly repulsive. Then, one year, they bought a tent. That really offended my sensibilities. I saw p.296 the tent as everything we'd evolved beyond. We had spent millennia overcoming nature, and here we were, voluntarily returning to it."

ARIC CHEN
Curator, writer and director of the Zaha Hadid Foundation
E.A.T. 2018: Side Country Side, Zuoz

DISTORTION

"Always be in transit –
a stream of data,
a constant scroll.
To feel human p.143
we are fed the image p.146,
the meme,
and we consume p.53.
We are both the viewer and
the viewed,
the subject and the
object p.217.
In this house p.142

we are constantly
rearranged,
distorted into something
we might not even
recognise.[p.277]"

JOANA DE LA FONTAINE
Architect
2024: E.A.T. × Kunsthalle Zürich,
Zurich

DNA

"Epigenetics explores the regulation of genome activity that occurs without any changes[p.43] in the underlying DNA sequence. This regulation can involve biochemical modifications to DNA or its associated proteins, as well as RNA molecules (small and long). These epigenetic factors act like multiple softwares directing the DNA's hardware, responding[p.284] dynamically and being influenced by conditions like diet, stress or toxins. They can have lasting effects on genome activity and gene expression and, ultimately, health."

ISABELLE MANSUY
Professor in neuroepigenetics
in the Medical Faculty
of the University of Zurich
and the Department of Health
Science and Technology
of ETH Zurich
E.A.T. 2022: Matter and Memory,
Zuoz

DOG

"For me, the alpine[p.28] pasture is also something rebellious. You're suddenly transported back to the Middle Ages – no hot water, sometimes not even any water in the hut. And you get used to it. You learn[p.199] from the dog to make do with as little as possible. The dog is ready in the morning, while the tourist takes three hours to get going."

LEO TUOR
Author in the Romansh language
E.A.T. 2021: Longue Durée,
livestream

DOMESTICITY

"I often ask myself: how can we, as architects, pursue ideals[p.145] like equality and democracy, yet end up with generic buildings? The answer might lie in our failure[p.121] to recognise[p.277] how personal and shifting[p.296] the concept of 'domesticity' really is. We try to define[p.64] standards, but those standards flatten the complexities of individual[p.189] lives."

TATIANA BILBAO
Architect
E.A.T. 2020: Silent – Listen, Zuoz

DOUGHNUT

"That little criss-cross curve[p.61] of supply and demand – it's an icon[p.144]. It slips past our analytical minds[p.207] and embeds itself deep in our thinking. It makes the market appear to be the natural centre of the economy, but it completely leaves out the state, the household and the commons. That's why we need new images[p.146]. 'The Doughnut Economy', my framework[p.128] for a 21st-century economy, starts with the planet – not with money[p.210], not with interest rates – and asks: what are the ecological[p.113] boundaries[p.39] we must not overshoot, and what are the social foundations no one should fall[p.122] below? It's about finding[p.125] a balance[p.34]: meeting the needs of all people within the means of the planet."

KATE RAWORTH
Economist, creator of theDoughnut of social and planetary boundaries, and co-founder of Doughnut Economics Action Lab
E.A.T. 2021: Longue Durée, livestream
→PLATE 32 p.97

DRINKING

"The drinking of alcohol refers to a kind of cathartic emotional behaviour[p.35], but also to the deadening of the material[p.204] spirit. Like all socially complex substances[p.302], alcohol is both a great emancipator and a psychological oppressor[p.219]."

HELEN MARTEN
Artist
E.A.T. 2012: Vision for the Alps, Zuoz

DURATION

"We live in a civilisation[p.47] that is impatient, where everything is expected to happen quickly. This speed is often seen as a victory, as something positive. We are an invasive generation[p.133], happy to travel far by moving fast. But in doing so, we have killed the pleasure of traveling. We don't really travel anymore; we simply go from one point to another. That is not a voyage. A true voyage is about duration – why? Because it gives you the opportunity to have experiences."

ETEL ADNAN
Artist
E.A.T. 2021: Longue Durée, livestream
→ PLATE 33 [p.98]

DUST

"The Russian interdisciplinary scientist Chizhevsky believed[p.36] that every 11 years, at the start of each new solar cycle[p.61], major historical[p.140] events occurred. He found[p.125] correlations between solar activity and revolutionary[p.286] movements. We're now trying to understand[p.313] how planetary rhythms[p.286] relate to cosmic dust. In an experiment[p.120] at the University of Chicago, we played 'Ziggy Stardust' at a higher frequency to levitate cosmic dust – material[p.204] from outer space – to see how these rhythms might shape[p.295] planetary formation. After all, we started as dust."

TOMÁS SARACENO
Artist
E.A.T. 2021: Longue Durée, livestream

E

EARTH

"We know that we are eating our lovely[p.202] planet Earth, and we don't know how to get out of that, because our society[p.299] is based on consuming. We consume[p.53] all the time, and through consumption we move the economy, but it spreads o ut very unequally. Some people consume far more of the Earth than others. There is hunger, poverty, and many wars. This situation is really ... big. And then there is the idea[p.145] of sustainability[p.304], which is already changing[p.43] something in our spirit. But the habits[p.139] that we have, we need to begin changing now."

ERNESTO NETO
Artist
E.A.T. 2023: Hoffnung? Hoffnung!, Zuoz
→ PLATE 34 [p.99]

ECOLOGY

"When we opened during COVID, we were still in the construction[p.53] of Atelier LUMA. LUMA is always in progress – constantly evolving. There's always something happening somewhere. One of our biggest successes is the park designed by landscape architect Bas Smets. It shows clearly the possibility of lowering temperatures[p.307] through ecological design, which is now being studied at Harvard's GSD. We're helping develop models[p.208] for the Mediterranean's[p.205] hottest cities[p.47]. LUMA is deeply plugged into the Mediterranean – it's not static, it's a living experiment[p.120]."

MAJA HOFFMANN
Executive president and founder of Luma Foundation and Luma Arles
2025: E.A.T. × St. Moritz, St. Moritz

ECOSYSTEM

"For over 40 years, water has leaked from supply and sewage pipes into the historic[p.140] buildings of the Khalifa neighbourhood. It's damaging, yes – but it's also water, a scarce and precious resource[p.283] in Egypt. So we started harvesting it. In some cases, we installed pumps to extract it and use it to green[p.138] abandoned lots, transforming[p.310] them into community[p.51] gardens[p.131]. In one site of only 80 square metres, we extract 100 cubic metres of water per day. That's a huge amount. We're now using some of it for urban farming[p.122], fire[p.125] control and municipal cleaning. These interventions are creating a new ecosystem in a dry, neglected urban context[p.55]."

MAY AL-IBRASHY
Architect, founder and principal of Megawra and co-founder and chair of the Built Environment Collective
E.A.T. 2025: Form and Impact, Zuoz

EDUCATION

"In 2011, I found[p.125] myself in a juvenile prison, trying something that seemed absurd: offering contemporary[p.55] art[p.31] workshops to incarcerated youth –

many of whom already had children, had never attended school[p.291], and couldn't read[p.276] or write. What began as an experiment[p.120] became[p.35] a meaningful[p.204] alternative form of education. It led to theatrical performances[p.222] and concerts in the prison, art works created by the prisoners, artists and the collective Døcumatism, touring shows in other prisons, an exhibition at the National Museum[p.212] of Contemporary Art in Athens & Centre d'Art Contemporain in Geneva and a series of films. This practice[p.228], using workshops and artworks, gave rise to a temporary sense of freedom[p.128], a moment when even the prison guards joined in, and for one night, everyone forgot the confinement."

MENELAOS KARAMAGHIOLIS
Artist
E.A.T. 2024: Jenseits von Ohnmacht – Beyond Powerless, Zuoz
→ PLATE 35 p.100

EMPATHY

"I've been exploring empathy for about 15 years because I noticed a growing[p.138] lack of it in society[p.299] – increasing divisions between political groups, generations[p.133] and migrants versus non-migrants. The ability to put yourself in someone else's shoes and see[p.296] the world through their eyes – known as cognitive empathy – develops in all of us from an early age. This ability is essential for addressing social conflicts and building understanding[p.313]."

ROMAN KRZNARIC
Philosopher
E.A.T. 2021: Longue Durée, livestream
→ PLATE 36 p.101

ENCOUNTER

"Art[p.31] for me is always about an encounter – an encounter that lets you understand[p.313] who you are and how things affect you, good or bad[p.33]. When the opportunity came to exhibit in the beautiful[p.34] Chapel of San Bastiaun in Zuoz[p.324], I thought I'd make a show that helped me think through the life of Christ p.45. Religion p.280 once served as a compass for many, but when Nietzsche said 'God is dead', at least in America p.28, consumerism p.53 became p.35 the new North Star. You're no longer a citizen – you're a consumer. And I'm a consumer too. That shift p.296 profoundly shapes p.295 how we see ourselves."

ALVARO BARRINGTON
Artist
E.A.T. 2025: Form and Impact, Zuoz
→PLATE 37 p.102

ENDURANCE

"Like Manuel Herz, who talked about 10 years of engagement p.116, I began to think about environmentalism not as a short-term campaign, but as something that lasts at least 25 years. In one essay I called this 'Long Environmentalism'. The struggle to create and protect p.232 the Arctic p.30 National Wildlife Refuge has been going on for eight decades, and it's a form of endurance, a generational p.133 commitment that blends art p.31, activism and scholarship."

SUBHANKAR BANERJEE
Photographer, writer, curator and environmental humanities scholar
E.A.T. 2017: Snow and Desert, Zuoz

ENERGY

"Energy has been present p.230 in my work for a long time p.308, often intuitively, as I've tried to slow p.298 it down or make it accessible p.23 in unfamiliar ways. When I began working with cable fragments p.127, it was a shift p.296 in sculptural approach. These subaquatic cables – buried under the sea or underground – carry p.41 power and information p.190, yet we rarely see them. I was struck by how silent p.297 this enormous flow of energy is. Showing the cable as a severed object p.217 made it feel raw p.275 and uncomfortable – something usually fluid p.126 and connected p.53 suddenly inert. The more I learned p.199, especially from Nicole Starosielski's brilliant book *The Undersea Network* (2015), the clearer it became p.35: these infrastructures p.191 aren't neutral p.214 or global in any utopian p.315 sense. They're deeply territorial, politically charged[p.44], and entangled with power structures that shape[p.295] our world."

NINA CANELL
Artist
E.A.T. × St. Moritz, St. Moritz
→PLATE 38 p.103

ENGADIN ART TALKS

"For over 10 years, Engadin Art Talks have been a key event in the Swiss[p.305] cultural[p.60] landscape. It has earned a reputation that extends far beyond national borders. Given the proximity of Zuoz[p.324] to Davos, the press has even dubbed it the 'World Economic Forum of the Arts'. I am delighted that a prestigious Swiss initiative has found[p.125] its place in Paris – the European metropolis par excellence – and, even more so, at the invitation of the Centre Pompidou[p.41], a leading[p.198] institution for art and culture. I truly cannot imagine[p.146] a more fitting venue."

ROBERTO BALZARETTI
Ambassador of Switzerland
to France 2020–2024
2023: E.A.T. × Centre Pompidou, Paris

ENGAGEMENT

"In Burkina Faso, temperatures[p.307] can reach[p.276] up to almost 50 degrees Celsius. To cool the classrooms in a simple and sustainable[p.304] way, we designed a special window unit. It consists of a bench made from eucalyptus wood[p.323]; a fast-growing species that was introduced to improve the soil, but has since proven invasive, increasing the desert[p.105]. Still, instead of discarding it, we decided[p.63] to make use of what's available. Underneath the bench, there's a small container[p.54] of water. As air[p.27] flows through the window, it passes over the water, adding moisture and cooling the indoor space slightly. Very simple. That's what we do. We find[p.125] what is available, and use it in a sustainable way. I don't want my people to keep complaining about colonisation, about whatever. That was a long time ago. This is our time[p.308] to engage ourselves and change[p.43] our world."

FRANCIS KÉRÉ
Architect
E.A.T. 2017: Snow and Desert, Zuoz
→ PLATE 39 [p.150]

ENOUGH

"To move beyond powerlessness[p.228], I believe[p.36] we need anger and courage. Artists like Zanele Muholi, who celebrates queer communities[p.51] in South Africa[p.26], show how vital it is to disrupt the status quo. The dominant elites maintain power through deference, but real change[p.43] will only come when young people say: 'enough is enough'. Respect[p.284] alone won't move the needle."

PAOLA AUDREY NDENGUE
Content producer, entrepreneur and media personality
E.A.T. 2024: Jenseits von Ohnmacht – Beyond Powerless, Zuoz

EPHEMERALITY

"Flowers are actually the sexual[p.295] organs of plants. That means that each time you offer someone a bouquet, you're basically giving them a bunch of dicks and vaginas – disposable ones at that – with a seasonal, ephemeral[p.117] nature[p.213]. Imagine[p.146] if your own sexual organs functioned[p.129] like your hair, nails, or even worse, like pimples – something that grows[p.138] independently[p.189] of you, and falls[p.122] away once used. This is what sex looks like for plants: the constant regrowth and shedding of organs, depending entirely on atmospheric[p.31] conditions. It's a very different conception of the body[p.38] – of life as a form of continuous[p.55] DIY."

EMANUELE COCCIA
Philosopher, lecturer and author
E.A.T. 2020: Silent – Listen, Zuoz

EPIC

"The epic of Dhat al-Himma is largely forgotten – even in the Arab world; most know only the name. It's about a woman warrior who didn't want to marry[p.203], preferring to be wedded to her sword. She eventually did marry and had a black child, which caused scandal. It also includes a queen of the Uyghurs who loved[p.202] taking lovers. The themes – gender[p.132], race, sexuality[p.295] – were all there, written in a bold and crude language[p.198] that you don't see today. I made sculptures based on the characters[p.43]: Dhat al-Himma, the queen, her lover, the horse that everyone tried to steal. These epics embody the entire culture[p.60] of a people."

SIMONE FATTAL
Artist
E.A.T. 2024: Jenseits von Ohnmacht – Beyond Powerless, Zuoz

ERASURE

"One of the archival[p.30] photographs I worked with shows two children sitting beside a sign that reads[p.276]: 'Each worker must bring 50 flies in order to receive his daily ration.' The image[p.146] dates back to 1929 and reflects[p.279] the colonial[p.50] obsession with sanitation and control. It wasn't enough[p.117] for Congolese workers to extract minerals – they were also forced to participate[p.221] in fly-hunting campaigns to 'clean' the city[p.47]. I traced[p.309] the history[p.140] of these campaigns and even located boxes of collected flies in Lubumbashi's entomology museum[p.212], labelled by name and location. I then photographed these materials[p.204] and made aerial images of the physical boundaries[p.39] that once separated the white and Black parts of the city. All of this came together in a work I titled *Essay on Urban Planning*, which was shown at the 2015 Venice Biennale. It's a way of confronting[p.52] how colonial violence[p.317] is embedded not only in architecture[p.29] and infrastructure[p.191], but in everyday acts of erasure and control."

SAMMY BALOJI
Artist
E.A.T. 2025: Form and Impact, Zuoz

EROSION

"In Venice, in the little-visited garden[p.131] behind the Biennale's main pavilion, we built a model[p.208] city[p.47] from unbaked clay[p.47], knowing the climate would slowly[p.298] wash it away. As the clay eroded, plants took root – not the cultivated local garden species already there, but invasive newcomers from abroad. We treated them like in a botanical garden, giving each its scientific name on a label. The result was an open garden shaped[p.295] by time[p.308] and chance, raising questions[p.275] about what is considered native or foreign in a landscape, and how identities[p.146] shift[p.296]."

GÜNTHER VOGT
Landscape architect and professor emeritus
2024: E.A.T. × Kunsthalle Zürich, Zurich

ETERNITY

"The Moon[p.210] is drifting away from us. Once, it was far closer to Earth[p.112], its gravitational pull slowing[p.298] our planet's rotation and lengthening our days. In the distant future[p.130], an Earth day will last an entire month, as the Moon and Earth become[p.35] tidally locked in an eternal embrace. This celestial ballet reveals: even the most constant things in our lives – the sunrise, the gentle moonlight – are but fleeting moments in an unending, cosmic transformation[p.310]."

BEN MOORE
Professor of astrophysics, author, musician and director of the Center for Theoretical Astrophysics and Cosmology at the University of Zurich
E.A.T. 2021: Longue Durée, livestream

EVIDENCE

"It's important to reclaim[p.277] the public and political power of forensics as a citizen science. Our investigations[p.196] are never limited to the courtroom, we also work with political groups and communities[p.51]. Every case is designed to operate across multiple forums: legal, public and cultural[p.60]. We insist that evidence must circulate widely, never in isolation."

EYAL WEIZMAN
Architect, founder and director of Forensic Architecture and professor of Spatial and Visual Cultures at Goldsmiths, University of London
E.A.T. 2016: Traces and Fragments, Zuoz

EXCHANGE

"Matthew-Lutz Kinoy and I began researching motifs[p.211] we found[p.125] in Hispano-Moorish pottery – floral patterns, decorative shapes[p.295] – and tried to trace[p.309] their origins. Some motifs appeared in Chinese[p.44] pottery, others in Iran. We realised these were travelling motifs, carried[p.41] across regions through trade, migration and cultural[p.60] exchange. Our collaboration[p.49] started to focus on uncovering those historical[p.140] moments where style[p.302] and technique merge. Ceramics[p.42] have always been vessels for such exchanges – they were the first packaging, carrying not just goods, but stories."

NATSUKO UCHINO
Artist
E.A.T. 2023: Hoffnung? Hoffnung!, Zuoz
→ PLATE 40 [p.151]

EXILE

"Mountains[p.211] are often seen as places for tourism, nature[p.213] and health; a voluntary, mostly temporary escape for a better life. What was once harsh and forbidding now feels more familiar and domesticated[p.110]. Yet, there is a counter-narrative to tourism and leisure trips: the history[p.140] of exile and imprisonment. Forced exile stands in contrast to self-chosen refuge – in other words[p.324], the mountain as a prison."

NIKOLAUS HIRSCH
Architect, curator and educator
E.A.T. 2011: Mapping the Alps, Zuoz

EXPERIMENT

"What we appreciate is a certain fragility – in materials[p.204], in construction[p.53] – that speaks to how far we can push the limits of norms and standards. Architecture[p.29] is often governed by strict regulations, almost like a recipe. But we like to experiment, take risks, and in doing so reveal another kind of beauty[p.34] – one that comes from exploring the expressive potential of materials."

STÉPHANIE BRU
Architect and co-founder of Paris-based architectural studio Bruther
2023: E.A.T. × Centre Pompidou, Paris

EXPOSURE

"Exposure refers to contact with environmental factors and life experiences such as diet, stress, medication, chemicals or pollutants – each of which can influence every cell in the body p.38 and impact p.148 overall health. If germ cells are affected, these changes p.43 may be transmitted to future p.130 generations p.133. For instance, when a pregnant woman is exposed to stress or pesticides not only can her baby be affected, but so are the baby's germ cells – suggesting that three generations can be exposed simultaneously. Whether some of the epigenetic changes can be maintained and permanently p.223 inherited p.191 remains a central question p.275 in the study of epigenetic inheritance."

ISABELLE MANSUY
Professor in neuroepigenetics in the Medical Faculty of the University of Zurich and the Department of Health Science and Technology of ETH Zurich
E.A.T. 2022: Matter and Memory, Zuoz

F

FAILURE

"It all starts with a curiosity about how things are made. Whenever I decide p.63 to work with a specific material p.204 or process – whether it's steel or how neon light is produced – it feels right to go directly to the source. But it has become p.35 increasingly complex: it's hard to trace p.309 where materials come from, how they're made, who is involved, and what the social implications are. Sometimes, during production, things go wrong – failed attempts or leftover pieces. Going back and asking how those failures happened can be just as interesting."

RAPHAEL HEFTI
Artist
E.A.T. 2021: Longue Durée, livestream

FAITH

"The human p.143 tendency towards hope p.142 needs anchors – something the fragile seedlings of hope can cling to and grow p.138 from. Looking back, it might sound like

I had everything figured out, but that wasn't the case. As a child grows and begins to think, faith wavers. The world is too cruel, and the one who guides the heavens feels too distant. Yet somehow, something in me continued[p.55] to seek trust[p.312], comfort and a sense of belonging[p.36] – even in a world shaped[p.295] by dictatorship and fear[p.123]."

JOACHIM GAUCK
Former Federal President of Germany (2012–2017)
E.A.T. 2023: Hoffnung? Hoffnung!, Zuoz

FALLING

"In 2009, science fiction[p.291] writer Bruce Sterling coined the term 'dark euphoria' to describe the coming decade. And that's the decade we've just lived through: things falling apart, endless possibilities we somehow dread. It's like falling towards Earth[p.112] at 900 kilometres per hour and suddenly realising there's no Earth there. That's dark euphoria."

EMILY SEGAL
Artist and writer
E.A.T. 2018: Side Country Side, Zuoz

FARMING

"Precision farming, in the name of efficiency, systematically eliminates anything deemed unnecessary; trees[p.311], grass[p.137], even entire farmhouses. The result is a kind of desert[p.105], where digital[p.107] logic manifests physically as absence[p.23]. It's a stark landscape in which the virtual becomes[p.35] devastatingly real."

REM KOOLHAAS
Architect and writer
E.A.T. 2018: Side Country Side, Zuoz
→ PLATE 41 p.152

FASHION

"I went to my first live fashion show – this was before you could see them online – and I was just blown away by the theatre of it. It felt more theatrically powerful than anything I was seeing in the theatre at that time[p.308]. Around the same period, I also attended my first voguing[p.319] ball. After seeing both, I couldn't put myself back together. They affected me deeply, filled me with thoughts I couldn't articulate. And ironically, I had a performance[p.222] scheduled at Judson Church – the epicentre of conceptual dance[p.61] – so I created a piece out of that inspiration[p.192]. It was minimalist voguing: walking[p.320], posing and gazing, just that. I performed it to *Ode to Boy* by Yazoo, and to my surprise[p.303], the room erupted in applause. I was so stunned, I just left. I didn't know anyone there. But I knew I had touched[p.308] on something new."

TRAJAL HARRELL
Choreographer and dancer
2023: E.A.T. × Centre Pompidou, Paris

FEAR

"One of the characteristics[p.43] of hope[p.142] that I find most interesting is how intangible and invisible it is. Like the flame of a candle in the dark[p.62], I think we can only understand[p.313] what hope truly means in a desperate situation. For me, German philosopher Ernst Bloch's *The Principle of Hope* (1954) was a huge inspiration[p.192] – and also an encouragement – in making artworks, because it proposes a very essential idea[p.145]: the enemy of hope is not despair; the enemy of hope is fear."

CAMILLE HENROT
Artist
E.A.T. 2023: Hoffnung? Hoffnung!, Zuoz

FEMALE

"I got bored with the conversation[p.56] about criticising. I was like, come on, who are these mega-humans we supposedly had in the past? A woman comes up and they're like, 'There's a lot of problems with her.' Really? That's just the inherent flaw in the female: that she's not quite a full human. I think we were poised to have a female leader[p.198] in the USA. And then came this global pushback: Russia, the FBI, and the Voting Rights Act softened. A three-pronged assault to make a woman not become[p.35] president[p.230]."

EILEEN MYLES
Poet, novelist and art journalist
E.A.T. 2017: Snow and Desert, Zuoz

FEMININE

"The feminine is not simply the gendered[p.132] opposite of

the masculine. In phallocentric culture[p.60], it represents[p.281] the unspoken – like death[p.63] and trauma[p.311] – that is overwritten by social norms. This is not about inserting women into the existing canon[p.39], but about uncovering what has been deposited in culture that resists[p.282] phallic (male-dominated) structures."

GRISELDA POLLOCK
Art historian, cultural analyst, and Professor emerita of Social and Critical Histories of Art at the University of Leeds
E.A.T. 2021: Longue Durée, livestream

FICTION

"I feel intensely relaxed about language[p.198] models[p.208] hallucinating. Wikipedia itself is a hallucination – a collectively agreed fiction. The Wikipedia page on the Tamil Revolution is made up, but so is all history: a fiction (often concocted by nation states to tell the story of their existence) that we've collectively decided[p.63] to believe[p.36] in. My work is not a documentary; it's my own hallucination of stories I remember[p.281] growing[p.138] up, reconstructed from fragments[p.127] of things I'd piece together but that my parents wouldn't really talk about."

CHRISTOPHER KULENDRAN THOMAS
Artist
E.A.T. 2024: Jenseits von Ohnmacht – Beyond Powerless, Zuoz

FIGHT

"To me, being alive means having hope[p.142]. One cannot truly live if one believes[p.36] oneself to be entirely without hope – that's impossible. It's like working with wood[p.323]: if the wood is dead, you can't do anything with it. Hope is part of us, even if we don't realise it. And thankfully so, because we face terrible circumstances every day. In my own work I make these large standing warriors, the upright figure. He truly wants to fight for a better future[p.130]. That's what he stands for."

SIMONE FATTAL
Artist
2023: E.A.T. × Centre Pompidou, Paris

FINDING

"You can search and look forever. Let's say you want to build a house[p.142] here, but maybe over there it's better. Nietzsche once said, 'Since I grew[p.138] tired of searching I taught[p.306] myself to find.' That's how it happens. You find. For example, in the Amazon I saw[p.296] land from a boat; it looked perfect. We approached, and of course, it was for sale. If you believe[p.36] in it, it's easy. But if you have even 1% doubt, don't do it. You need a portion of naivety."

NOT VITAL
Artist
E.A.T. 2017: Snow and Desert, Zuoz

FIRE

"A volcano erupts here in Iceland about every five years. You're always kind of ready. And people in that area still say 'before the fire' and 'after the fire' – they never say 'the eruption'. That's beautiful[p.34]: it's just 'the fire'."

RAGNAR KJARTANSSON
Artist
E.A.T. 2021: Longue Durée livestream
→ PLATE 42 p.153

FLEEING

"When I received the question[p.275] about my childhood in Algeria in relation to hope[p.142], I thought to myself, quite directly: hope is something I do not know. And already, you're using the word[p.324] 'hope' and not 'expectation'. That's significant. In French, we have both 'espoir' and 'espérance' – they're not the same at all. In German, I think there's only one word. But in French, 'espérance' refers to a theological virtue, like faith[p.121] and charity. Whereas 'espoir' – that's something entirely different. As a child in Algeria, I abandoned all hope. I didn't imagine[p.146] we could hope for anything from that country, so devoured it was by demons, hatred and racism. I told myself, very young, that it was a place to flee. And I did. As soon as I turned 18, I fled – because I had no hope."

HÉLÈNE CIXOUS
Writer, playwright and literary critic
2023: E.A.T. × Centre Pompidou, Paris

FLUID

"You call it a house[p.142]
but it is not
architecture[p.29],
not in any traditional sense.
There is no foundation.
No permanence[p.223].
It is an architecture of
images[p.146] –
a constant reconfiguration,
a collapsing and expanding
of space and form
that is fluid."

JOANA DE LA FONTAINE
Architect
2024: E.A.T. × Kunsthalle Zürich,
Zurich
→ PLATE 43 p.154

FOLK

"Growing[p.138] up, I thought folk songs[p.299] were just beautiful[p.34] music. We heard them on the radio, or maybe your grandmother sang them to you. But when I started researching Igbo culture[p.60], I discovered that these songs weren't just for entertainment – they were used to communicate[p.51], educate[p.113] and pass on morals. Traditional societies used them to teach[p.306] history[p.140], to instruct and to help children observe[p.217] and communicate. Many are call-and-response songs that draw you in. You're not just listening – you're participating. And through that, knowledge is passed on."

EMEKA OGBOH
Artist
E.A.T. 2020: Silent – Listen,
Zuoz

FOREST

"La Défense in Paris is as artificial[p.31] as it gets – a mineral, wind-swept, reflective environment. I understood[p.313] its climatic conditions are similar to that of a mountain[p.211] range and thought: what makes mountains comforting? It's the tree line. That's what we introduced – we planted as many trees as possible on this floating deck, in only 53 centimetres of soil. Every centimetre was a negotiation[p.214]. We prepared the trees in nurseries for two years, used sensors[p.294] to monitor moisture, designed metal cages to anchor them – in order not to touch[p.308] the waterproofing. The trees[p.311] create a continuous[p.55] canopy in between skyscrapers and are suspended above an urban boulevard, growing[p.138] slowly[p.298] into a new kind of urban forest."

BAS SMETS
Landscape architect
E.A.T. 2023: Hoffnung? Hoffnung!, Zuoz

FORMAT

"The format often tells you what's needed. When I developed something beyond a traditional exhibition – with music, scent, and movement in space – it called for a very particular kind of music, which I then created. The more I explored new formats, the more they pushed me to collaborate[p.49] with people from fields beyond my own, and that led to some truly fascinating conversations[p.56]."

ISABEL LEWIS
Artist, professor, artistic director of Tanzquartier Wien
E.A.T. 2021: Longue Durée, livestream

FOSSIL

"Perhaps the best compliment my work has ever received came when a drone photographed a piece we made in 2010. Since it wasn't labelled or identified as art[p.31], people assumed it was a fossil; some lost whale or dinosaur[p.108]. That, to me, was incredibly important. It meant the work had lost[p.201] its agency as art and was being read[p.276] through other lenses. I'm proud of that. I don't like the word[p.324] 'art' very much, and I've always mined how people interface with my work. When a piece is mistaken[p.208] for a natural relic, that's when it really succeeds."

ADRIÁN VILLAR ROJAS
Artist
E.A.T. 2018: Side Country Side, Zuoz
→ PLATE 44 p.155

FRAGMENT

"Built with fragments.
Memes, data points,
pixels[p.224].
This house[p.142] has no walls.
Only screens that reflect[p.279]
and refactor us,
reshape[p.295] us,
until we no longer know
what part of us is still[p.301]
alive.
Like standing in a maze,

surrounded by ourselves.
We reach p.276 out,
but the mirror p.208 pushes
back.
There is no depth, only an
illusion of depth."

PAMELA ROSENKRANZ
Artist
2024: E.A.T. × Kunsthalle Zürich,
Zurich

FRAMEWORK

"With *SOMETHING art space*, which opened in Abidjan in 2022, I created a place that had not previously existed on the continent, dedicated p.64 to video p.316, digital p.107 art and critical p.58 thought. It is an independent p.189 platform p.225, both locally anchored and globally oriented. Once again, collaborations p.49 proved decisive: Wolfgang Tillmans in conversation p.56 with Simon Njami for the first time; the inaugural exhibition with the Musée d'Art Moderne de Paris; Emeka Ogboh, then Carsten Höller exhibiting for the first time in Côte d'Ivoire for one, in Africa p.26 for the other, as well as emerging artists who we have supported p.303. What interests me is offering a framework to think about contemporary p.55 art differently, outside of established institutional models p.208."

ANNA-ALIX KOFFI
Creative director and founder of SOMETHING art space in Abidjan, SOMETHING WE AFRICANS GOT and OFF the wall
2023: E.A.T. × Centre Pompidou, Paris

FREEDOM

"When the Berlin Wall fell p.122, I felt an overwhelming sense of relief. Freedom became p.35 my most important value, and it still is. Yet today, I see our Western p.321 societies prioritising safety over freedom. That shift p.296 worries me."

MICHAEL SCHINDHELM
Author, filmmaker and curator
E.A.T. 2016: Traces and Fragments, Zuoz
→ PLATE 45 p.156

FRIENDSHIP

"What stayed with me the most, were the hugs with residents of Forest Houses – sometimes repeated, sometimes long and intense – 10 years later. I was moved by these gestures[p.134] of friendship and recognition[p.277], gestures that showed that the work done together had not been forgotten. The re-distribution of the substantial *Gramsci Monument* catalogue with the Forest Houses residents' contributions about their experience in 2013, made it even more meaningful[p.204]."

THOMAS HIRSCHHORN
Artist
2023: E.A.T. × Centre Pompidou, Paris

FUNCTION

"I remember[p.281] being asked by gallerist Claes Nordenhake what function means to architecture[p.29]. Inspired[p.192] by good food at the table I came up with this definition[p.64]: function to architecture is what health is to cooking. It is important but doesn't produce the taste of food, nor the form of the building. It seems to me that the theory of functionalism revitalised 20th-century design to no lesser degree than the notion of healthy food, our daily diet. One might be tempted to reflect[p.279] on this subject in this place of uncompromised beauty[p.34] and healthy environment that Engadin Art Talks[p.116] provides."

ZVI HECKER
Architect
E.A.T. 2013: Ghosts and the Uncanny, Zuoz
→ PLATE 46 p.157

FUNGUS

"Fungi have shaped[p.295] life on Earth[p.112] for more than a billion years. All of us – animals, plants and other microbes – have evolved in and around fungi, and these fungal relationships[p.280] have again and again helped redefine[p.64] biological possibility. The long influence of these relationships is a good reminder[p.281] that all the species we see today have long evolutionary roots[p.289] that stretch deep into the past, tangling and entwining with the roots of countless other species."

MERLIN SHELDRAKE
Biologist and author
E.A.T. 2021: Longue Durée, livestream
→ PLATE 47 p.158

FURNITURE

"To strictly follow sustainability p.304 guidelines, we would have to abandon the open plan and spatial continuity p.55 achieved during modernity and return to the 19th-century practice p.228 of separating each room with walls and doors. But instead of regressing, we propose not to draw plans based on rooms and spatial boundaries p.39, but to fix the furniture and define p.64 its uses according to specific temperatures p.307 and light intensities – much like a natural landscape, where you take refuge under a tree p.311 when it rains or sit in the shade of a rock p.288 when it gets too hot."

PHILIPPE RAHM
EPFL architect, Ph. D.
(Paris-Saclay University, 2019)
E.A.T. 2010: The Crystal Chain,
Zuoz
→ PLATE 48 p.159

FUSION

"I hate fusion food where someone has to explain what you're eating. I want the dish my grandmother made. But today, we're destroying memory p.206, erasing difference and forcing everything into one bland global culture p.60. That's more dangerous than anything. Let people go their own way, even if it leads p.198 to their own kind of failure p.121."

AI WEIWEI
Artist
E.A.T. 2023: Hoffnung? Hoffnung!,
Zuoz

FUTURE

"Chilean-French filmmaker Alejandro Jodorowsky says you must not talk about the future; the future is a con. The Tarot is a language p.198 that speaks of the present p.230. If you use it to predict the future, you become p.35 a charlatan. Nothing is a matter p.204 of probability. But if you set your spirit to something, that phenomenon will happen. When you enter the dimension he calls the 'dance of reality', the world begins to dance around you and gives you what you seek."

EMILY SEGAL
Artist and writer
E.A.T. 2018: Side Country Side,
Zuoz

G

GAP

"Katherine Dunham, an influential African[p.26] American[p.28] dancer, choreographer and anthropologist,was a remarkable and amazing woman. I mean the things she did, the travelling she did. They've tracked her, and she went all over the world. She stayed in Japan for years. It still amazes me that there I was at her deathbed, and I didn't have the question to ask her: did she meet Hijikata, the founder of Butoh? What did they talk about? So my piece 'deathbed' is really about this gap in history[p.140] – the questions[p.275] you couldn't ask. And it's not about answering them, but dealing with the fact that there's a gap I can never quite fill. That creates something that to me is close to art[p.31]."

TRAJAL HARRELL
Choreographer and dancer
E.A.T. 2021: Longue Durée, livestream

GARDEN

"Talking about gardens may seem far-fetched in the age of the anthropocene[p.29], but the garden of Senegalese artist, playwright, poet and philosopher Issa Samb holds[p.141] an answer for where to begin in rethinking museums[p.212], biennales and exhibitions. Gardens and museums share a history[p.140] of enclosure – for kings, for the elite – but in other traditions, such as Arabic and Persian[p.223] cultures[p.60], gardens were paradises[p.221] without sin. In contrast to Western[p.321] notions of nature[p.213] as something separate and ruined by man, these gardens were integrated[p.192], holistic spaces for pleasure, contemplation and coexistence[p.49]."

RASHA SALTI
Researcher, writer, producer and curator of art and film
E.A.T. 2024: Jenseits von Ohnmacht – Beyond Powerless, Zuoz

GATHERING

"The Àmà – the traditional public square in Igbo communities[p.51] of southeastern

Nigeria – is not just a place where people gather. It's also like a parliament. It's where meetings are held[p.141], and sometimes it functions[p.129] as a market. But what's very interesting is that these are also spaces where a lot of social activities take place: music, masquerades, singing, weddings, rituals. So when I was invited to create this installation at the Cleveland Museum, I became[p.35] more interested in how to take a gathering space and connect[p.53] it to something deeper. That's how I came up with the idea[p.145] of working with the Igbo concept of Àmà."

EMEKA OGBOH
Artist
E.A.T. 2020: Silent – Listen,
Zuoz

GAZE

"I've always been interested in anthropology as a tool, especially for its ability to be self-reflective and critical[p.58]. But what's fascinating is that anthropology itself has recognised[p.277] its own impossibility: the impossibility of neutrality[p.214], of being both the examiner and the subject. That's also the fundamental problem of painting – and even more so of filmmaking, where the point of view is embedded in the technology[p.306]. The question[p.275] is always: where is the gaze coming from?"

CAMILLE HENROT
Artist
E.A.T. 2023: Hoffnung? Hoffnung!,
Zuoz

GENDER

"Hilma af Klint, a Swedish artist and pioneer of abstract art, chose the snail as her emblematic animal – the creature[p.58] with the spiral[p.300] shell that inspired[p.192] the design of the Guggenheim Museum[p.212]. What fascinated af Klint was the snail's unique quality[p.274] of being hermaphroditic; possessing both male and female[p.123] traits simultaneously. She did not believe[p.36] in rigid gender boundaries[p.39] at all."

JULIA VOSS
Journalist
and scientific historian
2021: E.A.T. × Kunsthalle Zürich,
Zurich

→ PLATE 49 p.160

GENERALISATION

"What some people call the anthropocene p.29 really starts when human p.143 life begins to dominate the planet, but that's the problem. We can't generalise. We are not all the same. It's important to say some humans – not all humans – are responsible for the crises we're facing. Many are suffering the consequences. Every time I mistakenly p.208 use 'humans' in a generalised way, I try to stop and correct myself. It's crucial to shake that off and think differently."

TOMÁS SARACENO
Artist
E.A.T. 2021: Longue Durée, livestream

GENERATION

"Emerging research indicates that traumatic p.311 experiences, diet and exposure p.121 to endocrine-disrupting chemicals can have effects that span multiple generations. One study found p.125 that the great-granddaughters of men who began smoking during adolescence tended to have higher fat mass. While the data are correlative, they suggest that environmental exposures p.121 may leave biological signals that persist through four generations, challenging p.42 the traditional principle of genetic inheritance p.191."

ISABELLE MANSUY
Professor in neuroepigenetics in the Medical Faculty of the University of Zurich and the Department of Health Science and Technology of ETH Zurich
E.A.T. 2022: Matter and Memory, Zuoz

GEOPOLITICAL

"From a geopolitical and world-system perspective p.223, Argentina has always been positioned as the countryside p.57 of the planet. After Latin America was drained of gold and silver, it was restructured to provide food, minerals and oil for first-world economies. This continues p.55 today. So when I'm asked about memories of the countryside, it's complicated. I live on a continent that functions p.129 as the countryside for the rest of the world, producing raw[p.275] materials[p.204] while receiving manufactured goods in return."

ADRIÁN VILLAR ROJAS
Artist
E.A.T. 2018: Side Country Side, Zuoz

GESTURE

"What interests me is the relationship[p.280] between the gestures of the human[p.143] body[p.38], nature[p.213] and materials[p.204]. At the Venice Biennale, we wanted to install a black, highly polished lime floor. Initially, the masons were supposed to do the work, but they found it difficult to sit on the floor in the specific posture required for the technique. Surprisingly[p.303], only the carpenters – who were not originally part of this task – were able to perform it successfully. That experience made me realize that once we lose certain ways of sitting and our connection[p.53] to the ground, the ability to practice[p.228] specific techniques can disappear with them."

BIJOY JAIN
Architect, founder of Studio Mumbai and Norman R. Foster Visiting professor at Yale University
E.A.T. 2010: The Crystal Chain, Zuoz

GHOST

"We – performers, listeners and everyone present[p.230] – must activate the 'ghosts' in the room. These ghosts are already there, waiting to be awakened. I am optimistic that this can happen, but it requires time[p.308]. It's not something you can achieve instantly by simply sitting and listening briefly. The process is similar to the experience of a James Turrell installation: when you enter a dark[p.62] room, you must sit quietly[p.275] for about ten minutes as your eyes gradually adjust to the subtle light. Only then do you begin to perceive the structure, and understand[p.313] the artist's intention[p.193]. Sound[p.300] works in much the same way – the room responds[p.284] to specific sounds and pitches over time."

FRITZ HAUSER
Drummer, percussionist and composer
E.A.T. 2021: Longue Durée, livestream
→ PLATE 50 p.161

GOODBYE

"In my work, the bow is not just a moment for the audience to tell you how good you are. It's a goodbye. And that's always a sad moment for me. Saying goodbye is never easy – and that's partly why I try to extend the time p.308 I spend with people, whether it's through gestures p.134 during the piece or even physically greeting them after. It's a form of care p.40."

TRAJAL HARRELL
Choreographer and dancer
2023: E.A.T. × Centre Pompidou, Paris

GORILLA

"In the 1880s, when gorillas in the Western p.321 world still existed only as myth, there were depictions based purely on rumour – like Fremiet's sculpture *Gorilla Abducting a Woman* (1887), which fused p.130 European fears p.123 of the so-called Black Continent with voyeuristic male fantasies. It's interesting that this mythologising of 'authentic wilderness' arose at the exact same time as the construction p.53 of the first modern high-rises, around 1885, suggesting that the modern metropolis required a binary counterpart: the idea p.145 of untouched, ancestral nature p.213. This culminates in pop culture p.60 with the clash of the high-rise and the gorilla in King Kong."

NIKLAS MAAK
Architectural historian, journalist and lecturer
E.A.T. 2018: Side Country Side, Zuoz

GRACE

"The location of a public artwork p.273 is very important – it's half the work itself. I love p.202 French philosopher Simone Weil's quote: 'Grace fills, but it can only enter where there is a void p.320 to receive it – and it is grace that creates this void.' In Wiesbaden, I made a work in public space, *Sperr*, in which furniture p.130 and other household[p.142] belongings[p.36] were put out on the street as if they could be taken away. The word[p.324] 'Wirklichkeit' was written on the items. Two residents, present[p.230] 24 hours a day for 10 days, embodied the letters 'E' and 'I'. What I hadn't anticipated was that this spot, just in front of the sculpture, was a gathering[p.131] place for heavy drinkers[p.111]. 'Wirklichkeit' therefore truly challenged[p.42] the work. Over time[p.308], a kind of complicity[p.51] developed between us – them and the 'I's and 'E's. A shared presence[p.229], face to face, day and night."

THOMAS HIRSCHHORN
Artist
2023: E.A.T. × Centre Pompidou, Paris

GRADIENT

"We don't always realise how much acoustics contribute to the overall experience of a space, and that an overall comfort depends on the alignment of the visual and aural. When it's too quiet[p.275] in a large hall – too dull acoustically – you might actually feel more uncomfortable than if there's ambient noise[p.215]. In designing these buildings, especially the last one with its central hall, we had to explain to the client that a sense of spatial comfort comes through transitions[p.310] – gradients of acoustical experience. From a reverberant central space to quieter, more private rooms, these layers[p.198] allow people to feel part of a larger system, not isolated from it."

JEANNETTE KUO
Architect and founding partner of architectural firm KARAMUK KUO
E.A.T. 2020: Silent – Listen, Zuoz
→PLATE 51 p.162

GRAPHIC DESIGN

"I had to support[p.303] myself, so I called myself a graphic designer, not an artist. In those days, I could never have supported myself as an artist. But as a graphic designer, they paid me like an architect. And when American[p.28] architects Charles Moore and Bill Turnbull built the Swim and Tennis Club at Sea Ranch,

I saw[p.296] the raw[p.275] wooden[p.323] walls and said, 'Paint them white, and I'll create something.' I treated it like a three-dimensional canvas, starting with a huge wave on one wall – and just kept going."

BARBARA STAUFFACHER SOLOMON
Artist and graphic designer
E.A.T. 2023: Hoffnung? Hoffnung!, Zuoz
→PLATE 52 p.163

GRASS

"English society[p.299] has an erotic relationship[p.280] with grass. In front of the Tate, there are no benches. People lie on the lawn. When we proposed benches for the European visitors[p.318], the British said no – they want to touch[p.308] the grass. I've never experienced a society[p.299] so intimately[p.195] connected[p.53] to this element of a landscape."

GÜNTHER VOGT
Landscape architect and professor emeritus
2024: E.A.T. × Kunsthalle Zürich, Zurich
→PLATE 53 p.164

GRAVITY

"For me, it's essential how a sculpture connects[p.53] to the ground. The horse hooves I use sometimes turn into hybrid[p.144] forms, phantasmagorical architecture[p.29]. They become[p.35] replacements for pedestals, shoeboxes of ideas[p.145]: substitutes that can act as vessels for desire[p.106] while also standing in the 'firing line' of its violence[p.317]. Early in my practice[p.228], I worked with fibreglass, which is very much about gravity – how things sag, how weight behaves[p.35]. I need everything to be grounded, even when the form resists[p.282]. Perhaps what I'm also trying to invoke is the emotional terrain of a youthful, almost adolescent passion – one that appears to draw near to its object[p.217] of affection but, in reality[p.277], remains curiously distant or detached. Travesty plays a role, too; maybe that is the part where 'play' is most at work."

LENA HENKE
Artist
E.A.T. 2019: Grace and Gravity, Zuoz

GREEN

"The 1960s marked the birth of the green movement, although the term 'green' hadn't yet been coined. A number of pivotal influences converged: American p.28 marine biologist Rachel Carson's *Silent Spring* (1962) exposed p.121 the damage of pesticides on ecosystems p.113; the Apollo missions gave us the first image p.146 of Earth p.112 from space, revealing its fragile protective p.232 layer p.198; and thinkers like American architect Buckminster Fuller published p.273 *Operating Manual for Spaceship Earth*. Our architectural practice p.228 was born out of this moment – a utopian p.315 vision p.317 of architecture responding p.284 to emerging ecological p.113 challenges p.42. Early projects explored solar energy p.115, desalination and sustainable p.304 tourism. At the time p.308, this was all very fringe – decades ahead of today's mainstream environmental concerns."

NORMAN FOSTER
Architect, founder and executive chairman of Foster + Partners
E.A.T. 2025: Form and Impact, Zuoz
→ PLATE 54 p.165

GROWTH

"We tend to want things to be simple, clean and seamless – but real growth happens in the murky, tense p.307 spaces. When you're trying to move things forwards, not everything will be pretty. There's mess p.206, conflict and struggle. But that's part of the work. I embrace that. It's how the practice p.228 evolves – through discomfort p.109 and challenge p.42."

RICK LOWE
Artist
E.A.T. 2025: Form and Impact, Zuoz

GUIDANCE

"In Switzerland p.305, we've been trying very hard to control natural forces. But now we're beginning to realise that perhaps we can't control them as much as we thought. So the strategy for the future p.130 should be less about control and more about guidance – guiding natural forces. That shift[p.296] opens up the possibility of creating new forms of nature[p.213] and new relationships[p.280] with water and natural processes. Especially with climate change[p.48], where we face more frequent material[p.204] washouts and, at the same time, increasing droughts, we need to find[p.125] a different attitude – one that embraces dialogue[p.107] with these dynamics rather than opposing them."

MARTINA VOSER
Landscape architect and co-founder of landscape architecture and urban planning studio Mavo Landschaften
E.A.T. 2024: Jenseits von Ohnmacht – Beyond Powerless, Zuoz

H

HABIT

"A long time[p.308] ago I ate a lot of meat. I made a lot of barbecues. But around seven[p.294] or eight years ago – since I gained an awareness that a steak or a hamburger are equivalent to 15,000 litres of water and are major contributors for deforestation and global warming – I began to stop. Now I don't eat meat; I eat fish and vegetables and many other things. Habit is something we can change[p.43], if we want to. But in my view, it's not something we should force by saying, 'From now on, I'll never do this or that again.' We should change little by little. Be gentle to our bodies[p.38] – as gentle as we can be to the Earth[p.112]."

ERNESTO NETO
Artist
E.A.T. 2023: Hoffnung? Hoffnung!, Zuoz

HABITAT

"In 1951, we had a lot of snow[p.298] here in the Engadin. My brother and I built a tunnel[p.312] in front of our house[p.142] in Sent. He went off to school[p.291] – I was too little – and I spent a lot of time[p.308] in that tunnel. I still remember[p.281] how the light came through the snow, how it smelled. But the most important thing was the coziness. Even though I was too young to be conscious of it then, I think that's when I understood[p.313] I would always be searching to build my own habitat – someplace, somewhere, somehow."

NOT VITAL
Artist
E.A.T. 2017: Snow and Desert, Zuoz

HERITAGE

"We created a virtual museum[p.212] to keep this low-tech heritage alive and accessible[p.23]. It's a transmedia project – with text, audio design, 3D[p.307] models[p.208] – all aimed at giving new life to forgotten innovations. By revisiting these stories and making them visible again, we build a bridge between past experiments[p.120] and today's ecological[p.113] challenges[p.42]. The idea[p.145] is not to preserve nostalgia, but to activate memory[p.206] as a tool for resilience."

LOÏC ROGARD
Researcher in the field of renewable energies at Atelier 21
E.A.T. 2023: Hoffnung? Hoffnung!, Zuoz

HIERARCHY

"There may be no hierarchy when traces[p.309] are placed in an indeterminate, generic context[p.55]. For instance, footprints on the sand are quite different from the footprint on the Moon[p.210]. A sign that represents[p.281] an apple or a rectangle establishes a hierarchy; it replaces the apple or the rectangle. But a sign that only represents itself – like the mark of a brush – does not have a fixed hierarchy."

GIORGIO GRIFFA
Artist
E.A.T. 2016: Traces and Fragments, Zuoz

HISTORY

"Whether we like it or not, and regardless of the limited evidence[p.119] future generations may have of our actions[p.24], today's contemporary[p.55] art[p.31] will become[p.35] the art history of the future. This also means we need to consider initiating processes in our work that anticipate a long-lasting temporal impact[p.148] – one that includes its own obsolescence p.218 – and reflect p.279 on what will follow after."

RAQS MEDIA COLLECTIVE
Artist collective,
media practitioners, curators,
and researchers
E.A.T. 2012: Vision for the Alps, Zuoz

HOLD

"It's tricky to talk about hope p.142. The geopolitical p.133 situation across the Sahel and West Africa p.26 is chaotic. My hometown Gao, along with Timbuktu and much of central Mali, was occupied for 11 months in 2012–2013. When I visited last July, I had to fly from Bamako – the first time I've done that in 30 or 40 years. To speak of hope amid this reality p.277 feels like denial. And yet, we must construct p.53 new narratives p.213 – stories that help us hold on to what is slippery, intangible and yet vital."

MOHOMODOU
HOUSSOUBA
Writer and literary scholar
E.A.T. 2023: Hoffnung? Hoffnung!,
Zuoz

HOME

"Torre David, a Caracas 45-STORY office building, has become the makeshift home for over 750 families living in a precarious p.229, unofficial settlement often called a vertical slum. Though only temporarily tolerated, the residents have transformed p.310 this ruin p.289 into a home. While some view it as a failed p.121 development, we see Torre David as a laboratory to study informal settlements. We believe p.36 informal communities p.51 worldwide hold p.141 potential for innovation and experimentation p.120, and our goal is to design towards a more equitable and sustainable p.304 future p.130."

HUBERT KLUMPNER
Architect and co-founder of the
interdisciplinary design practice
Urban-Think Tank
E.A.T. 2012: Vision for the Alps, Zuoz
→ PLATE 55 p.166

HONOUR

"When I saw p.296 the Dinh Nguyen vinyl collection – 14,000 records of mostly Afro-Caribbean music once belonging p.36 to a French-Vietnamese man – it wasn't just about preserving it. It was about honouring the spirit in those records. These aren't 'found[p.125] objects[p.217].' That language[p.198] was always wrong. These are spiritual vessels that need care[p.40], need someone to charge[p.44] them so they can radiate their full energy[p.115]. That's what we tried to do – with love[p.202], respect[p.284] and purpose[p.274]."

THEASTER GATES
Artist
2025: E.A.T. × St. Moritz, St. Moritz

HOPE

"I don't like the word[p.324] 'hope'. I don't like the word 'freedom'[p.128] either – they're the most empty words we use. When my father was exiled[p.120], he said to my mother: 'We must imagine[p.146] we were born here.' He was cleaning toilets in minus 30 degrees, a poet who had never done physical work. He told me: if you don't have hope, you will not feel hopeless. That was my first lesson."

AI WEIWEI
Artist
E.A.T. 2023: Hoffnung? Hoffnung! Zuoz

HORIZON

"French novelist and literary critic Marcel Proust wrote a short prose text called *Présence Réelle*, describing two landscapes: the Silsersee at six in the evening and the view of the Puschlav valley from Alp Grüm. Both show deep, layered[p.198] horizons – a sense of long duration[p.111] in the landscape that fascinated Proust. This connects[p.53] to painters like Ferdinand Hodler, Giovanni Segantini, and Arnold Böcklin, who similarly captured time[p.308] and emotional depth through layered landscapes."

LUZIUS KELLER
Scholar for Romance languages, translator, and lecturer
E.A.T. 2021: Longue Durée, livestream
→ PLATE 56 p.167

HOUSING

"British architect and theorist John F.C. Turner's work helps build a different understanding[p.313] of the role of the architect and architectural education[p.113]. The first is his acknowledgement[p.24] that the barrios[p.34] taught[p.306] him to see housing not as a noun but as a verb – what housing does and how it contributes to people's livelihoods. Housing needs to work, especially in financial terms. Self-built[p.293] homes may be precarious[p.229] but inexpensive, and allow families to save money[p.210] and progressively improve them with better materials[p.204]."

ELISA SILVA
Architect and founder and principal of Enlace Arquitectura and Enlace Foundation
E.A.T. 2024: Jenseits von Ohnmacht – Beyond Powerless, Zuoz

HUB

"There are seven[p.294] co-founders involved at the development of the Swiss InnHub La Punt, combining expertise in sports, digital[p.107] innovation, hospitality and holistic health. Together, we're building a space with hotel rooms, restaurants, a co-working and co-creation[p.58] hub, and facilities for altitude training[p.309]. The goal is to empower individuals[p.189] and groups to find[p.125] new solutions for human[p.143] and planetary health. But nothing happens without the community[p.51]. We want to work closely with the local community and help them discover new ways to innovate within tourism. La Punt has always been a historically[p.140] important place – a bridge where people from the north, south, east and west once converged. Merchants and tradesmen met the locals there. We want to revive that spirit by inviting global business leaders[p.198] to come to La Punt and co-create new solutions."

REGULA CURTI
Musician, entrepreneur and philanthropist
E.A.T. 2025: Form and Impact, Zuoz
→ PLATE 57 [p.168]

HUMAN

"I don't really have a favourite material[p.204], but if I had to choose one, it would be the human being. That's what I'm most fond of, what fascinates me. What interests me is understanding[p.313] how they function[p.129]. You could say that humans are both creator and material."

PASCALE MARTHINE TAYOU
Artist
E.A.T. 2016: Traces and Fragments, Zuoz

HYBRID

"I started feeding the ceramic p.42 descriptions from our book Keramikos 3 into DALL·E – a family of AI p.31 models p.208 developed by OpenAI that can generate images p.146 from textual descriptions – and asking it to generate plates based on those texts. Since our real-world plates are historic hybrids, using AI felt like a natural next step. It's both research and production. A lot of people ask, 'Who made this plate?' – but for us, it's about shared authorship p.32. In that sense, AI became p.35 the fourth player in our collaboration p.49, alongside us and the material p.204."

MATTHEW LUTZ-KINOY
Artist
E.A.T. 2023: Hoffnung? Hoffnung!, Zuoz

I

ICON

"When invited to conceive an outdoor intervention for the 2016 edition of Engadin Art Talks p.116 in Zuoz p.324, I immediately envisioned a sculpture made of ice. The crystalline p.59 nature of the material p.204 lends it an almost immaterial presence p.229, underscored by its inherent ephemerality p.117. For me, an ice sculpture in the form of an oversized perfume bottle functioned p.129 as a metaphor: a seductive p.292, immaculate object p.217 that gradually disappeared even as its image p.146 persisted – transformed p.310 into an icon, like the ghostly p.134 traces p.309 of advertisements weathered by time p.308."

SYLVIE FLEURY
Artist
E.A.T. 2016: Traces and Fragments, Zuoz

→ PLATE 58 p.169

ICONOCLASM

"Iconoclasm is part of the process of making heritage p.140. Every society p.299 shapes p.295 its heritage by deciding what to preserve and what to discard. Iconoclasm makes that decision[p.63] visible – sometimes violently – by declaring: 'This must go away.' It's one way in which societies shape[p.295] what they pass on to future[p.130] generations[p.133]."

DARIO GAMBONI
Professor emeritus of art history at the University of Geneva
E.A.T. 2021: Longue Durée, livestream

IDEA

"Landscape is a cultural[p.60] production. When I'm saying it's a cultural production, you have to go close to this culture. Sometimes it's not so easy – even in the UK or in London it wasn't so easy for me. I'm trained[p.309] in Mediterranean[p.205] traditions: trees[p.311] are in a line, trees are in a grid. In London they said, 'Oh God, we want to see[p.296] nature[p.213], not your Frenchy approach.' Therefore you see the little birch forest[p.126] in front of the Tate – the result of two or three years of working together to understand[p.313] their idea[p.145] of nature."

GÜNTHER VOGT
Landscape architect and professor emeritus
2024: E.A.T. × Kunsthalle Zürich, Zurich

IDEAL

"I'm interested in understanding[p.313] how architecture[p.29] could be a platform[p.225] for people to design their own lives, rather than imposing a way of living. The 20th century gave us functionalist ideals – that everyone needs a kitchen, a labelled sleeping room, a labelled living room. But not all of us live the same way, and not all of us need those same spaces. We started to design open-ended houses[p.142], self-constructed with minimal budgets, where any space could become[p.35] a kitchen, bedroom or gathering[p.131] space. It's difficult to design for seven[p.294] billion different people, but that's exactly why architecture should become a medium, not an authoritarian script."

TATIANA BILBAO
Architect
E.A.T. 2020: Silent – Listen, Zuoz

IDENTITY

"The Hinzert camp, located in the Hunsrück upland, was a Nazi concentration camp holding[p.141] political prisoners from over 20 countries. Prisoners lived in barracks built for 208 people, later expanded to 560, enduring harsh weather conditions. Families received no news about their loved[p.202] ones. The code name 'NN' stood for both 'Nacht und Nebel' (Night and Fog) and nullum nomen ('without name'), reflecting[p.279] the camp's aim to erase[p.118] individual[p.189] identity[p.146]. This anonymity opposes tourists' desire[p.106] for personal stories. The mountains[p.211] became[p.35] a place of loss[p.201] of identity. Today, the Hinzert Document Centre is a topological building that houses[p.142] archives[p.30], seminar rooms and exhibition spaces, giving voice[p.319] to objects[p.217] and histories[p.140] as the survivors fade away."

NIKOLAUS HIRSCH
Architect, curator and educator
E.A.T. 2011: Mapping the Alps, Zuoz

IMAGE

"We used deep-sea footage from German research institutes – shot by robotic[p.287] submersibles at 5,000 metres. These images were never shown outside the realm of science, but looked like Hollywood productions. We transferred and reframed them in the exhibition space to ask how these images shape[p.295] legal, ecological[p.113] and economic debates. Who owns the ocean floor? Who can extract rare minerals or patent microbes found[p.125] at black smokers? Concepts like 'mare liberum' by Hugo Grotius or the UN Convention on the Law of the Sea are no longer sufficient. New visual tools are needed to reflect[p.279] this legal vacuum."

ARMIN LINKE
Artist
E.A.T. 2022: Matter and Memory, Zuoz

IMAGINATION

"Our obsession with reality[p.277] – what's immediate[p.147], what's now – is dangerous.

It's an ideology rooted p.289 not just in technology p.306 but in religion p.280, especially Protestantism. Social media intensifies this by demanding transparency p.311, and that undermines hope p.142. Because to hope, you need to project p.232 into the future p.130. And to do that, you need rest, time p.308 off – space to imagine alternative possibilities."

CAMILLE HENROT
Artist
E.A.T. 2023: Hoffnung? Hoffnung!, Zuoz

IMMEDIACY

"What attracted Michel Auder to the video format is its immediacy. It allows him to record almost everything happening in daily life. While some scenes might be slightly staged, much of it captures life as it unfolds; people, views, real moments around him. Alongside this, he incorporates pre-recorded material p.204, such as television footage, which he films and filters with a subversive perspective p.223."

ADAM SZYMCZYK
Curator, writer and editor
E.A.T. 2021: Longue Durée, livestream

IMMIGRATION

"I can't think of the desert p.105 without thinking about immigration and the word p.324 'coyotes' for those who ferry immigrants. I had to resist p.282 including the word 'illegal' right there, meaning p.204 I've been hypnotised. It's almost knee-jerk when I see 'immigrant' in America p.28 to say 'illegal.' Media and language p.198 work that way. It's an emotional word. But this is not an animated version of the world. I'm borrowing the power of animation. Because isn't animation inherently propaganda? I realise how much snow p.298 stands in for feeling. How delightful; fat flakes pouring down on someone who died p.63 in the desert, just to change p.43 the subject."

EILEEN MYLES
Poet, novelist and art journalist
E.A.T. 2017: Snow and Desert, Zuoz

IMPACT

"Being a landscape architect is always about impact[p.148]. When we begin shaping space, we initiate ecological[p.113] and social processes. A slope affects wetness, which influences soil conditions, vegetation and the other co-inhabitants of our world – birds, insects, animals, plants. It's always about creating connections[p.53] between spaces. Even hedges meant to divide areas become[p.35] habitats[p.139] themselves. So, every action[p.24] in our work leads[p.198] to reactions – intended[p.193] or not."

MARTINA VOSER
Landscape architect and co-founder of landscape architecture and urban planning studio Mavo Landschaften
E.A.T. 2024: Jenseits von Ohnmacht – Beyond Powerless, Zuoz

IMPRINT

"People always say clay[p.47] has memory[p.206] – and it really does. Depending on how you shape[p.295] it, even after you turn it, re-wedge it, and remix[p.281] it, when you fire[p.125] it in the kiln, it tends to go back to that memory shape. Because I was deeply invested in performance[p.222] and live work, ceramics[p.42] felt like a logical extension. It became[p.35] a way to communicate[p.51] movement and touch[p.308] through an object[p.217], one that maintains an imprint over time and can be passed on – like a performance frozen in clay."

MATTHEW LUTZ-KINOY
Artist
E.A.T. 2023: Hoffnung? Hoffnung!, Zuoz

PLATES
39–76

→ENGAGEMENT p.116

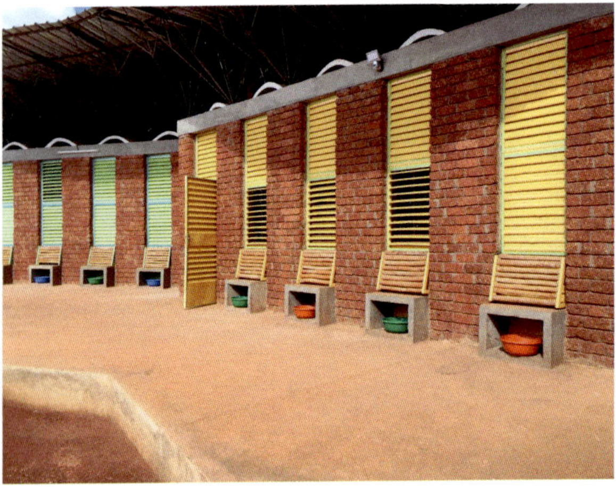

FRANCIS KÉRÉ
Water containers at Lycée Schorge, Koudougou, Burkina Faso.
© Kéré Architecture.

PLATE 40
→EXCHANGE p.120

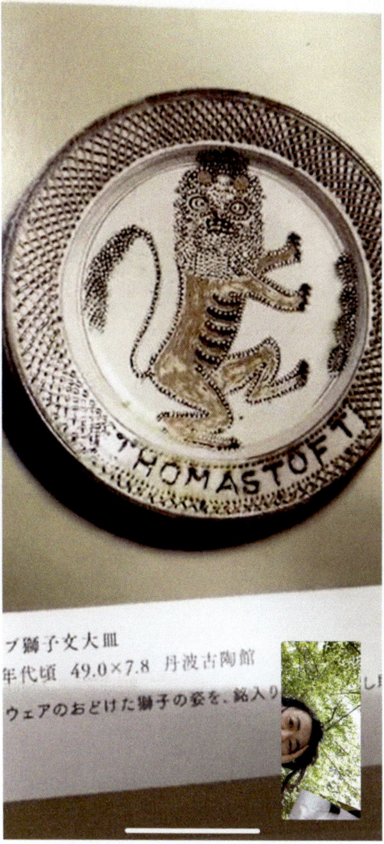

NATSUKO UCHINO
Research image for *Keramikos 4*.

PLATE 41

→FARMING p.122

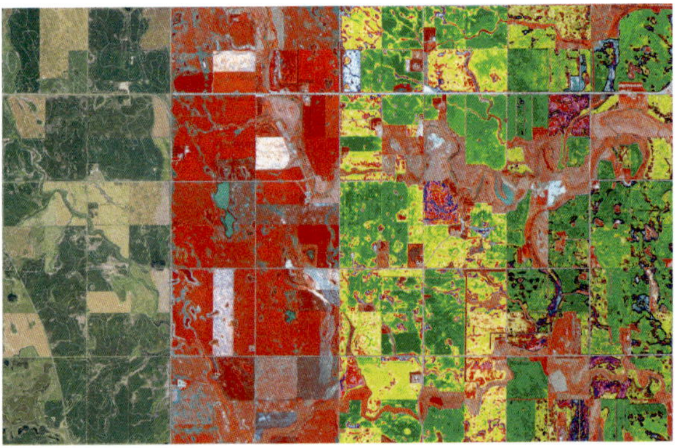

REM KOOLHAAS
Precision Farming, American Midwest.
Courtesy of AMO.

PLATE 42

→FIRE p.125

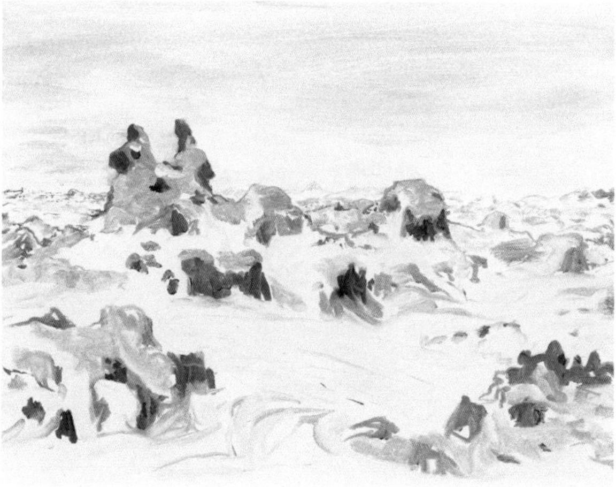

RAGNAR KJARTANSSON

Ragnar Kjartansson, *Eldhraun*, 2019,
oil on canvas, 80 × 105 cm.

PLATE 43
→FLUID p.126

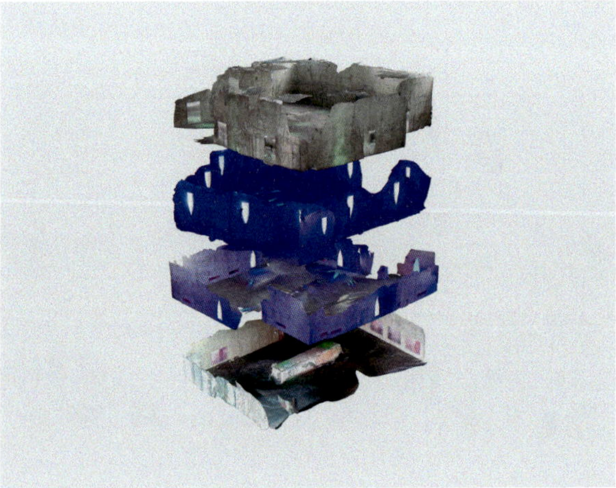

JOANA DE LA FONTAINE
Pamela Rosenkranz, *House of Meme*, 2021.
3D scan by Joana de la Fontaine.
© Courtesy of Pamela Rosenkranz.

PLATE 44
→FOSSIL p.127

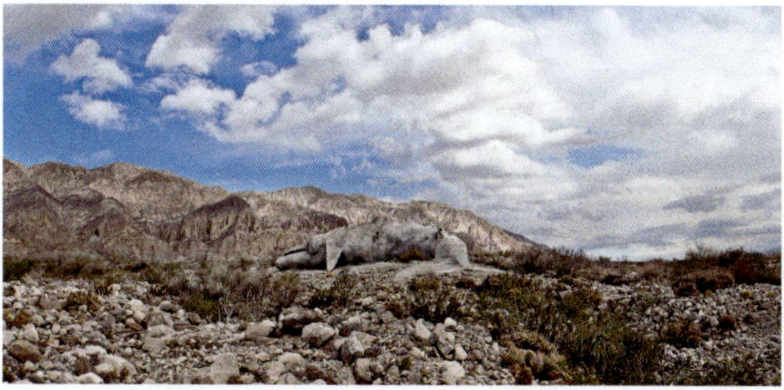

ADRIÁN VILLAR ROJAS
Adrián Villar Rojas, *Mi familia muerta (My Dead Family)*, 2010, unfired local clay, cement, 3 × 27 × 4 m. Installation view in Sierra Chica de Zonda, San Juan, Argentina.
© Photo by Alan Legal. Courtesy of the artist.

PLATE 45
→FREEDOM p.128

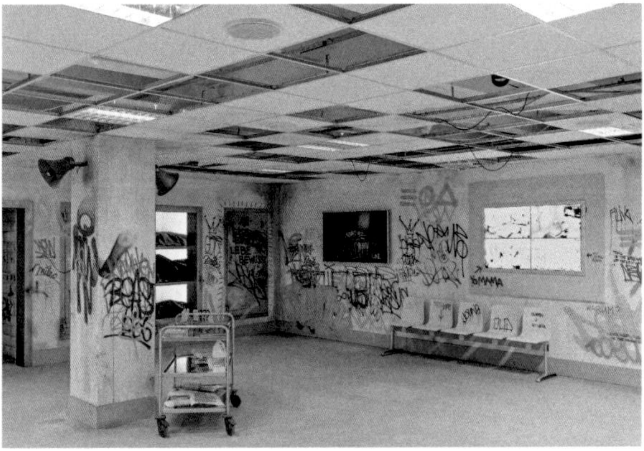

MICHAEL SCHINDHELM
Exhibition view of *THE END OF AGING* by Michael Schindhelm, *Reception*, Kulturstiftung Basel H. Geiger | KBH.G, 2024.
© Photo by Kulturstiftung Basel H. Geiger | KBH.G.

PLATE 46
→FUNCTION p.129

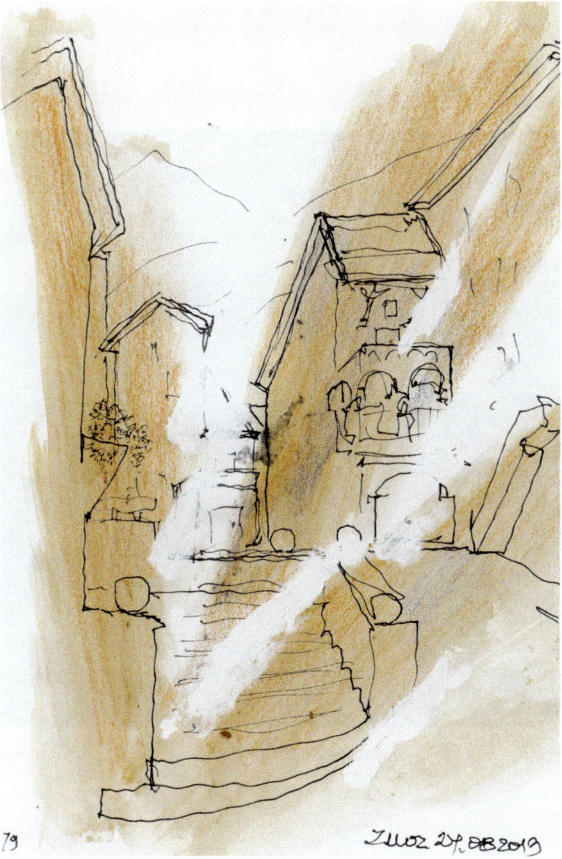

ZVI HECKER
Drawing by Zvi Hecker.
Courtesy of Ella Zimmerman and Zvi Hecker Architektur und Kunst Stiftung.

PLATE 47
→FUNGUS p.129

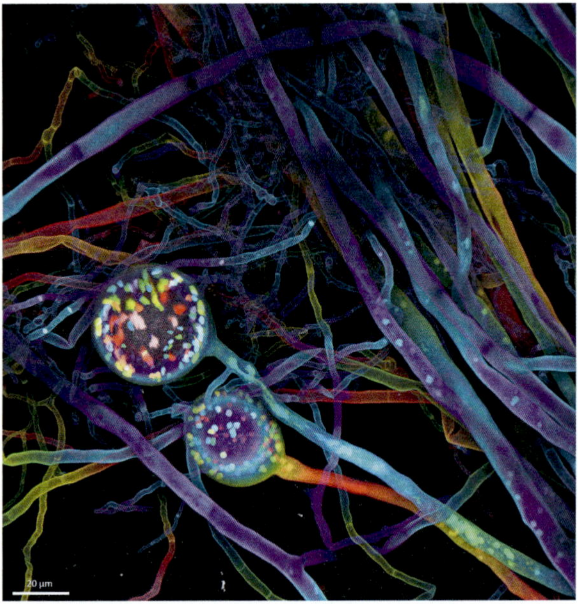

MERLIN SHELDRAKE
Microscopic image of fungal spores.
© Photo by Vasilis Kokkoris, VU Amsterdam.

PLATE 48

→FURNITURE p.130

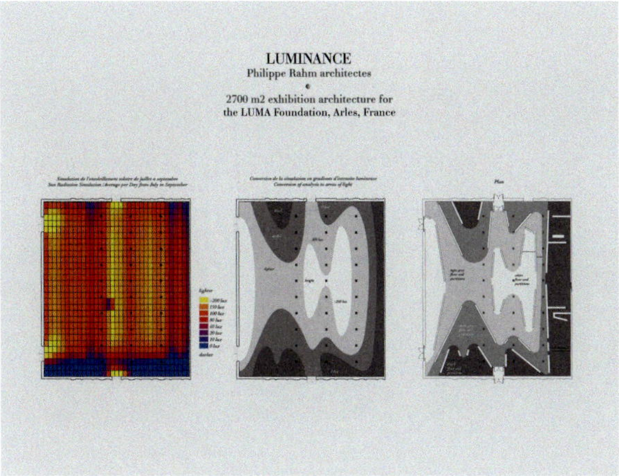

PHILIPPE RAHM
Philippe Rahm architectes, *Luminance*, exhibition design, LUMA Foundation, Arles, France, 2016.
© Photo by Philippe Rahm architectes.

PLATE 49
→GENDER p.132

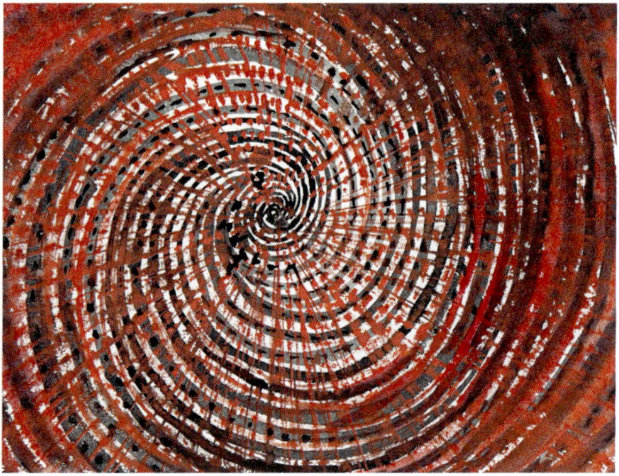

JULIA VOSS
Hilma af Klint, *On the Viewing of Flowers and Trees*, 1922, watercolor, 18 × 25 cm, HAK 612.

PLATE 50
→GHOST p.134

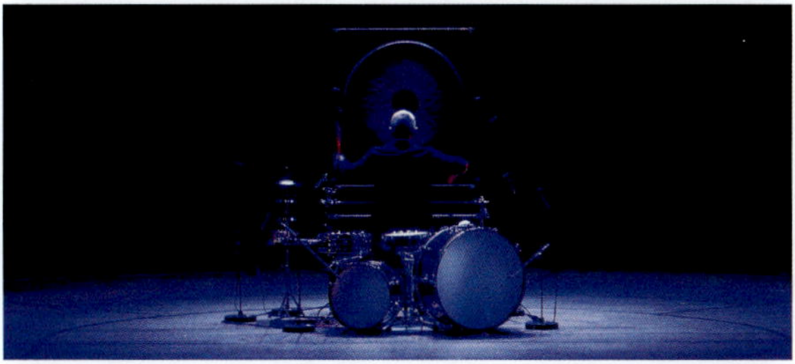

FRITZ HAUSER
Videostill from *SPETTRO* at KKL Lucerne, 2018.
© Video by Erich Busslinger.

PLATE 51
→GRADIENT p.136

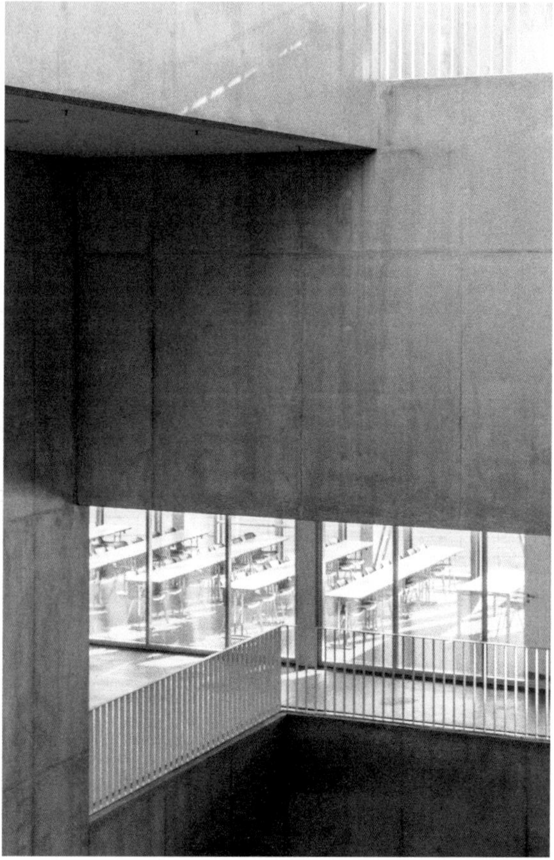

JEANNETTE KUO
Weiden Secondary School by Karamuk Kuo.
© Photo by Adrien Comte.

PLATE 52
→GRAPHIC DESIGN p.136

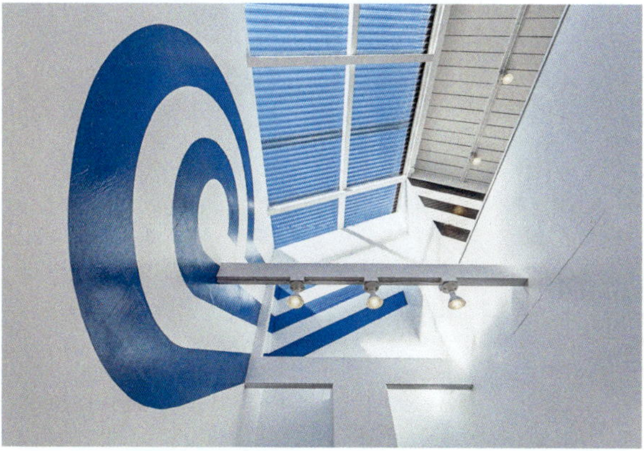

BARBARA STAUFFACHER SOLOMON
Supergraphic by Barbara Stauffacher Solomon at Moonraker Recreation Center, The Sea Ranch.

PLATE 53
→GRASS p.137

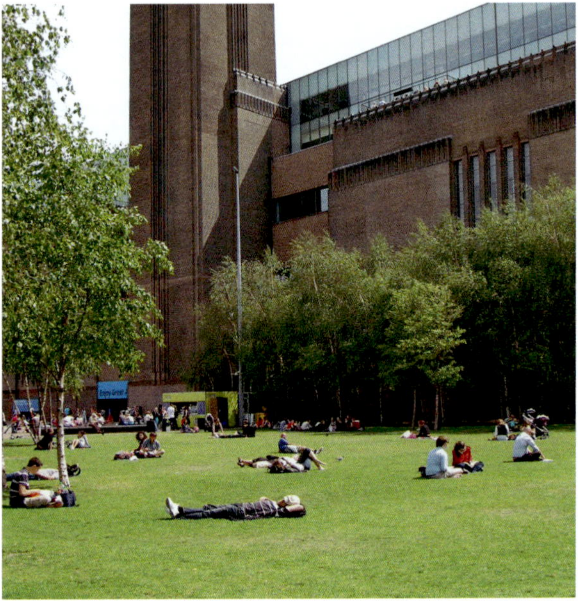

GÜNTHER VOGT
Public landscape design for the Tate Modern site by VOGT Landscape Architects.

PLATE 54

→GREEN p.138

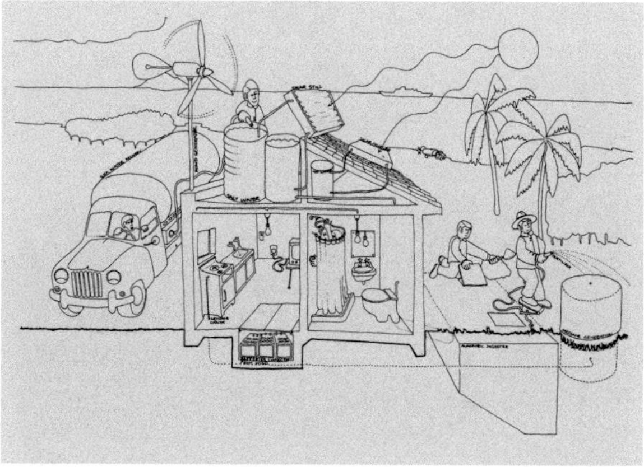

NORMAN FOSTER

Gomera Regional Planning Study. Drawings by Pedro Guedes illustrating energy self-sufficient houses: the house on the left relies on conventional services, while the one on the right is supported by natural resources – wind power generates electricity for lighting, sea-water deliveries allow drinking water to be distilled in solar stills, and anaerobic generators digest household waste to create methane gas for cooking.

PLATE 55
→ HOME p.141

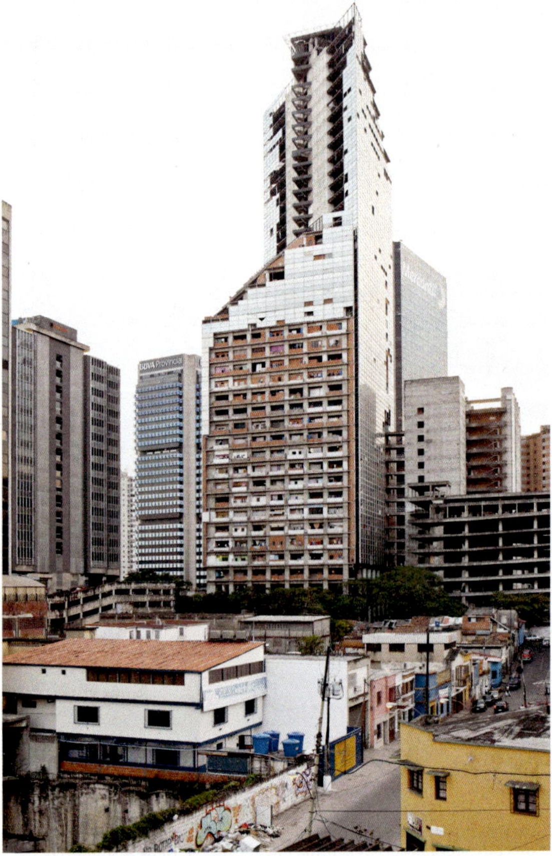

HUBERT KLUMPNER
Centro Financiero Confinanzas (Torre de David), Caracas.
© Photo by ETH Zurich, Urban-Think Tank / Daniel Schwartz.

PLATE 56

→HORIZON p.142

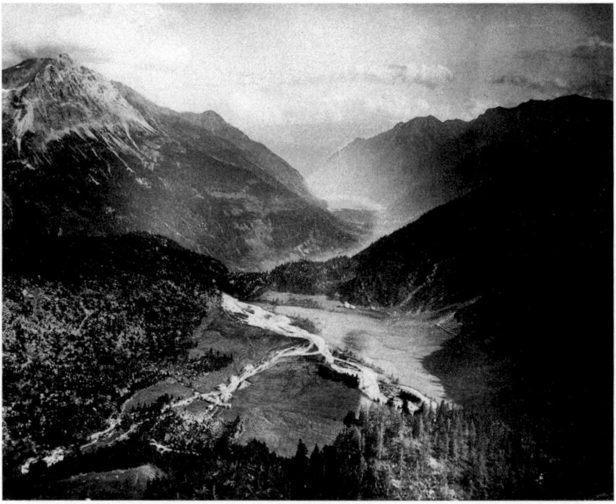

LUZIUS KELLER
View from Alp Grüm into the Puschlav, around 1880–1900.
© Photo by Elizabeth Main.

PLATE 57
→HUB p.143

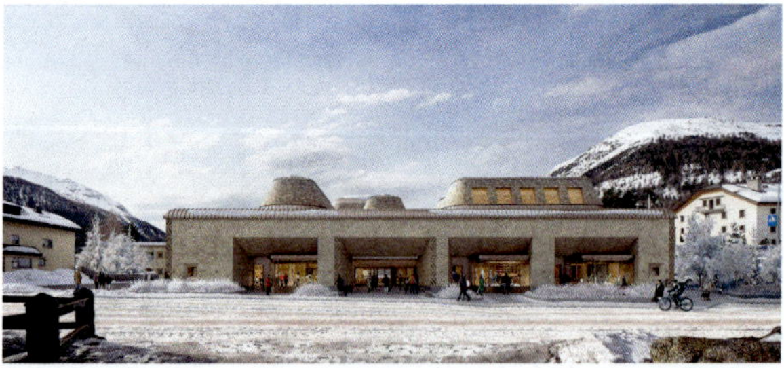

REGULA CURTI
Rendering of the proposed innovation centre InnHub La Punt in La Punt, Switzerland, by Foster + Partners.
© Foster + Partners.

PLATE 58
→ICON p.144

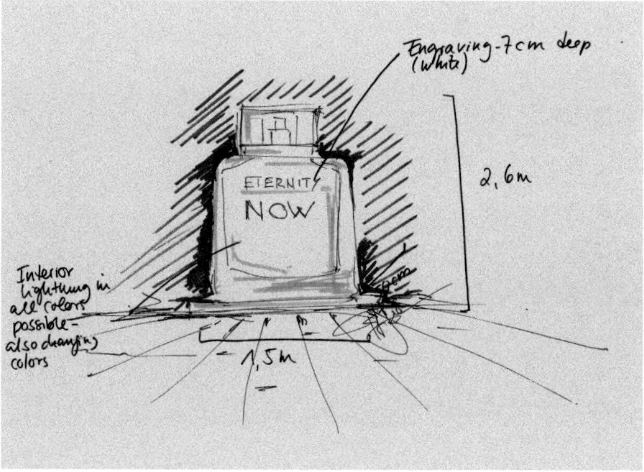

SYLVIE FLEURY
Sketch for the ice sculpture *Eternity Now* by Sylvie Fleury, presented by Gübelin at the 2016 edition of Engadin Art Talks.

PLATE 59

→INFINITY p.190

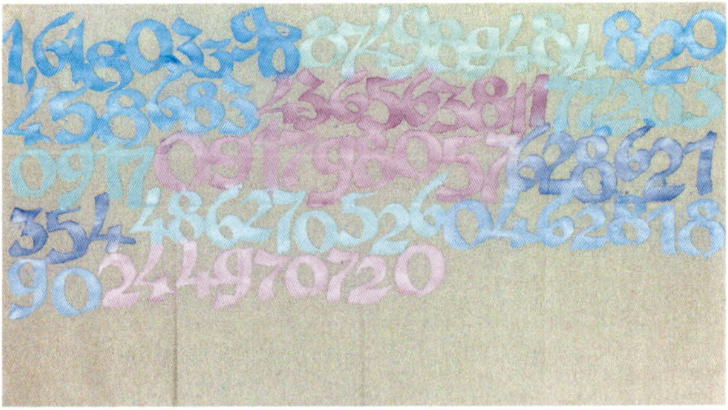

GIORGIO GRIFFA

Giorgio Griffa, *Canone aureo 720*, 2016, acrylic on canvas.

PLATE 60

→INTEGRATION p.192

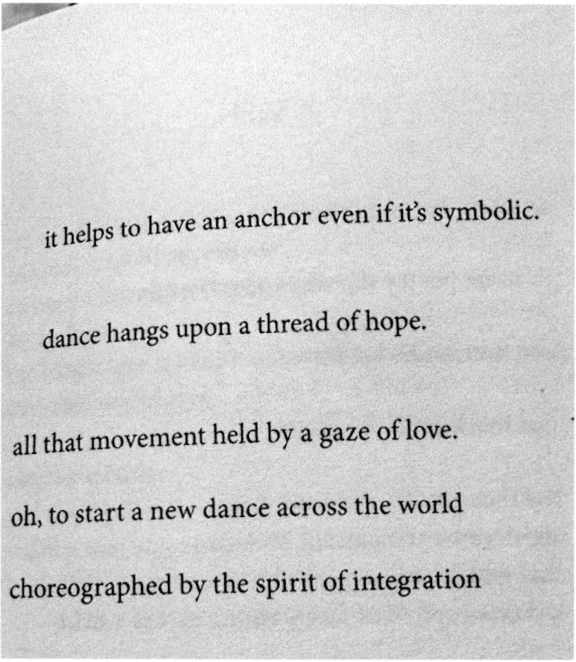

it helps to have an anchor even if it's symbolic.

dance hangs upon a thread of hope.

all that movement held by a gaze of love.

oh, to start a new dance across the world

choreographed by the spirit of integration

BEN OKRI

Excerpt from *Ballet of the Unseen* by Ben Okri.

PLATE 61
→INTENTION p.193

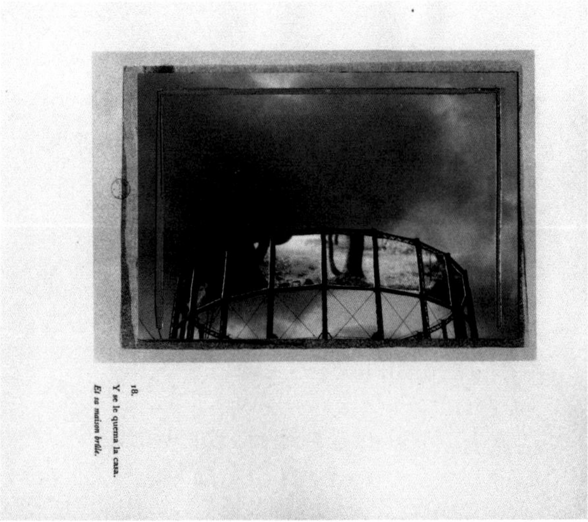

BETHAN HUWS
Bethan Huws, *Untitled*, 1985. Black-and-white photomontage from a set of 21 sheets. 17.5 × 20.5 cm/each.
Courtesy of the artist. Kunstmuseum St.Gallen, Donation Erika and Otto Friedrich, Basel 2013.

PLATE 62
→INTIMACY p.195

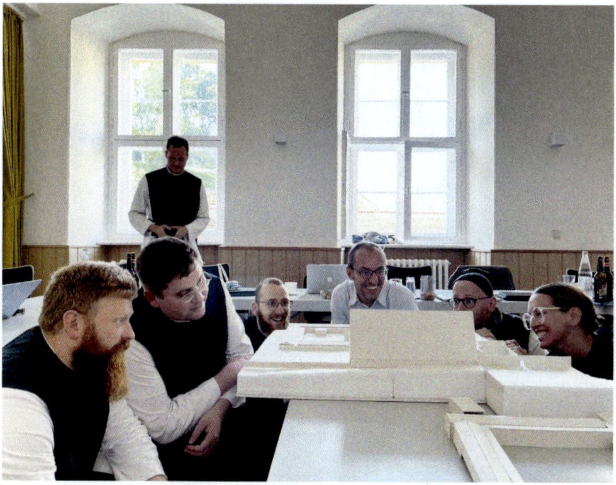

TATIANA BILBAO
Design workshop at Maria Friedenshort Convent, Neuzelle, Brandenburg, Germany, 2020.

PLATE 63
→JUSTICE p.196

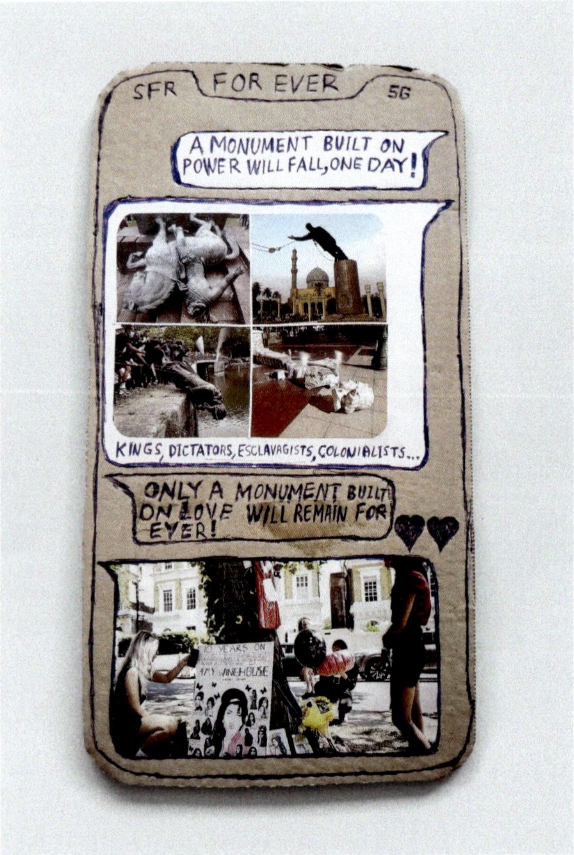

THOMAS HIRSCHHORN
Thomas Hirschhorn, *POST (56)*, 2023, cardboard, prints, felt pen, 37 × 21 cm.

PLATE 64

→LAYER p.198

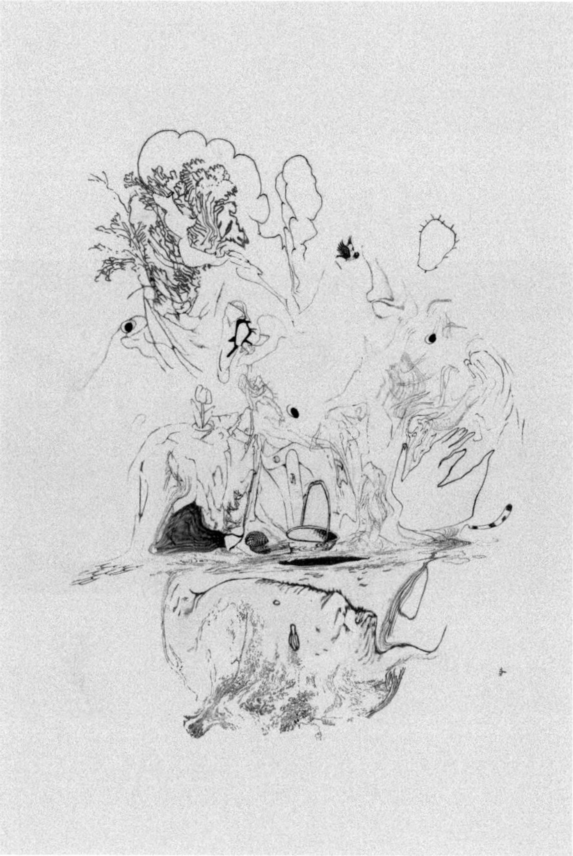

RACHEL ROSE

Rachel Rose, *The Sandbox*, 2023.

PLATE 65
→MAPPING p.203

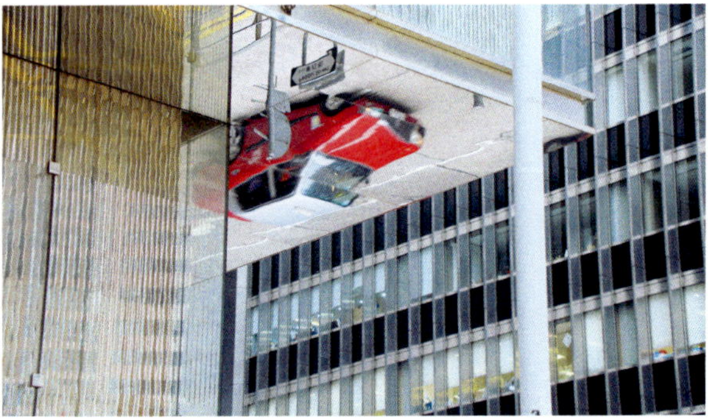

SARAH MORRIS
Film still of *ETC* by Sarah Morris, 2024,
HD Digital, 79:17 minutes, 16:9

PLATE 66

→MARRIAGE p.203

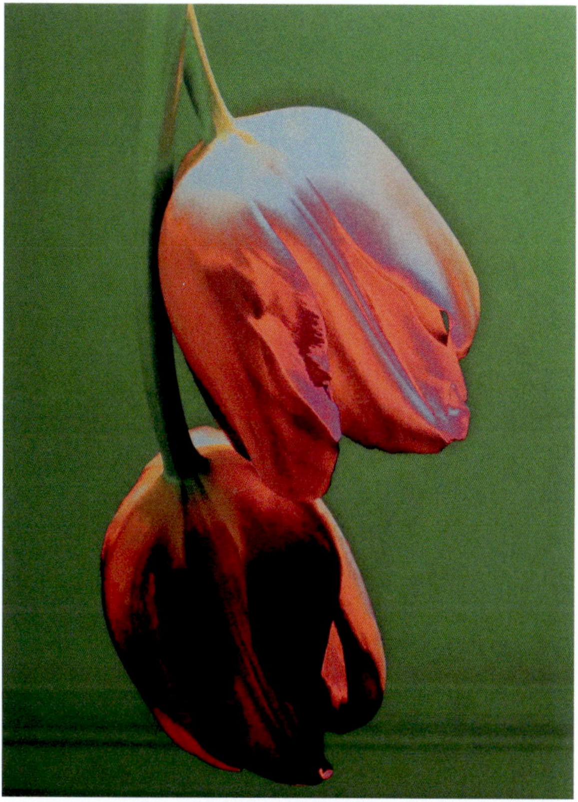

MIREILLE WUNDERLY
Mireille Wunderly, *Floral Unterwegs*.

PLATE 67
→MATERIAL p.204

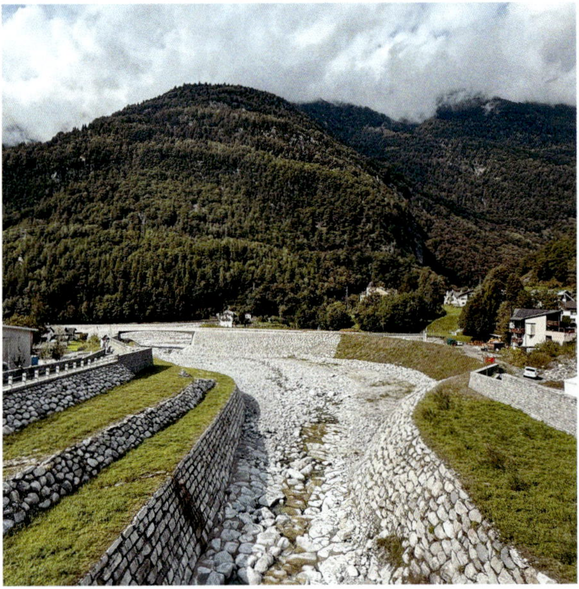

MARTINA VOSER
Strata, 2023.
Client: Comune di Bregaglia and Canton of Grisons.
Authors: ARGE 'strata'; overall management and civil structures by Conzett Bronzini Partner, Chur; hydraulic engineering by Eichenberger Revital, Chur; road engineering by Caprez Ingenieure, Silvaplana; landscape architecture by mavo Landschaften / Müller Illien, Zurich; architecture by Conradin Clavuot, Chur.
© Photo by mavo Landschaften.

PLATE 68

→MISTAKE p.208

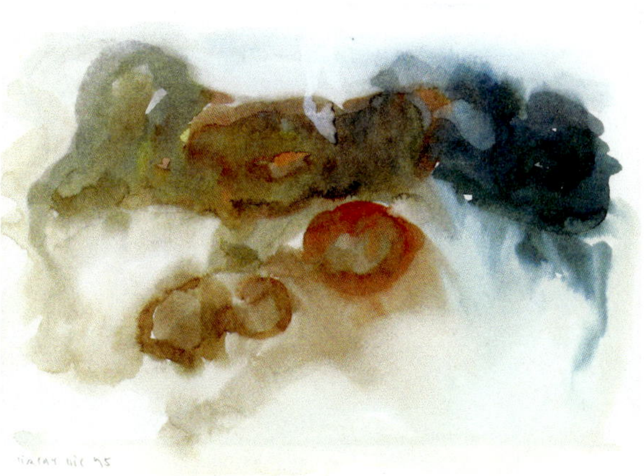

SMILJAN RADIC
Watercolour by Smiljan Radić, preparatory work for his installation for the Céline fashion show, Paris, 2017.
Courtesy of Smiljan Radic.

PLATE 69
→MUTE p.213

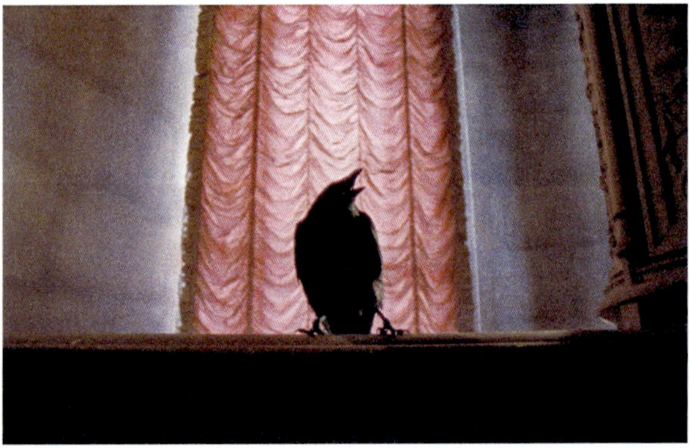

MARIANNA SIMNETT
Film still of *The Bird Game* by Marianna Simnett, 2019.
Courtesy of the artist, Société, Berlin, FVU,
the Rothschild Foundation, and Frans Hals Museum.

PLATE 70
→NEUTRALITY p.214

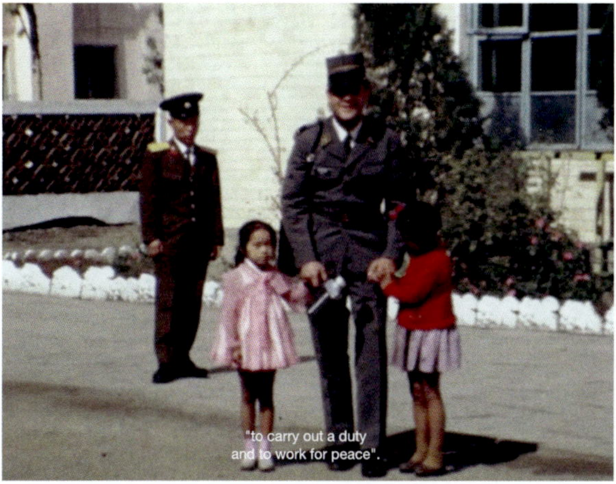

DENISE BERTSCHI
Film still of *STATE FICTION. Neutral Only On The Outside* by Denise Bertschi, 2021, 70 min.
Courtesy of the artist.

PLATE 71
→NOTE p.216

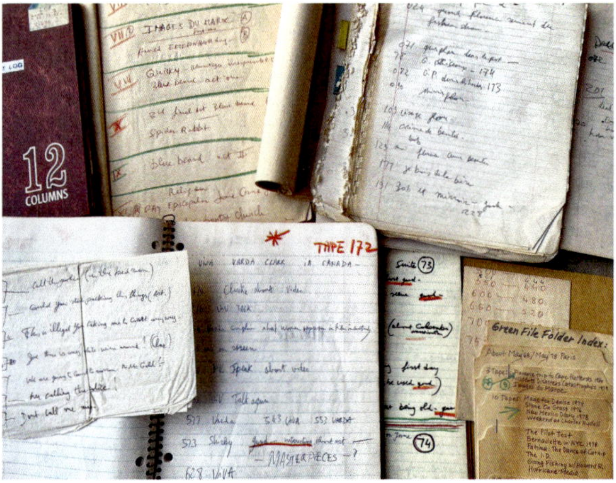

MICHEL AUDER
Editing notes by Michel Auder, 1970s.
Courtesy of Michel Auder and Karma International.

PLATE 72
→NOTRE-DAME p.216

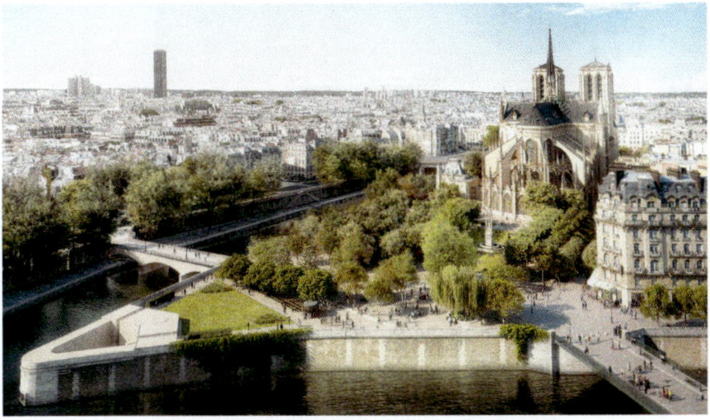

BAS SMETS
Notre-Dame, Paris, rendering by Studio Alma for Team Bureau Bas Smets.

→OBJECT p.217

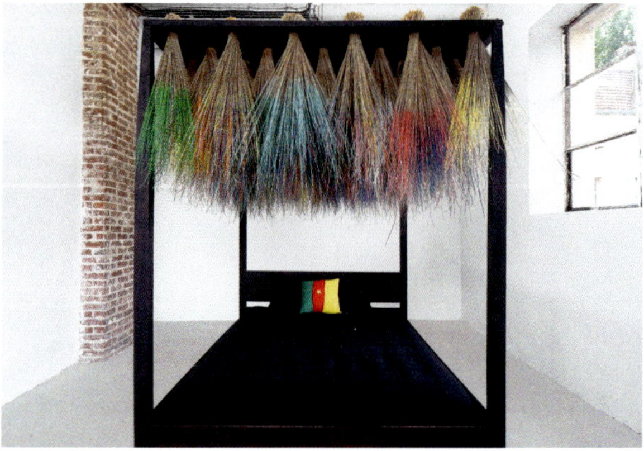

PASCALE MARTHINE TAYOU
Pascale Marthine Tayou, *Balais Citoyens*, 2025,
unique work, wood, veins of palm leaves, paint, fabrics.
© ADAGP, Paris. Courtesy of the artist and GALLERIA CONTINUA.
Photo by Hafid Lhachmi.

PLATE 74
→OPERA p.218

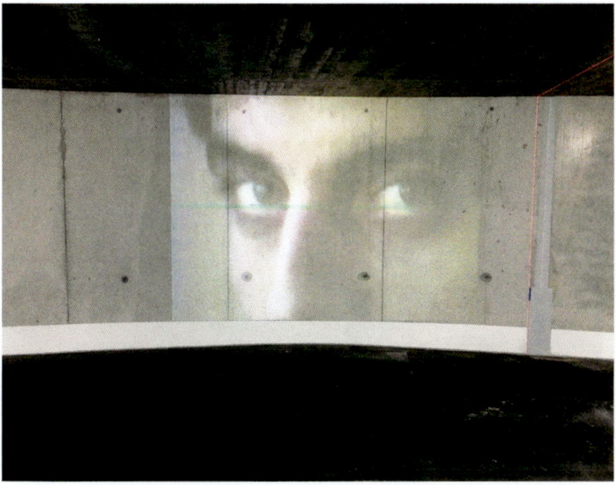

ADAM SZYMCZYK
Michel Auder, *Champfèr Garage Opera*, 2019,
two-channel video installation.

PLATE 75
→OWNERSHIP p.221

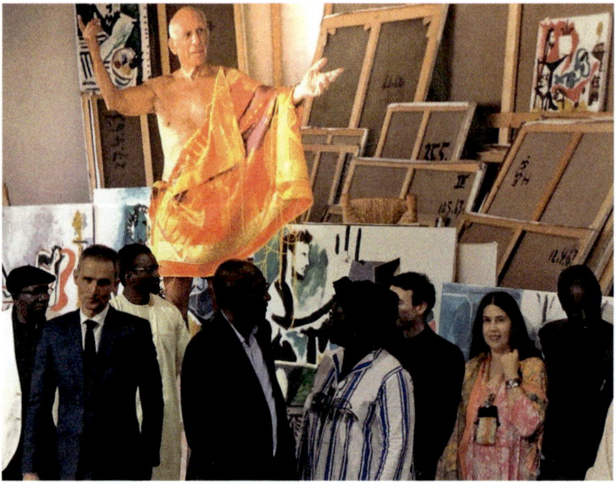

CHRIS DERCON
Visitors of the *Picasso à Dakar, 1972–2022* exhibition
at the Museum of Black Civilisations in Dakar, Sénégal, 2022.
© Photo by Chris Dercon.

PLATE 76
→PARADISE p.221

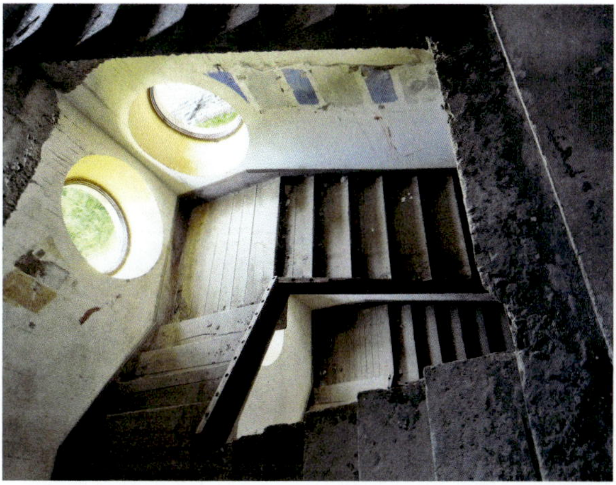

TOBIAS REHBERGER
Ruins of the former Hotel Paradiso, Martelltal Valley, originally designed by Gio Ponti between 1933 and 1935.
© Photo by Tobias Rehberger.

INCLUSION

"Inclusion isn't about numbers or political correctness – it's about action[p.24]. We've learned[p.199] that true inclusion is a monumental task that must be approached collectively, beginning with how we behave[p.35], who we hire and how we communicate[p.51], not just what we programme. It demands profound cultural[p.60] change[p.43], not superficial gestures[p.134]. Without that depth, any effort remains shallow and ineffective."

LAURENT LE BON
Curator and president of the Centre Pompidou, Paris
E.A.T. 2022: Matter and Memory, Zuoz

INDEPENDENCE

"Autocracy thrives on obedience[p.217]. Art[p.31] is rooted[p.289] in independence. The artistic process affirms that people can shape[p.295] their own world. It reflects[p.279] a freedom[p.128] that dictators, no matter how ruthless, cannot eliminate. That's why they fear[p.123] it. As long as we can create, we hold[p.141] the seeds of freedom – and that terrifies them."

KENNETH ROTH
Former ED of Human Rights Watch
E.A.T. 2023: Hoffnung? Hoffnung!, Zuoz

INDIVIDUALISM

"The Sistine Chapel is really about God giving individual identity[p.146] to man, and that's a fundamentally Western[p.321] idea[p.145]. It's one of the reasons the West clings so tightly to the concept of individualism. Without the Sistine Chapel, maybe even democracy wouldn't exist. It's our North Star – we shape[p.295] our collective decision-making around it."

ALVARO BARRINGTON
Artist
E.A.T. 2025: Form and Impact, Zuoz

INDUSTRY

"The carbon[p.40] footprint of the art[p.31] world is horrific, and yet it is probably one of the industries least studied in terms of ecological[p.113] toxicity. We should really pay attention to that."

RASHA SALTI
Researcher, writer, producer and curator of art and film
E.A.T. 2024: Jenseits von Ohnmacht – Beyond Powerless, Zuoz

INEQUALITY

"In Lubumbashi, the city[p.47] was deliberately designed to enforce racial segregation during Belgian colonial[p.50] rule. A so-called 'neutral[p.214] zone' was created to avoid close contact between White and Black populations: an almost empty area measuring[p.205] at least 500 metres, based on the distance a malaria-carrying mosquito could fly. This sanitary corridor physically separated the white 'European city' from the Black 'indigenous city' and was used to justify keeping white residents 'safe' – not only from disease but also from what colonial authorities called the 'rowdy activities' of the Black population. Urban planning in Lubumbashi thus became[p.35] a tool of control, containment[p.54] and exclusion – promising each race the chance to live according to their own 'needs', while in reality[p.277] reinforcing a deeply violent system of inequality."

SAMMY BALOJI
Artist
E.A.T. 2025: Form and Impact, Zuoz

INFINITY

"In one of my recent works, there is the number – the golden number – which I think is very important because it never finishes. In time[p.308], it's similar to poetry[p.226] that lives beyond its own era. And what is incredible is that this number continues[p.55] infinitely, but becomes[p.35] smaller and smaller, because of the decimals. Sixteen will never become seventeen, but it continues without end. In my opinion, it is something similar to a form that moves through the air[p.27], towards a result that never arrives. The golden number steps into the unknown[p.313] like Orpheus."

GIORGIO GRIFFA
Artist
E.A.T. 2016: Traces and Fragments, Zuoz
→ PLATE 59 p.170

INFORMATION

"Imagine[p.146] if every material[p.204] had a digital[p.107] tag such as an RFID chip leading to a database[p.62] that tells you what it is, when and where it was made, what condition it's in, and where it's been. That would allow us to design with real information. For the Dome Pavilion at ETH Zurich, we engraved QR codes on each beam, so anyone could scan them and access p.23 all the specifications to enable true reuse p.285."

CATHERINE DE WOLF
Professor, civil engineer, architect, and founder and director of the chair of Circular Engineering for Architecture (CEA), ETH Zurich
E.A.T. 2023: Hoffnung? Hoffnung!, Zuoz

INFRASTRUCTURE

"Right now, infrastructure is designed to deliver perfect protection p.232, perfect roads, perfect systems. But I'm convinced that identity p.146, culture p.60, and poetry p.226 are just as vital. Future p.130 infrastructure must be designed not just for monofunctional efficiency, but to support p.303 the multifaceted well-being of society p.299. That means embracing complexity – where protection meets meaning p.204, and engineering meets care p.40."

MARTINA VOSER
Landscape architect and co-founder of landscape architecture and urban planning studio Mavo Landschaften
E.A.T. 2024: Jenseits von Ohnmacht – Beyond Powerless, Zuoz

INHERITANCE

"We must engage p.116 with the past. We need to understand p.313 the legacies that we've inherited. We've also inherited negative legacies – legacies of slavery, colonialism p.50 and racism creating deep inequities that must now be repaired, legacies of economies that have been structurally addicted to endless economic growth p.138, and fossil fuels that must now be transformed p.310. If we don't understand that long history p.140, particularly the social and economic history we've inherited, we can't really pinpoint in what ways we need to change p.43 the way we think about the future p.130."

ROMAN KRZNARIC
Philosopher
E.A.T. 2021: Longue Durée, livestream

INJUSTICE

"You know that I was particularly shaken as a child because my father, when I was eleven, was abducted by the communists and sent to Siberia. Together with others from Rostock, he was secretly sentenced to two terms of 25 years of forced labour. For two and a half years, we had no ideap.145 whether he was alive. At schoolp.291, I was learningp.199 songsp.299 about the beautyp.34 of socialism and the godlike father of humanityp.143, Joseph Stalin. You recite those texts, then come homep.141, look into your mother's eyes, and know the truth: this is injustice."

JOACHIM GAUCK
Former Federal President of Germany (2012–2017)
E.A.T. 2023: Hoffnung? Hoffnung!, Zuoz

INSPIRATION

"We need to stop criticising what is and start inspiring what could be. Humanp.143 beingsp.36 always want to innovate. We want to move forwards, not stay stillp.301. So let's be inspired by the impossible mission: to stop this seemingly unstoppable train of destruction that is climate changep.48. We made this messp.206. Why wouldn't we be able to fix it?"

CYRILL GUTSCH
Designer and founder of Parley for the Oceans
E.A.T. 2020: Silent – Listen, Zuoz

INSTINCT

"In performancep.222, you surrender to the unknownp.313; to the energyp.115 the visitorp.318 brings, to how they move through space, how they might react. That surrender is unsettling, even frightening, but it heightens your senses. It wakes you up; like an animal instinct."

ISABEL LEWIS
Artist, professor, artistic director of Tanzquartier Wien
E.A.T. 2021: Longue Durée, livestream

INTEGRATION

"the politics of the
powerlessp.228 who sing
strength
with their bodiesp.38,
of the prayersp.228 for truth...
it helps to have an anchor

even if it is symbolic[p.305].
dance[p.61] hangs upon a
thread of hope[p.142].
all that movement held[p.141]
by a gaze[p.132] of love[p.202].
oh, to start a new dance
across the world
choreographed[p.45] by the
spirit of integration."
(Excerpt from Ballet of the Unseen.*)*

BEN OKRI
Poet and novelist
E.A.T. 2020: Silent – Listen, Zuoz
→PLATE 60 p.171

INTENTION

"For the 2013 edition of Engadin Art Talks[p.116] centred around the theme of *Ghosts and the Uncanny*, I showed a series of black-and white photomontages from my BA Fine Art[p.31] portfolio, which had never been shown publicly before. Many of the images[p.146] combine architectural[p.29] elements from London with rural[p.289] scenes from my native Wales – where interiors suddenly become[p.35] exteriors and vice versa, often creating a sense of disorientation. For example, behind a building where we expect to see[p.296] the sky, we see an extreme close-up of a door; in a second image, we see a large, looming sky with a row of gable-roof, terraced houses[p.142] slowly[p.298] sinking into the earth[p.112] beneath; in a third, we see an ethereal forest[p.126], fragmented[p.127] through the eight frames of a Victorian gasholder. In college at this time[p.308], I was known as 'the surrealist' – a term that I disliked a lot because my form of surrealism was unintentional – the images just turned out that way."

BETHAN HUWS
Artist
E.A.T. 2013: Ghosts and the Uncanny, Zuoz
→PLATE 61 p.172

INTERNET

"When Sri Lanka got its first Internet Service Provider in 1995, the Sri Lankan government didn't know how to censor[p.41] the internet, so the Liberation Tigers of Tamil Eelam immediately saw the potential of the World Wide Web – not just to circumvent censorship, but also to coordinate the Tamil diaspora worldwide. To me these lost histories p.140 – that didn't get to play out – are like sci-fis p.291 that offer a glimpse of alternate possible realities. p.277"

CHRISTOPHER KULENDRAN THOMAS
Artist
E.A.T. 2024: Jenseits von Ohnmacht – Beyond Powerless, Zuoz

INTERSECTION

"Rick Lowe spoke about the importance of both Joseph Beuys und John T. Biggers in shaping p.295 *Project Row Houses* – one a canonical figure, the other more obscure, largely because he's regional. That intersection is powerful. In the U.S. p.28, I find regional artists to be a deep well of knowledge. The vitality of civic and artistic practice p.228 doesn't only come from New York or L.A. or the big museums p.212 – it comes from the regions. And the regional artist might be a professor, a studio artist or someone without a formal title at all – just someone embedded in their community p.51. They cross p.59 the professional and institutional silos we often see in the art world. What unites p.313 them is a textured, sustained relationship p.280 to place and people. That's what gives their practice strength, and that's what revitalises the field – not just what's visible in the centre."

SIDDHARTHA MITTER
Writer, critic and journalist
E.A.T. 2025: Form and Impact, Zuoz

INTERTWINE

"We normally p.215 think of polyphony p.227 as a musical form, and as such a human p.143 art p.31. But it's also a powerful analogy for biological systems. In polyphonic music, melodies intertwine without ceasing to be many. And yet, when listening p.200 to polyphonic music, several streams of consciousness commingle in the mind p.207, and a multitude of parts can coalesce into a single piece of music that doesn't exist in any one of the parts alone[p.28]. I've come to think of fungal mycelium – which is both a multitude of growing[p.138] tips and a single interconnected[p.53] entity – as polyphony in bodily form. Mycelium is what happens when elongating fungal cells, which are streams of embodiment rather than streams of consciousness, commingle."

MERLIN SHELDRAKE
Biologist and author
E.A.T. 2021: Longue Durée, livestream

INTIMACY

"When I began working with the Cistercian monks outside Vienna, I found[p.125] myself unable to understand[p.313] their way of life through my own rational lens. Their life is devoted to a spiritual process – an intimacy with God that's hard to grasp. But I learned[p.199] that their architecture[p.29] isn't about function[p.129] or representation[p.281]. The robe is their first external expression. Then comes the cell. The cell becomes[p.35] the building block of the community[p.51]. If the community loses balance[p.34], the monastery ceases to exist. After listening[p.200] to Pater Kilian, I began to understand silence[p.297] not as emptiness, but as a precious and fragile presence[p.229] – the purest form of love[p.202], where everything is clear. Designing for that level of intimacy – that became my next obsession."

TATIANA BILBAO
Architect
E.A.T. 2020: Silent – Listen, Zuoz
→PLATE 62 p.173

INVENTION

"What you see[p.296] on our website today is just the beginning – nearly 100 inventions made freely available, ranging from solar energy and wind power to sustainable[p.304] mobility. But it's not just about technology[p.306]. Our work includes science fiction[p.291], speculative art[p.31] and overlooked narratives[p.213]. We translate these archives[p.30] into multiple languages[p.198] to make them truly public – because innovation should be a common resource[p.283], not a closed system."

LOÏC ROGARD
Researcher in the field of renewable energies at Atelier 21
E.A.T. 2023: Hoffnung? Hoffnung!, Zuoz

INVESTIGATION

"In 2008, we had designed the Bird's Nest to be the nation's glamour. But I was the first to criticise[p.58] it openly. The state told people: the best way to support[p.303] the Olympics is to stay home[p.141] and watch TV. Migrants were forced to leave the city[p.47], foreigners were restricted. I realised I could no longer be part of this machine[p.202]. Then came the Sichuan earthquake – 90,000 lives lost[p.201]. I found out over 5,000 students had died[p.63] because the government schools[p.291] collapsed while neighbouring buildings stood. That's when I began my investigation. I realised the most powerful thing I could do was to investigate. We found the names, birthdays, schools and classes of 5,219 of the students who died. We interviewed their parents. The point was to ask central questions[p.275], to insist on real numbers and to tell people: life must be respected[p.284]. We must not forget."

AI WEIWEI
Artist
E.A.T. 2023: Hoffnung? Hoffnung!, Zuoz

J

JUSTICE

"Monuments must fall[p.122]. All monuments established by authority, power and those honouring[p.141] oppressors[p.219], colonialists[p.50], tyrants, dictators, corrupt politicians. To destroy them is a form that problematises justice and gives a new form. By contrast, I cannot agree with the defilement of an artwork only because it is famous. There is a crucial distinction: toppling a monument for what it represents[p.281]: yes! But attacking art[p.31] solely because it is a powerful artwork in a museum[p.212], in order to get media reactions[p.24] focused on other issues, is just stupid and inefficient. It's a no-go, simply because it doesn't create a new form."

THOMAS HIRSCHHORN
Artist
2023: E.A.T. × Centre Pompidou, Paris
→ PLATE 63 p.174

K

KAFKA

"One thing I adore in Kafka, which Montaigne doesn't have, is fable. Montaigne stays grounded in reason. Kafka constantly stages parables. When he writes that Frau Ohnemacht (Madame Fainting) came to visit him – he lives it that way. And I, too, experience things that only take form for me through figuration. It's through figures – embodied metaphors – that I interpret the inexplicable. Is this paralysis? Powerlessness [p.228]? It becomes [p.35] fabulous. Kafka is like that all the time."

HÉLÈNE CIXOUS
Writer, playwright and literary critic
2023: E.A.T. × Centre Pompidou, Paris

KISS

"In one of my pieces, *Dancer of the Year,* I blow a kiss to every person in the audience – it can be 80 to 150 people. You just sit there, waiting for your turn. It's absurdly cheesy, I know. Even I think to myself: how dare you do this? But people respond [p.284]. They wait, they smile, they kiss me back. Somehow, it means something to them. Maybe it works because it's so cheesy. But it's also a gesture [p.134] of genuine connection [p.53]. No one's forced to participate [p.221] – and yet, everyone is drawn in."

TRAJAL HARRELL
Choreographer and dancer
2023: E.A.T. × Centre Pompidou, Paris

L

LABOUR

"These materials [p.204] used to transport cocoa – they are only allowed for one-time use due to international hygiene regulations. But in Ghana, after their official use, they start to circulate [p.46] again. They're reused p.285 by local merchants, by migrants, by workers. You find them all over: in markets, in trains, in slums, on people's backs. They travel far beyond their original function p.129. The longer they circulate, the more they acquire traces p.309 of the hands that touched p.308 them. They become p.35 part of an economy of residue, an economy of memory p.206. The value isn't just symbolic p.305 – it's material and social. The object p.217 becomes a document of movement and labour."

IBRAHIM MAHAMA
Artist
E.A.T. 2016: Traces and Fragments, Zuoz

LANGUAGE

"Even a dead language is like a fossil p.127. It's precious, like lithium or cobalt. Ancient p.29 Egyptian, Greek – it was through the Rosetta Stone that we could decode the hieroglyphs and access p.23 that rich p.286 legacy p.199 of philosophy p.224, literature and science. In the same way, languages like Songhay, Bambara, Fula or Tamashek have been around for centuries – and even if they seem marginal or forgotten, they hold p.141 deep cultural p.60 and historical p.140 significance."

MOHOMODOU HOUSSOUBA
Writer and literary scholar
E.A.T. 2023: Hoffnung? Hoffnung!, Zuoz

LAYER

"In *Palisades in Palisades* (2014), I used sound p.300 to collapse different historical p.140 moments, layering elements like a bullet ricocheting, birds squawking, the breath p.39 of a body p.38 or a steamboat engine. Each sound is tied to a different time p.308, but when overlaid, they allow you to feel multiple eras at once."

RACHEL ROSE
Artist
E.A.T. 2016: Traces and Fragments, Zuoz
→PLATE 64 p.175

LEADERSHIP

"I believe p.36 art can drive political change p.43. Think of the AIDS crisis – its cruelty, and the fact that it emerged at a time[p.308] when homosexuality was taboo and criminalised in many so-called democracies. Were it not for the painters, the poets, the writers, the filmmakers, the singers – people living with HIV would not have reclaimed[p.277] their humanity[p.143] and dignity[p.108]. It was the artists who led the way; everyone else followed."

RASHA SALTI
Researcher, writer, producer and curator of art and film
E.A.T. 2024: Jenseits von Ohnmacht – Beyond Powerless, Zuoz

LEARNING

"When I said I needed to make money[p.210] after my husband died[p.63], friends[p.128] told me to go to Swiss[p.305] graphic designer[p.136] Armin Hofmann. He and his wife Dorle were marvellous – they met me at the train station, brought chocolates for my daughter and found[p.125] us an apartment right on the river[p.287] in Basel. Armin told me, 'Just keep your mouth shut – I'll do the talking.' And he got me into the school by pretending I could speak German. He was an angel. I had been a painter, I knew about colour[p.50], about working large – big dripping group paintings. But I had no idea[p.145] how to do what Armin was trying to teach[p.306] me. I just went into the classes and learned[p.199]. I didn't say a word[p.324]. At first, no one spoke to me. I didn't speak German. But once I started to draw and think in Helvetica, suddenly everyone spoke English – except Armin, whose English was terrible, but we managed."

BARBARA STAUFFACHER SOLOMON
Artist and graphic designer
E.A.T. 2023: Hoffnung? Hoffnung!, Zuoz

LEGACY

"The museum[p.212] should really be a holistic place that reflects[p.279] contemporary[p.55] everyday reality[p.277], political and social discussions, while also dealing with history[p.140] as an ongoing process. Museums do not just store and activate objects[p.217]; they think about the legacy of those objects and what they mean today."

ANN DEMEESTER
Director of Kunsthaus Zurich
E.A.T. 2022: Matter and Memory, Zuoz

LEGITIMACY

"Autocrats[p.32] have tried to mimic democracy through 'managed elections' – rigging the system by silencing[p.297] media, banning protests[p.273], and suppressing opposition. But even that backfires. People still vote against them when they can. So they end up risking only an electoral charade – elections with no legitimacy, hollow rituals of power designed to fake popular support[p.303]. But these zombie democracies don't fool anyone."

KENNETH ROTH
Former executive director of Human Rights Watch
E.A.T. 2023: Hoffnung? Hoffnung!, Zuoz

LINK

"We architects have a reputation for being control freaks. But from our perspective[p.223], being an architect often feels like being chained by contradicting[p.56] demands – and then being asked to release ourselves from them like a magician[p.202]. What we do involves conceptualising relationships[p.280], finding[p.125] links between things that may not seem connected[p.53] – how people live or work, cultural[p.60] traditions or a site's specific conditions – and translating those into space. Our medium is the physical environment, with all its complexities, contradictions and chaos. With every project, we're asked to imagine[p.146] possible futures[p.130] for constantly evolving contexts[p.55], while using mostly static materials[p.204]."

JEANNETTE KUO
Architect and founding partner of architectural firm KARAMUK KUO
E.A.T. 2020: Silent – Listen, Zuoz

LISTEN

"We are all very good listeners – it's part of our evolution. 40,000 years ago, humans[p.143] were living communially[p.51] in caves, whether in alpine[p.28] valleys, Ethiopia or the Kalahari. At night, when saber-toothed tigers or hyenas entered a cave, some people would wake up because they heard them and escape. We are descended from those who listened and survived. Those who didn't wake up didn't pass on their genes."

CHRIS WATSON
Musician and sound recordist
E.A.T. 2020: Silent – Listen, Zuoz

LONGING

"The Engadine: a high alpine p.28 valley stretching for around one hundred kilometres, named after the Inn – the river p.287 that rises here, and flows all the way to the Black Sea, bringing distant breezes into this landscape. Shaped p.295 by departure, return and permanence p.223, the valley is a place of longing, and also the everyday environment of those living here."

RICO VALÄR
Literary scholar and cultural mediator
E.A.T. 2021: Longue Durée, livestream

LOOM

"To me, the grid structure on a loom is like an empty piece of paper ready to be drawn on. The magic p.202 happens once you take the work off the loom when the tension p.307 is released, and it is transformed p.310 into its relaxed state. It is a work as well as a material p.204 with its own characteristics."

CHRISTINA FORRER
Artist
E.A.T. 2021: Longue Durée, livestream

LOSS

"Language p.198 is like biology or chemistry – it's a fundamental material p.204. After returning to Mali in 2000, I didn't want to keep working on African-American literature. I wanted to do something that could give back. A Canadian linguist told me: 'Your language had the historical p.140 chance to be part of world literature – written in Arabic script – but now the key is not to miss the next technological p.306 shift p.296.' If our languages are absent p.23 from digital p.107 spaces, then future[p.130] generations[p.133] will lose all connection[p.53] to them."

MOHOMODOU HOUSSOUBA
Writer and literary scholar
E.A.T. 2023: Hoffnung? Hoffnung!, Zuoz

LOVE

"I began with poetry[p.226] because, like everyone, I went to school[p.291], and there we were introduced to poets and poems. For me, it was love at first sight[p.296] – a deep, enduring love. Poetry has accompanied me through every stage of life. It must always be present[p.230]; it is a companion that gives you hope[p.142], even when the poem is sad or the poet has led a difficult life – which they often have. But these are words[p.324] that are absolutely essential to life."

SIMONE FATTAL
Artist
2023: E.A.T. × Centre Pompidou, Paris

M

MACHINE

"In London we had to design for a rare bird, the black redstart, which lives on abandoned gravel sites (Laban Dance Centre). We couldn't plant trees[p.311] – they would attract predators – and we weren't allowed to remove the contaminated[p.54] soil. So we shaped[p.295] it into mounds, created habitat[p.139] on the theatre roof, and used plants that extract toxins from the ground. It looks like a simple park, but it's a hidden ecological[p.113] machine, designed as much for a bird's survival as for the neighbourhood's enjoyment."

GÜNTHER VOGT
Landscape architect
and professor emeritus
2024: E.A.T. × Kunsthalle Zürich, Zurich

MAGIC

"American[p.28] philosopher David Abram was performing[p.222] card tricks at a restaurant. Days later, five guests filed complaints: 'The magician must've spiked our drinks – the sky looked too blue, the posters too vivid.' But David replied, 'I didn't spike anything. I just disrupted what they expect from a coin – and with that, what they expect from the sky.' We don't actually see[p.296] the colour[p.50] of the sky – we see the colour we expect it to be. That's where magic has power: it unsettles our assumptions, and in doing so, opens a door to change[p.43]."

ES DEVLIN
Artist
E.A.T. 2022: Matter and Memory, Zuoz

MAPPING

"For me, mapping means seeing[p.296] things 'simultaneously from many perspectives[p.223]'. It is like a schizophrenic process where you view coordinates from inside, outside and through different people's perspectives within a city[p.47]. You shift[p.296] constantly between tiny details and the entire panorama – there's no fixed viewpoint. In this context[p.55], Charles and Ray Eames's film *Powers of Ten* (first version 1968, final version 1977) was very influential, as it zooms out and in, challenging[p.42] and expanding our sense of perspective."

SARAH MORRIS
Artist
E.A.T. 2011: Mapping the Alps, Zuoz
→PLATE 65 p.176

MARRIAGE

"For 40 years, painting was my dominant practice[p.228]. I always took photographs on the side, but never with true intent. Then I compiled all my paintings into a book – and after that, I found I could no longer paint. That marked the moment I truly turned to photography[p.224]. Now, for the first time, I'm combining the two: the logic of painting with the tools of photography. It's a wonderful marriage, opening up a new possibility – to create images[p.146] that feel painted, yet are captured through the lens."

MIREILLE WUNDERLY
Artist
E.A.T. 2022: Matter and Memory, Zuoz
→PLATE 66 p.177

MATERIAL

"We found it absurd to mine stone from mountains p.211 while the Cengalo Peak had just sent us a massive quantity of material. Yet working with this material meant relearning p.199 old techniques – cracking, not sawing stone – to avoid high water and energy p.115 use. We built test walls, using the rounder granite from the landslide material. The result: walls that are clearly new but in respectful p.284 dialogue p.107 with the old. Transforming p.310 the protecting p.232 wall into a terraced garden p.131 landscape was essential for grounding the new infrastructure p.191 in place and memory p.206, and to allow new life to grow p.138."

MARTINA VOSER
Landscape architect and co-founder of landscape architecture and urban planning studio Mavo Landschaften
E.A.T. 2024: Jenseits von Ohnmacht – Beyond Powerless, Zuoz
→ PLATE 67 p.178

MATTER

"To live is to breathe p.39 – and in breathing, we embrace the matter p.204 of the world. With every breath, an animal and the cosmos p.57 are joined. We draw in the world and make it part of our body p.38; we release our body back into the world. Breathing is not just a function p.129 – it is the place where life and the planet become one."

EMANUELE COCCIA
Philosopher, lecturer and author
E.A.T. 2020: Silent – Listen, Zuoz

MEANING

"I have certain expectations of architecture p.29: there are timeless constants – construction p.53, topography and materials p.204. Beyond these, however, there are other aspects that are just as important: meaning, emotions and lived experience. I long p.201 for an architecture that turns away from pure objectivity and embraces events, emotions and the courage to fall p.122 out of time p.308."

GION CAMINADA
Architect
E.A.T. 2021: Longue Durée, livestream

MEASURE

"German geographer and naturalist Alexander von Humboldt tried to measure everything: altitude, latitude, humidity, wind speed – even the blueness of the sky. He translated all this data into beautiful p.34 images p.146, to understand p.313 and represent p.281 the systemic logic of an enivronment. We call this a designerly way of thinking. For me, that's deeply inspiring. Unlike Humboldt, I don't explore natural environments; I'm asked to intervene in artificial p.31 sites – to bring nature p.213 back into the man-made. And in doing so, I try to understand these environments as interconnected p.53 systems, as microclimates p.207 where life can return."

BAS SMETS
Landscape architect
E.A.T. 2023: Hoffnung? Hoffnung!,
Zuoz

MEDITERRANEAN

"When Matthew-Lutz Kinoy and I first arrived at the Los Arrayanes factory in Granada, I think they expected us to hand them a design to reproduce. Instead, we wanted to paint ourselves – drawing inspiration p.192 from their repertoire and from the region's historical p.140 and geographic context p.55. Of course, part of the reason we came to the factory was their capacity for volume and large series, so we worked on their bisqueware. They gave us a small workspace inside the factory, and what fascinated me most was the convergence of motifs p.211: traditions from the Middle East, North Africa p.26 and Southern Europe all meeting in that region. It felt like a living synthesis of the Mediterranean trade routes. I initially came with an interest in ecology p.113 and material p.204 culture p.60, but what we discovered was a visual language p.318 that embodied a cross-continental, transhistorical p.140 decorative ecosphere."

NATSUKO UCHINO
Artist
E.A.T. 2023: Hoffnung? Hoffnung!,
Zuoz

MELT

"When you think the mountains[p.211] are so resistant[p.282] – they are not. In the canton of Glarus people recently saw that the shape[p.295] of their mountain had changed[p.43]. Melting glaciers and permafrost make slopes unstable. In 70 years we will have around 2,000 more lakes in Switzerland[p.305]. If global warming is continuous[p.55], even the Matterhorn could lose its form as the permafrost melts. That means our national identity[p.146] may shift[p.296] from the mountains to the lakes, as you can already see[p.256] in the national assembly room, mountains and a lake, in a huge painting. Yet hardly anyone outside science, geology or art[p.31] is working on this."

GÜNTHER VOGT
Landscape architect and professor emeritus
2024: E.A.T. × Kunsthalle Zürich, Zurich

MEMORY

"The walls of *House of Meme* are alive – breathing[p.39] with data, shimmering with light that mimics leaves, water and soft sunlight. The floors, the ceilings, every surface is infused with memory: traces[p.309] of what is, what was and what could be. This house is a body[p.38] of consumption[p.53], absorbing[p.23] and reflecting[p.279] our voices[p.319], gestures[p.134] and desires[p.106]."

JOANA DE LA FONTAINE
Architect
2024: E.A.T. × Kunsthalle Zürich, Zurich

MESS

"Might today's architects resemble Philibert de l'Orme's 'bad architect' – blind and ungrounded, surrounded by gates and fortified buildings? If we embrace the messiness of reality[p.277] as a field of practice[p.228], and see ourselves as facilitators and interpreters rather than designers of objects[p.217], we could unlock powerful ways of living and building together."

ELISA SILVA
Architect and founder and principal of Enlace Arquitectura and Enlace Foundation
E.A.T. 2024: Jenseits von Ohnmacht – Beyond Powerless, Zuoz

MICROCLIMATE

"I call it biospheric urbanism – thinking of the built layer[p.198] as the interface between an uncertain atmosphere[p.31] above and an underused geology below. If we manage to turn our cities[p.47] into microclimatic ecologies[p.113], we can do two things at once: reduce the causes of the climate crisis, and mitigate its effects. That is my hope[p.142]."

BAS SMETS
Landscape architect
E.A.T. 2023: Hoffnung? Hoffnung!, Zuoz

MIND

"In his 1968 essay *A Sedimentation of the Mind: Earth Projects*, American[p.28] artist Robert Smithson aligns humidity with stifling sentimentality, and conversely, aridity with mental clarity. He derides modern[p.209] art[p.31], especially abstract expressionism: 'The wet mind enjoys pools and stains of paint. The artist or critic with a dank brain is bound to end up appreciating anything that suggests saturation[p.290]. They prefer art in a dewy green[p.138] setting – say, the hills of Vermont – rather than the painted desert[p.105]. When the artist goes to the desert, he burns the water or paint on his brain. The slush of the city[p.47] evaporates from the artist's mind as he installs his art.'"

EMILY-ELIZA SCOTT
Interdisciplinary scholar, artist and former park ranger
E.A.T. 2017: Snow and Desert, Zuoz

MINORITY

"Europe has many minority languages[p.198] – taken together, they are not a minority, but a reality[p.277]. They interact and benefit from each other. Romansh[p.288] has also absorbed[p.23] impulses from other regions. Historically[p.140], the language was at times marginalised, but today there is a growing[p.138] understanding[p.313]: to all those who speak[p.300] it or learn[p.199] it actively, it opens wide doors – to Italian, Spanish, and other Romance languages, and even to English through its Latin roots[p.289].

It is a small language with a wide horizon."

RICO VALÄR
Literary scholar
and cultural mediator
E.A.T. 2021: Longue Durée,
livestream

MIRROR

"For German artist Gerhard Richter, I think there are two kinds of perfect images p.146: the photograph and the mirror. The photograph is more well-known, of course, because of his photo-based paintings. But the mirror is always present p.230 too. In his studio, he always had this steel ball rolling around. It fascinated him – this polished sphere that reflects p.279 everything around it. It's the perfect mirror. When he was in the Engadin, he conceived the idea p.145 of producing a series of steel balls, each engraved with the name of a mountain p.211. It's not a depiction of nature p.213, but it symbolises p.305 how nature overwhelms you here – how it throws you back on yourself, just as the mirror-like ball throws your image back. This isn't an intimate p.195 or sentimental view of nature; it's external, overpowering and inaccessible."

DIETER SCHWARZ
Curator
E.A.T. 2024: Jenseits von
Ohnmacht – Beyond Powerless,
Zuoz

MISTAKE

"After a month of trying to design a clean, soft, wrinkle-free bubble for an eight-minute fashion p.122 show, I decided p.63 to abandon the technology p.306. Instead, we inflated a giant, plain bag – a banal geometry. As it grew p.138, it settled into the surrounding space and conformed to the structure around it. The fabric, sewn like a garment, gave it a sensual, textile presence p.229. It was a mistake turned graceful p.135."

SMILJAN RADIC
Architect
E.A.T. 2019: Grace and Gravity,
Zuoz
→ PLATE 68 p.179

MODEL

"American p.28 architect Buckminster Fuller once said: 'To change p.43 something, build a new model that makes the existing model obsolete.' That's how I see circular[p.46] construction[p.53]. It's a new model, but one that actually revives ancient[p.29] knowledge. We need to make the linear model – extract, use, dispose – obsolete. And we can only do that by making circular methods faster, cheaper and easier to implement."

CATHERINE DE WOLF
Professor, civil engineer, architect, and founder and director of the chair of Circular Engineering for Architecture (CEA), ETH Zurich
E.A.T. 2023: Hoffnung? Hoffnung!, Zuoz

MODERNISM

"*Stop Painting* (2021) is an exhibition that traces[p.309] five moments of rupture in Modernism – from French painter Paul Delaroche to today – when painting was interrupted by iconoclastic[p.144] gestures[p.134]. These gestures often reflect[p.279] shifts[p.296] in values, driven by political or technological[p.306] change[p.43]. I was interested in how these moments didn't end painting, but reshaped[p.295] it. Especially now, we see the canon[p.39] of Modernism being deeply questioned[p.275]. That's not just academic – it shapes how we see images[p.146], how we understand[p.313] history[p.140] and how we connect[p.53] to the present[p.230]."

PETER FISCHLI
Artist
E.A.T. 2021: Longue Durée, livestream

MODESTY

"I obtained a PhD in Physical Chemistry before studying Art History, and studying science can sometimes be quite challenging[p.42] and humbling. I think that's a good thing, because it makes you question[p.275] your intellect – and a bit of modesty is always valuable in life. Over the past year, for example, we've seen how COVID has made us more modest, which I believe[p.36] is very important."

ZIBA ARDALAN
Founder and director of Parasol unit foundation for Contemporary Art
E.A.T. 2021: Longue Durée, livestream

MODULARITY

"One of our recent projects with the United Nations is a modular container[p.54] that functions[p.129] as a school[p.291] during the week – equipped with low-tech renewable energy[p.115] systems – and transforms[p.310] into a space for art[p.31], music and community[p.51] exchange[p.120] on weekends. The aim is to stop separating technology[p.306] from culture[p.60]. Education[p.113], creativity and energy transition[p.310] must go hand in hand."

CÉDRIC CARLES
Designer and founder of Atelier 21
E.A.T. 2023: Hoffnung? Hoffnung!, Zuoz

MONEY

"I always say art[p.31] and money have sex[p.295] together but they don't sleep in the same bed. Because Dürer, Albrecht, Rembrandt, Rubens – there's a whole long history[p.140] of artists, that had an intimate[p.195] relationship[p.280] with cash. Even da Vinci was involved in lawsuits for leaving one commission behind when a better one presented itself. So I don't think that art and money is a new relationship. The levels of money today are vastly increased, but the connection[p.53] itself is very old."

KENNY SCHACHTER
Artist, writer and lecturer
E.A.T. 2021: Longue Durée, livestream

MOON

"What colour[p.50] really is the Moon? Actually, it is a dark[p.62] grey colour. It appears white to our eyes because of an optical illusion. This observation[p.217] tells us something profound – that our perception of the universe is shaped[p.295] not just by what exists, but by how we see[p.296] it. The Moon itself hasn't changed[p.43], but our understanding[p.313] of it has. This is true of much of science: it is a journey from illusion to deeper reality[p.277]."

BEN MOORE
Professor of astrophysics, author, musician and director of the Center for Theoretical Astrophysics and Cosmology at the University of Zurich
E.A.T. 2021: Longue Durée, livestream

MOTIF

"My photographs look benign – nothing like American[p.28] artist Robert Mapplethorpe's – yet I was censored[p.41] at the Smithsonian and called a liar by a U.S. Senator. That's when I began to understand[p.313] colour[p.50] not as a medium, but as a political motif. Colour became[p.35] a visual language[p.318] to challenge[p.42] the reductive labels pro-drilling politicians used to describe the Arctic National Wildlife Refuge; phrases like 'barren wasteland' or 'flat white nothingness'."

SUBHANKAR BANERJEE
Photographer, writer, curator and environmental humanities scholar
E.A.T. 2017: Snow and Desert, Zuoz

MOTION

"In the 1960s, the artists of postmodern dance[p.61] revolted against their predecessors. Embracing the ideals[p.145] of the avant-garde, they believed[p.36] that no special qualities or formal training[p.309] were needed to dance. Dance belonged[p.36] to everyone. With American[p.28] dancer and choreographer Yvonne Rainer's *No Manifesto – no to spectacle, no to virtuosity, no to magic* – they laced up their sneakers and radically expanded the dance vocabulary[p.318] to include every gesture[p.134] and movement, especially walking[p.320] and running. Performances[p.222] moved out of theatres and into galleries, gyms and city[p.47] squares, rejecting narrative[p.213], set design and often even traditionally understood[p.313] music. Dance became[p.35] a work of art[p.31] that revealed, above all, the complex beauty of the human[p.143] body[p.38] in motion – nothing more, nothing less."

JOANNA LEŚNIEROWSKA
Curator, dramaturge and performance maker
E.A.T. 2019: Grace and Gravity, Zuoz

MOUNTAIN

"The French architect and restorer Eugène Viollet-le-Duc took the analogy between architecture and geology very seriously[p.294]. He viewed mountains much like buildings. His theory proposed that, during the cooling of the Earth's[p.112] crust, its outer layer[p.198] crystallised[p.59] into geometric shapes[p.295], such as the basalt columns found[p.125] at the Giant's Causeway in Ireland. Viollet-le-Duc was convinced that mountains – like buildings – must have an internal, orderly structure."

JAN VON BREVERN
Art historian
E.A.T. 2011: Mapping the Alps,
Zuoz

MURDER

"A friend[p.128] told me that as the British female[p.123] MP Jo Cox was being stabbed, the man stood on the steps shouting, 'Britain first, Britain first.' And the media didn't make enough[p.117] of that. Yes, she was murdered because she was a woman, but the point my friend tried to make was that he was killing her for England. That's a new idea[p.145]. The single murder is equivalent to the wall. It was terrorism. And it was lethal for all of us not to call it that."

EILEEN MYLES
Poet, novelist and art journalist
E.A.T. 2017: Snow and Desert,
Zuoz

MUSEUM

"We are stuck, not because people like us lack ideas[p.145], but because politicians lack imagination[p.146]. The ways we communicate[p.51] are flawed. Institutions are collapsing under misguided, commercial funding logics. To justify a festival, you now need to quantify croissants sold. We don't need more exhibitions – we need more collective lunches, more poetry[p.226], more spaces of convening. Museums are fighting[p.124] to survive, but we must ask: should they survive in their current form?"

RASHA SALTI
Researcher, writer, producer
and curator of art and film
E.A.T. 2024: Jenseits von
Ohnmacht – Beyond Powerless,
Zuoz

MUTE

"Birdsong correlates with high levels of testosterone. Female p.123 birds that receive testo implants sing more – their songs p.299 become p.35 more male-like in frequency and structure. But in most species, there is only a very short period in their first year of life in which they can acquire their species' song. If deprived of this window through isolation, many will remain mute."

MARIANNA SIMNETT
Artist
E.A.T. 2020: Silent – Listen, Zuoz
→PLATE 69 p.180

N

NARRATIVE

"We must question p.275 the prevailing narrative of the city p.47 as a realm of freedom p.128 and progress, and the countryside p.57 as a zone of xenophobia, decline and despair. There's reason enough p.117 to be sceptical about romanticising either the countryside or refugee life, but in several cases, refugees have created parallel societies that function p.129 productively in rural p.289 areas – experimenting p.120 with new forms of coexistence p.49 and sometimes even echoing the utopian p.315 spirit of historic p.140 rural communes p.51."

NIKLAS MAAK
Architectural historian, journalist and lecturer
E.A.T. 2018: Side Country Side, Zuoz

NATURE

"The painting *Waterfall* by German artist Gerhard Richter, which I was able to acquire for the Kunst Museum Winterthur in 1997, appears at first glance to show nature in full bloom. But it's based on a photograph – a moment captured, then painted, and finally blurred. The result is flat, removed from nature. As Richter said, the sheen of nature in painting stands between us and reality p.277. It's not about experiencing nature directly – it's about the loss p.201 of that reality.

That's the core of these Engadin works: a landscape not as presence p.229, but as absence p.23. Beautiful p.34, yes, but deeply ambivalent."

DIETER SCHWARZ
Curator
E.A.T. 2024: Jenseits von Ohnmacht – Beyond Powerless, Zuoz

NEGOTIATION

"I don't like the word p.324 'negotiation'. I never use it, neither in my texts nor in my approach. Art p.31 is not a transaction. When I started working on the *Gramsci Monument*, I proposed an idea p.145, a vision p.317, a challenge p.42 – I didn't propose a trade. Clyde Thompson, the social worker of Forest Houses, understood p.313 that. He introduced me to Erik Farmer, president p.230 of the Tenant Association of Forest Houses. And only because Erik agreed to this challenge, to this vision and this idea, and because he fully agreed to share the experience – with its failure p.121 and its success – was it possible to build the work together. We did it in sharing conviction, love p.202 and competence. Not through 'trade'."

THOMAS HIRSCHHORN
Artist
2023: E.A.T. × Centre Pompidou, Paris

NEUTRALITY

"The soldiers stationed near the Korean DMZ after the ceasefire in 1953 filmed their surroundings in a way that appears innocent – going on weekend missions, recording daily life. But if you examine their zooms, their framings, their choice of subject matter p.204, you realise how the camera itself participates p.221 in a patriarchal and colonial p.50 gaze p.132. There is this quote from a soldier's diary I used in the book: 'What is so strangely touching here is not typically Swiss p.305, but typically human p.143.' And that's what struck me; how even in these images p.146 of leisure or flower picking or photography p.224 exchanges p.120 with villagers, there are layers p.198 of hierarchy p.140 and ideology. I often felt that if true neutrality exists, it would only be in death p.63. Because life is always in movement; thought, context p.55, desire p.106, bias p.37. Neutrality, then, becomes p.35 a fiction p.124. And maybe it's time p.308 we stopped hiding behind it."

DENISE BERTSCHI
Artist and scholar
2021: E.A.T. × Centre Culturel Suisse, Paris
→PLATE 70 p.181

NFT

"Looking back to artists like Sol LeWitt, who worked with certificates outlining a piece, while the actual execution – whether a drawing or sculpture – could vary p.316, we saw a clear parallel to NFTs. This was a key inspiration p.192: owning p.221 the concept itself, while the physical form can change p.43 or even be realised in the future p.130."

JOHANNES GEES
Artist
E.A.T. 2022: Matter and Memory, Zuoz

NOISE

"Pistol shrimps make some of the loudest natural underwater noises. They have asymmetrical claws – one normal p.215, one oversized – and when they snap the large claw shut, it creates cavitation and a bang that stuns prey. I've recorded them in every ocean, from the Arctic p.30 to the Southern Ocean. If this planet has a signature sound p.300, it's the sound of pistol shrimps. We should send that into space instead of more Blur tracks."

CHRIS WATSON
Musician and sound recordist
E.A.T. 2020: Silent – Listen, Zuoz

NORMAL

"We've normalised hopelessness to the point where resilience becomes p.35 dangerous. Resilience can mean spending all your time p.308 adapting p.24 to new forms of hardship instead of stopping, taking a hard look and saying, 'This is not normal.'"

PAOLA AUDREY NDENGUE
Content producer, entrepreneur and media personality
E.A.T. 2024: Jenseits von Ohnmacht – Beyond Powerless, Zuoz

NOTE

"I still rely on my notes. Until 1999, before computers, I kept piles of handwritten scripts which I have preserved until today. When creating new video p.316 works, I often revisit footage from decades earlier together with these notes. Sometimes, watching the tapes again reveals details more interesting than what I originally wrote – and sometimes an old notes help me see p.296 something new in the video. The material p.204 keeps revealing new meanings p.204 over time p.308."

MICHEL AUDER
Artist
E.A.T. 2021: Longue Durée, livestream
→ PLATE 71 p.182

NOTRE-DAME

"When asked to rethink the public space around the Notre-Dame in Paris, we didn't just redesign a plaza – we questioned p.275 what kind of city p.47 we want for the 21st century. We looked at the site from two angles: socially, how to invite Parisians as well as tourists; and climatically, how to lower perceived temperatures p.307. Using tools like wind modelling p.208, tree p.311 shade analysis and evaporative cooling, we reimagined p.146 the square not as an empty space, but as a place of comfort – shaded, cool, and generous."

BAS SMETS
Landscape architect
E.A.T. 2023: Hoffnung? Hoffnung!, Zuoz
→ PLATE 72 p.183

NOWHERE

"The desert p.105 is not a void p.320 but a site of erasure p.118; one shaped p.295 by the systematic forces of colonisation p.50 and militarisation. It is a terrain where 'nowhere' is actively produced to obscure tracks and histories p.140. The land itself can function p.129 as an indexical medium, much like film, bearing traces p.309 so subtle they strain the limits of perception. As Eyal Weizman has noted, evidence p.119 often exists at the threshold p.308 of detectability p.106, demanding high-resolution forms of analysis to be identified and understood p.313. Just as crucially, there is no clear separation between environments and the media through which they are apprehended."

EMILY-ELIZA SCOTT
Interdisciplinary scholar, artist and former park ranger
E.A.T. 2017: Snow and Desert, Zuoz

O

OBEDIENCE

"People should go back to nature p.213 because nature teaches p.306 them that time p.308 has to be long and that you cannot rush it. We are used to pushing buttons nowadays and having everything instantly. But nature does not obey that; it does not obey buttons. You have to take your time. If you have a garden p.131, that's the first lesson you learn p.199. It's wonderful to have a garden."

SIMONE FATTAL
Artist
E.A.T. 2021: Longue Durée, livestream

OBJECT

"Toïdism [Tayou's self-invented artistic term that reflects p.279 his practice p.228 of turning waste p.321, marginality and disorder into art p.31 and philosophy p.224] is my open secret – more than an aspirin. I ended up being a wanderer because I try to find p.125 healing through objects p.217. Objects allow me to get a closer look at what is essential in a city p.47."

PASCALE MARTHINE TAYOU
Artist
E.A.T. 2016: Traces and Fragments, Zuoz
→ PLATE 73 p.184

OBSERVATION

"It was really a wonderful experience working with the students of Lyceum Alpinum in Zuoz p.324. We tried something simple yet difficult – drawing a self-portrait using a small mirror p.208 placed flat on the table. Instead of aiming to draw yourself, you just draw what you see p.296. Then you realise it's actually a self-portrait. That moment when you stop controlling and start observing – it opens up a new mental space. It might seem like a small exercise, but I think it can be a big step."

ZILLA LEUTENEGGER
Artist
E.A.T. 2024: Jenseits von Ohnmacht – Beyond Powerless, Zuoz

OBSOLESCENCE

"You always have to think about obsolescence. From the original idea[p.145] to execution, the shortest timeframe is five years – more often, it's ten. Yet buildings are meant to last for decades, maybe even a century. So how do you design for a future[p.130] you can't know? For me, it's not about creating something timeless. I prefer to think of it as marking the time[p.308] you're in – responding[p.284] to the materials[p.204], the budget, the context[p.55], the urgency[p.314] of the moment – while leaving enough[p.117] room for others to re-script it later."

ELIZABETH DILLER
Architect and partner at Diller Scofidio + Renfro
E.A.T. 2019: Grace and Gravity, Zuoz

OCCUPATION

"Some of these materials[p.204] have been occupied and used in ways that reflect[p.279] their history[p.140]. The interventions I make with them are shaped[p.295] by the intense labour[p.197] involved in their production and reuse[p.285]. There's always a sense of migration embedded in them – of people moving, adapting[p.24], surviving. I'm interested in this idea[p.145] of occupation: how people leave traces[p.309], how spaces remember[p.281]. So when the material enters the art[p.31] world, it's not abstract – it already has a life."

IBRAHIM MAHAMA
Artist
E.A.T. 2016: Traces and Fragments, Zuoz

OPERA

"Michel Auder created and named his two-channel video[p.316] installation *Champfèr Garage Opera* (2017) specifically for an exhibition in Champfèr, Engadin. Why opera in relation to video? It suggests a larger concept like 'opera mundi'; the opera of the world. This refers to an expansive, almost limitless set of events happening everywhere, both near and far. Through material p.204 Auder gathered p.131 over 50 years, we are immersed in his life and those of others; some famous, like in the Warhol circle, others unknown p.313 and briefly filmed. These moments become p.35 the material from which Auder molds something larger, like this garage opera – a very singular way of working."

ADAM SZYMCZYK
Curator, writer and editor
E.A.T. 2021: Longue Durée, livestream
→ PLATE 74 p.185

OPPRESSION

"For want of justice p.196 or
soap or flowers
Instead of fears p.123, our
age is confused p.52:
The world runs ahead while
humanity p.143
falls p.122 behind, trampled
on by juggernauts
Whose names are the
fearsome powers.
Across borders and nations,
a new web
Of chains within the
greatest horizons p.142
The world has ever known.
Water itself
resists p.282 oppression."
(Excerpt from Finding The Present.*)*

BEN OKRI
Poet and novelist
E.A.T. 2020: Silent – Listen, Zuoz

ORGANISATION

"The shift p.296 from a welfare-state model p.208 towards private commissioning has made architecture p.29 more of a business than a social project. That forces us to rethink how we operate. If our agency is reduced to choosing colours p.50 and materials p.204, we're in trouble. So the question p.275 becomes p.35: how do we organise ourselves collectively to reclaim p.277 some power and transform p.310 our environment with the means available to us?"

ALEXANDRE THERIOT
Architect and co-founder of Paris-based architectural studio Bruther
2023: E.A.T. × Centre Pompidou, Paris

ORIENTAL ART

"At Portikus (the exhibition institution for contemporary[p.55] art[p.31] located in Frankfurt am Main), as in Venice, I wanted the exhibition to resonate[p.283] with the site. Portikus is a charming building on an island in the middle of the river[p.287], surrounded by trees[p.311] – nature[p.213] is everywhere. That led me to one of my favourite themes: ancient[p.29] oriental art. In the epic[p.117] of Gilgamesh, there is Humbaba, the guardian of the forest[p.126]. And what's the first thing Gilgamesh does, despite being a great hero? He kills the forest's guardian to access[p.23] the trees[p.311] – a reminder[p.281] that nothing has really changed[p.43] in 5,000 years."

SIMONE FATTAL
Artist
2023: E.A.T. × Centre Pompidou, Paris

OSCILLATION

"The countryside[p.57] issue got me thinking again about the ancient[p.29] question[p.275] of autonomy[p.33] and retreat – how as artists we constantly oscillate between engagement[p.116] and withdrawal. There's a drive to be in the world, to demonstrate, to be part of the collective. But also the urge to secede, to go inwards, to make abstract, mystical or spiritual work inspired[p.192] by things like Tantric art. That contradiction[p.56] – between inner retreat and outer fight[p.124] – is central to my practice[p.228]."

MAI-THU PERRET
Artist
E.A.T. 2018: Side Country Side, Zuoz

OVERVIEW

"From mountaintops, the overview lets us observe[p.217] the landscape from a bird's-eye perspective[p.223]. Looking down from 'high-up' viewing platforms[p.225] in the mountains[p.211] gives us the illusion of an endless, horizontal[p.142] landscape below, an illusion that is also part of any landscape in a desert[p.105] or by the sea."

NAIRY BAGHRAMIAN
Artist
E.A.T. 2011: Mapping the Alps, Zuoz

OWNERSHIP

"Museums p.212 must rethink what it means to own art p.31. Do we really need to possess artworks in the traditional sense, or can we imagine p.146 new ways to make them accessible p.23? Managing an artist's legacy p.199, for instance, doesn't always require holding p.141 the physical work. This shift p.296 calls into question p.275 how museums collect, care p.40 for and share art."

CHRIS DERCON
Art historian, curator and managing director of Fondation Cartier pour l'art contemporain
E.A.T. 2022: Matter and Memory, Zuoz
→PLATE 75 p.186

P

PARADISE

"Italian architect and industrial designer Gio Ponti realised one of his only Swiss p.305 hotel projects between 1933 and 1935; the Hotel Paradiso in the Martell valley. The hotel offered 100 beds, and amenities like a post office and sauna. It closed during World War II, was used by the German army, renovated in 1952, and shut down permanently p.223 in 1955. Now an abandoned ruin p.289, it fascinated me so much that I started a series of books about ruins titled *Paradise*. Besides this series, I'm working on two other books, including one about an abandoned Luna Park near Berlin. I'm intrigued by how joyful places like funfairs become p.35 melancholic, dying spaces."

TOBIAS REHBERGER
Artist
E.A.T. 2012: Vision for the Alps, Zuoz
→PLATE 76 p.187

PARTICIPATION

"My entry into community-engaged work came through the belief p.36 that impact p.148 is strongest when it's participatory and collaborative. My role as an artist became p.35 about creating the platform p.225 – connecting p.53 people so they could employ their own creativity. With *Project Row Houses*, it started with no money p.210, but endless creative resources[p.283]. We relied on people – from museum[p.212] workers to church groups – to help renovate 22 abandoned homes[p.141]. That collaboration[p.49] was the art[p.31]."

RICK LOWE
Artist
E.A.T. 2025: Form and Impact, Zuoz
→ PLATE 77 [p.234]

PARTICLE

"We had before a living world and a world of non-living; man, animals, creators on one side, materials[p.204] on the other. But now we know that particle work is everywhere. I saw in a book of a physicist that the diffusion of light happens because a photon – a particle of light – enters an electron in a particle of matter[p.204], and then that matter emits another photon. So there is communication[p.51], there is circulation between air[p.27] and matter. There is an intelligence that works everywhere. The artist, who used to give life to dead matter, must now look at the intelligence of matter. It is something like the hand of the poet, that puts itself at the service of the matter. That, for me, is a very beautiful[p.34] statement for the 21st century."

GIORGIO GRIFFA
Artist
E.A.T. 2016: Traces and Fragments, Zuoz

PERFORMANCE

"What really stayed with me after that performance wasn't just the applause – it was the fact that I didn't know anyone in the room. I had this moment, this breakthrough, and then I simply left. That experience marked me. Since then, I've tried never to leave the scene like that again. It shaped[p.295] how I approach performance today – with the intention[p.193] of truly being in contact with those in front of me. Especially as I grow[p.138] older, I'm aware that there's more time[p.308] behind me than ahead. So I try to make each moment as meaningful[p.204], as full of care[p.40] and possibility as I can. I'm constantly asking: who is in the room, and how can I be with them, here and now?"

TRAJAL HARRELL
Choreographer and dancer
2023: E.A.T. × Centre Pompidou, Paris

PERMANENCE

"Even after 40 years, tents remain central to Sahrawi compounds – not only because of their cultural p.60 significance or climatic advantages, but also because they send a message: 'This is not permanent.' The tent becomes p.35 an architectural expression of a political demand; a demand for return. It tells us that the Sahrawis have not accepted p.23 their displacement as final."

MANUEL HERZ
Architect
E.A.T. 2017: Snow and Desert, Zuoz

PERSIA

"I curated the Collateral Event *The Spark Is You*, which had two parts. The first part debuted in Venice during the 2019 Biennale, and a few days later, the second part opened at Parasol unit's gallery in London. The exhibition encouraged viewers to engage p.116 with the works of a selected group of Persian artists through the lens of poetry p.226, regardless of their generation p.133 or where they lived and worked. The idea p.145 was to highlight something about Persian culture p.60 to the younger generation, who might not have a clear understanding p.313 of who we are. Our extraordinary poetic heritage p.140, spanning over a thousand years, serves as our cultural cornerstone – much like classical music does in Europe or the Western p.321 hemisphere."

ZIBA ARDALAN
Founder and director of Parasol unit foundation for Contemporary Art
E.A.T. 2021: Longue Durée, livestream
→ PLATE 78 p.235

PERSPECTIVE

"When designing a building, you do so with an awareness of its past and the realities of the present p.230 day, but you are also attempting to anticipate a future p.130 that is essentially unknown p.313.

In that sense, it involves taking a very long-term perspective – looking back to the origins and history[p.140] of the building, while also looking far ahead into the future."

NORMAN FOSTER
Architect, founder and executive chairman of Foster + Partners
E.A.T. 2021: Longue Durée, livestream

PHILOSOPHY

"My approach to philosophy is deeply shaped[p.295] by French philosopher Henri Bergson's idea[p.145] that memory[p.206] is always an act of writing in the present. Memory does not retrieve a fixed past – it reactivates the past in the now. This view has profoundly influenced how I understand[p.313] philosophy itself: as something that is always contemporary[p.55], rooted[p.289] in the present[p.230], and helping us to think through our current condition."

SOULEYMANE BACHIR DIAGNE
Philosopher
E.A.T. 2022: Matter and Memory, Zuoz

PHOTOGRAPHY

"Photography once served to document reality[p.277], but now imaging[p.146] technologies define[p.64] it. At the High Performance Computing Center in Stuttgart, for example, engineers, designers and marketing teams use a 3D[p.307] theatre linked[p.200] to a supercomputer for modelling[p.208] and real-time decision[p.63] making. In car manufacturing, for instance, calculating costs, material[p.204] use or aerodynamic effects can be determined and controlled while designing. This similar logic of superimposed reality and virtuality manifested itself in the reconstruction[p.53] of Notre-Dame[p.216], where digital[p.107] models included data from the video[p.316] game Assassin's Creed."

ARMIN LINKE
Artist
E.A.T. 2022: Matter and Memory, Zuoz

PIXEL

"The Lidar model[p.208] of the Saint Gotthard that we built isn't just an image[p.146] or video[p.316]; it's the embodiment of the mountain's[p.211] physical structure through a topology of countless electronic points. Think of it as a digital[p.107] drape comprised of a multitude of tiny pixel dots, like dew drops, that merge together to describe the surface of the mountain. We have thus moved far beyond the conventions of perspective[p.223] inherited[p.191] from Alberti 500-years ago. The extraordinary geographical precision of point clouds opens an entirely new way to concieve, model and think landscapes in the future[p.130]."

CHRISTOPHE GIROT
Landscape architect, M.Arch M.L.Arch, BSA. Professor Emeritus of Landscape Architecture and former Dean of the Department of Architecture, ETH Zurich
E.A.T. 2012: Vision for the Alps, Zuoz

PLASTIC

"At the Ellen Macarthur Foundation, we deliberately chose plastics as a demonstration case back in 2013 – something ubiquitous that everyone on the planet touches[p.308]. We assumed there would be loads of data after 40–50 years of use, but there wasn't. That absence[p.23] of basic information[p.190] told us something profound: the global plastics system had grown[p.138] without anyone truly mapping[p.203] its flows and impacts[p.148]."

ANDREW MORLET
Former CEO of the Ellen MacArthur Foundation, chair of the UK Government CIRCULAR Economy Taskforce, lead of the CIRCULAR Economy Innovation Hub at Standard Chartered Bank
E.A.T. 2022: Matter and Memory, Zuoz

PLATFORM

"I still get messages from people asking why I would give someone like Kanye West a platform – especially within a respected[p.284] institution like Kunsthalle Zürich. But I honestly find that question[p.275] incredibly boring. If we talk about platforms, Kanye already has the biggest one imaginable. He's vastly bigger than the Kunsthalle and certainly bigger than me. So when you look at the constellation – Kanye West, Kunsthalle Zürich and me –

there's at least some kind of diversity in that combination. And that's more interesting to me than the simplistic idea[p.145] of validating or deplatforming someone."

HEJI SHIN
Photographer
E.A.T. 2019: Grace and Gravity, Zuoz

PLURALISM

"The idea[p.145] that philosophy[p.224] is inherently Western[p.321] is relatively recent. Greek philosophers never believed[p.36] philosophy belonged[p.36] exclusively to them – Plato, for instance, acknowledged[p.24] Egypt's influence on Greece. Descartes himself rooted[p.289] his thinking in algebra, a discipline that was foreign to Europe at the time[p.308]. The notion of philosophy as essentially European emerged through colonialism[p.50] and a belief in European exceptionalism, which served to legitimise colonial domination. That's why decolonising the history[p.140] of philosophy is essential: to pluralise it and to acknowledge and understand[p.313] its diverse, global traditions."

SOULEYMANE
BACHIR DIAGNE
Philosopher
E.A.T. 2022: Matter and Memory, Zuoz

POETRY

"I'd love a poet-in-residence in every city[p.47] and town in the United States[p.28], and I'd bring arts[p.31] programmes back. My dreams would be about education[p.113] and the arts, because they've been stripped away in the States. Poetry represents[p.281] freedom[p.128] of speech[p.300]; kids need that early on. We need a bombardment of dirty[p.108] language[p.198], of poetry, of kids being exposed[p.121] to absolute and utter freedom, so by the time they grow[p.138] up, they know how to speak and think."

EILEEN MYLES
Poet, novelist and art journalist
E.A.T. 2017: Snow and Desert, Zuoz

POLLUTION

"Places like this – with quietness[p.275] and stillness[p.301] – are becoming[p.35] rare, especially in Europe. Once noise p.215 pollution is introduced, you can't reverse it. It's not like planting trees p.311. These quiet places are valuable not only ecologically p.113, but psychologically. We need them to centre our thoughts. It's not silence p.297 we need, but a stillness that lets us rest mentally. This is essential for our health and well-being."

CHRIS WATSON
Musician and sound recordist
E.A.T. 2020: Silent – Listen,
Zuoz

POLYPHONY

"This harp is called *arpa doppia a tre registri* – a double harp with three rows of strings. 'Double' here simply means: more than one row. Looking at these three rows, I'd say it's actually a 3D p.307 harp. Unlike the modern pedal harp, where chromatic changes p.43 are made with the feet, I move my hands between the rows, constantly crossing p.59 over. The polyphony unfolds not only in sound p.300, but in space and in my body p.38. It's a physical dialogue p.107, because the music literally travels through my hands, across invisible layers p.198. It's not just vertical harmony or horizontal p.142 melody; it's architecture p.29 you play with your hands."

MARGRET KÖLL
Harpist
E.A.T. 2022: Matter and Memory,
Zuoz

PORTRAIT

"Of course I'm aware of other situations where portraits of controversial figures caused public reaction p.24. Just recently I was discussing Andy Warhol's show at the Whitney – huge portraits of Mao Zedong, the Shah of Iran, all these powerful and morally complex figures. This has always existed in art p.31. A portrait can be a time p.308 capsule, a sign of the times. It's never just about the person – it's about what the portrait activates in society p.299."

HEJI SHIN
Photographer
E.A.T. 2019: Grace and Gravity,
Zuoz

POWERLESSNESS

"It took me a long time[p.308] to come to terms with the meaning[p.204] of the word[p.324] 'powerlessness', but I never quite accepted[p.23] the word itself – especially in English, which is not the language[p.198] I use every day. In Greek, the term is ambiguous and far less precise. It includes both weakness and a lack of authority. In English, it points directly to an absence[p.23] of strength, an absence of power. That's what troubles me. When is power gained or lost[p.201], and how? Who is truly powerless: the one constrained by their circumstances, or the one who feels powerless despite their privileges? Can powerlessness become[p.35] a strength through art[p.31] and cinema[p.46]?"

MENELAOS KARAMAGHIOLIS
Artist
E.A.T. 2024: Jenseits von Ohnmacht – Beyond Powerless, Zuoz

PRACTICE

"Your relationship[p.280] with your practice is the only thing you can control. You can't control the market – it will do what it does – but the studio won't fail[p.121] you. I always tell young artists: be committed to your work, not to careerism. That's what lasts."

CHARLES GAINES
Artist
E.A.T. 2020: Silent – Listen, Zuoz

PRAYER

"You can visibly see[p.296] where the feet, where the knees go and where the hands would rest. Where the head rests is typically a little circular[p.46] dull space. The act of prayer is meant to reconstitute the internal world – because we say in Islam that we are in a state of forgetfulness and that it is your responsibility, through effort, to remember[p.281] who you truly are. At some point I wanted to unravel the prayer rags as an act of saying we all have to make our own Islam. I was going to undo the prayer rugs, make some thread with it, and then reweave my own Islam; my own prayer rug."

IGSHAAN ADAMS
Artist
E.A.T. 2022: Matter and Memory, Zuoz

PRECARIOUSNESS

"All the works I've made in public space – more than 70 works so far – are precarious. The definitionp.64, which I lovep.202 and think is strongest, is Italian philosopher Giorgio Agamben's: 'Precarious refers to what is obtained by means of a prayerp.228 (praex, a verbal request, as different from quaestio, a request that is made with all available means, even violent ones) and is, for this, fragile and adventurous. Literature – and here I replace 'literature' by 'art'p.31 – is itself adventurous and precarious, if it wishes to preserve the right relation with the mystery.' This beautifulp.34 quote helps me understandp.313 the dimension of 'precariousness' and helps me in my work every day."

THOMAS HIRSCHHORN
Artist
2023: E.A.T. × Centre Pompidou, Paris

PREJUDICE

"Physical lowness or horizontalityp.142 is often used as a metaphor for lacking control, for surrender. Phrases like 'taking something lying down' or 'sleeping on the job' imply a failurep.121 to be in command. This beliefp.36 that the Earthp.112 is a corrupt realm becomesp.35 conflated with lowness, carnality, sleep, deathp.63 and animality. In contrast, the sky becomes a symbolp.305 of divinity, eternityp.119, freedomp.128 and gracep.135. This prejudice – that all that is up is good – persists in the way grace is seen as a corrective to the offensiveness of gravityp.137."

ISABEL NOLAN
Artist
E.A.T. 2019: Grace and Gravity, Zuoz

PRESENCE

"These camps defyp.64 our assumptions. They are not spaces of passivity, where refugees simply receive aid. They are political projects, places where people practise running a nation in exilep.120.

They are also spaces of culture[p.60], daily life and normality[p.215]. Not, as Italian philosopher Giorgio Agamben would put it, states of exception, but spaces of presence, identity[p.146] and continuity[p.55]."

MANUEL HERZ
Architect
E.A.T. 2017: Snow and Desert, Zuoz
→ PLATE 79 p.236

PRESENT

"As the days passed walking[p.320] alone[p.28] towards the South Pole, I started to see[p.296] that it wasn't completely white after all. Colours[p.50] began to appear – bluish, greyish, yellowish tones grew[p.138] on me. It wasn't flat either. Slowly[p.298], I began to notice all the details, the structures in the ice and snow[p.298]. My body[p.38] no longer ended at my fingertips; it extended into the environment. Nature[p.213] started to send me ideas[p.145], and I began to live fully in the present. The future[p.130] and the past no longer mattered – because thinking is usually about the future or the past. But walking long distances connects[p.53] you to yourself, and that's how I began to understand[p.313] what silence[p.297] really is and how it can enrich our lives."

ERLING KAGGE
Explorer, publisher, author, philosopher, lawyer, art collector and entrepreneur
E.A.T. 2020: Silent – Listen, Zuoz

PRESIDENT

"My goal isn't just to build; I want to inspire[p.192] ideas[p.145]. So in the office, I was thinking: how do I convince the president of Burkina Faso to realise this new design for the parliament building? I had once met Obama, and someone from my team took a photo of that moment, then edited it to show the president of Burkina Faso shaking hands with Obama. We included[p.189] that image[p.146] in the presentation materials[p.204] for the parliament project. Someone said, 'If you show him this picture, he'll believe[p.36] that if he builds your design, Obama will come and shake his hand.' And it worked: the project was formally selected by Burkina Faso's government as the proposed new parliament building. That's how you work as an architect in my country; you have to be creative to inspire. Then later – I think it was November 2016 – I came back to the office and everyone was laughing. I asked, 'What's going on? What's wrong?' They said, 'Francis, the U.S. p.28 has a new president, we have to change p.43 the picture.' In the end we chose to keep Obama in the presentation images."

FRANCIS KÉRÉ
Architect
E.A.T. 2017: Snow and Desert, Zuoz

PRIMAL

"For me, drawing has this very primal quality p.274 that feels somewhat bare. I never know if the drawings are good or bad p.33 because they are simply a very honest expression of myself. It's an activity I love p.202 to do, and for me, it has that elemental quality. Recently, I started buying charcoal and pastel because they seem closest to what I want to achieve – a synthesis filled with the rawness p.275 of primal expression through these mediums."

GABRIEL CHAILE
Artist.
E.A.T. 2021: Longue Durée, livestream
→ PLATE 80 p.237

PRIORITY

"Whenever I build new houses p.142, I try to avoid making them look like old Engadin farmhouses. I think it is important to understand p.313 the original constructions p.53: these historic p.140 buildings have those characteristic p.43 small windows because people wanted to be protected p.232. Today, the priorities are different: we want a nice view, large windows to let the sunrays in to heat the house. So why are old Engadin farmhouses still often used as models p.208 for new houses?"

HANS-JÖRG RUCH
Architect
E.A.T. 2010: The Crystal Chain, Zuoz

PROJECTION

"Contemporary p.55 primatologists now argue that our assumptions about gorilla p.135 behaviour p.35 have long been coloured p.50 by human p.143 projections – such as male dominance hierarchies – which are not as fixed as once thought. A striking example came when a silverback was killed by lightning and researchers expected the group to choose the next strongest male. But instead, some females p.123 chose a young alpha, while others chose an elderly migrant who was physically weaker but a better groomer. This revealed an overlooked dimension: female choice. And it exposed p.121 the many clichés p.48 still present p.230 even in scientific research."

NIKLAS MAAK
Architectural historian, journalist and lecturer
E.A.T. 2018: Side Country Side, Zuoz

PROTECT

"For people in the remote mountain p.211 regions, it is not the word p.324 that comes first, but the mountain. The mountains have, of course, protected the language p.198 by isolating communities p.51 and limiting outside influence – my mother tongue is Romansh p.288. Without the mountains, this language would have disappeared. That is why, for me, mountain and language belong p.36 together. And it was because of the language that I ultimately became p.35 a writer."

LEO TUOR
Author in the Romansh language
E.A.T. 2021: Longue Durée, livestream

PLATES
77–114

PLATE 77

→ PARTICIPATION p.221

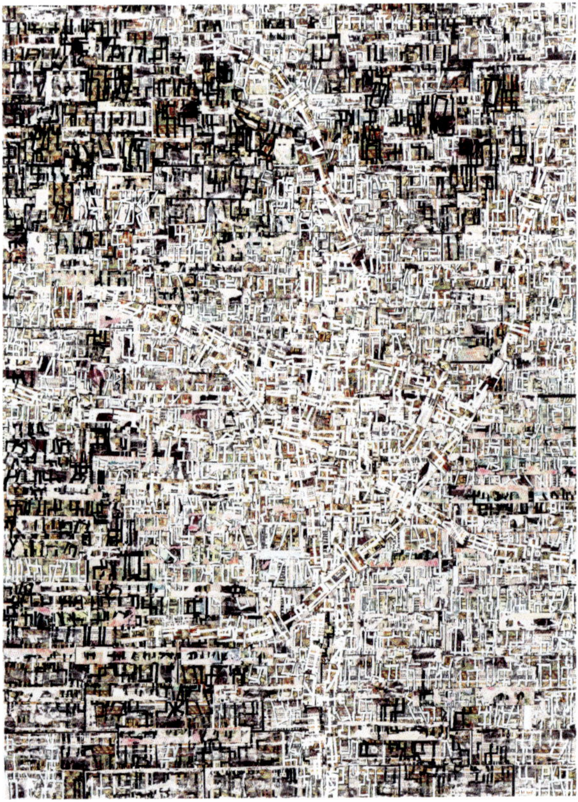

RICK LOWE

Rick Lowe, *Project Row Houses: Biggers and Beuys*, 2021.

PLATE 78
→ PERSIA p.222

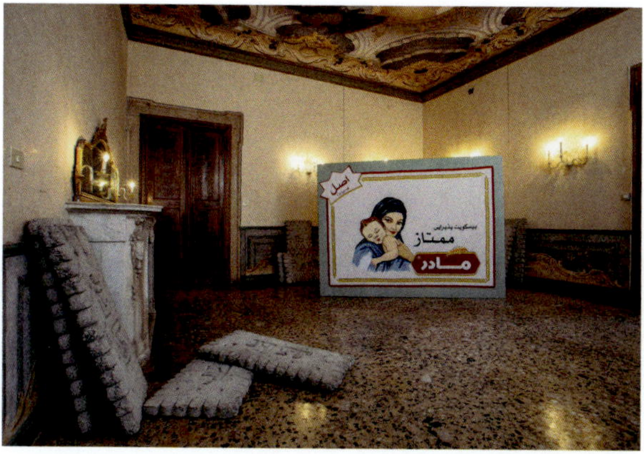

ZIBA ARDALAN
Installation view of *The Spark Is You: Parasol unit in Venice*, Conservatorio di Musica Benedetto Marcello di Venezia, 2019. © Photo by Francesco Allegretto. Courtesy of the artists and Parasol unit foundation for contemporary art.

PLATE 79
→PRESENCE p.229

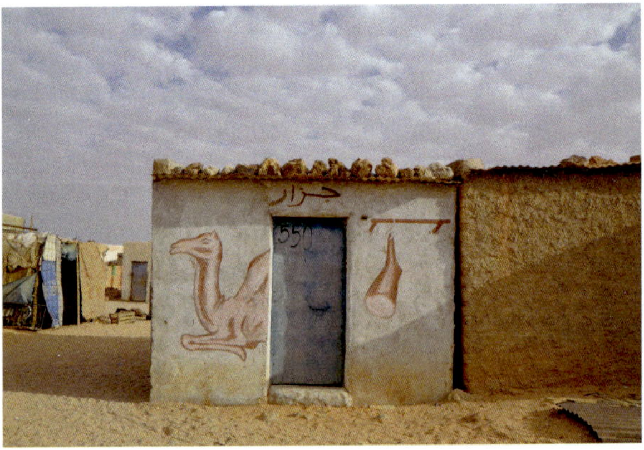

MANUEL HERZ
Camel meat shop in Camp Smara.
© Photo by Manuel Herz.

PLATE 80
→PRIMAL p.231

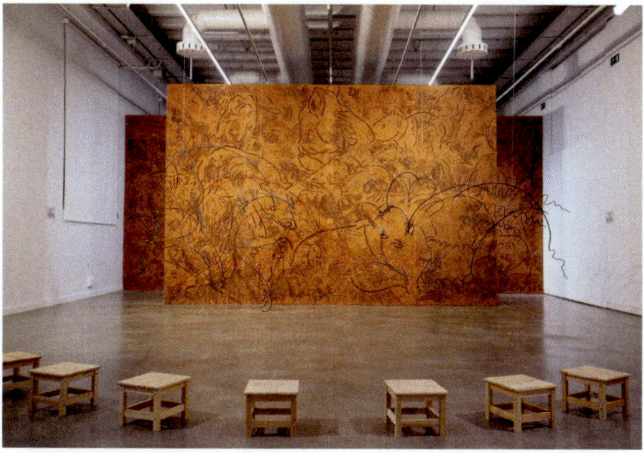

GABRIEL CHAILE
Installation view of *Contemplating is How We Have Been Changing* by Gabriel Chaile at Tabakalera – International Centre for Contemporary Culture, San Sebastián, Spain, 2024–2025.
Courtesy of ChertLüdde, Berlin, and Tabakalera – International Centre for Contemporary Culture, San Sebastián.

PLATE 81
→PROTEST p.273

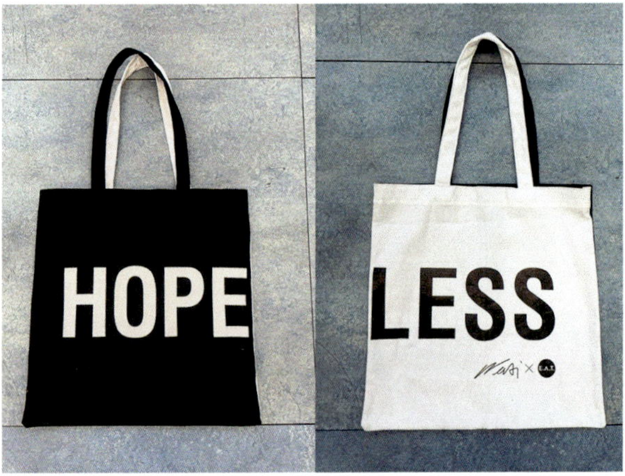

AI WEIWEI
Ai Weiwei, *Hope Less / Less Hope*, 2023,
100 % cotton bag, 40 × 40 cm, edition of 160.
Commissioned by Engadin Art Talks.
Courtesy of Engadin Art Talks and Ai Weiwei Studio.

PLATE 82

→QUIET p.275

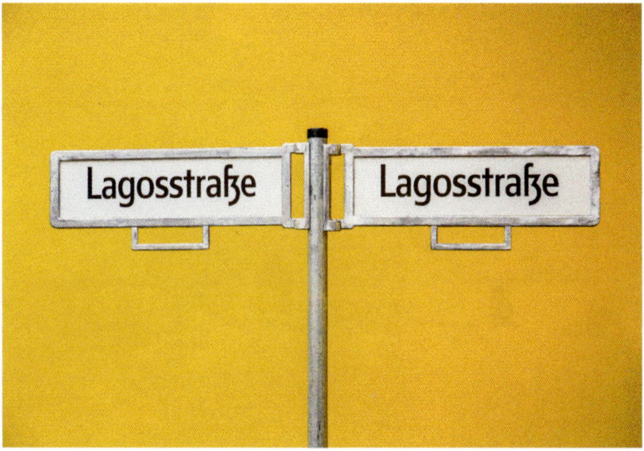

EMEKA OGBOH

Emeka Ogboh, *Lagos State of Mind III*, 2017/2020.

PLATE 83
→RAW p.275

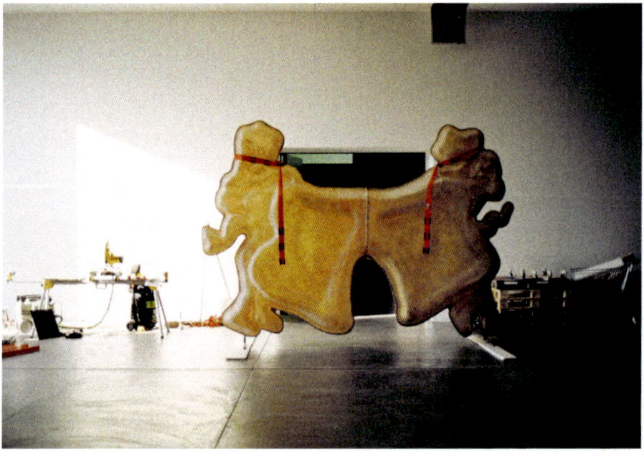

IDA EKBLAD
Installation progress of *FRA ÅRE TIL OVN* by Ida Ekblad.
Kunsthalle Zürich, 2019.

PLATE 84

→REACH p.276

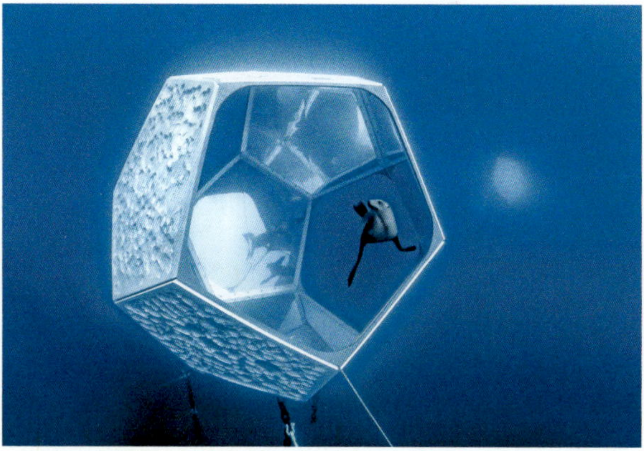

CYRILL GUTSCH
Doug Aitken, *Underwater Pavilions*, 2016,
produced by Parley for the Oceans.
© Photo by Shawn Heinrichs. Courtesy of Cyrill Gutsch.

PLATE 85

→RECOGNITION p.277

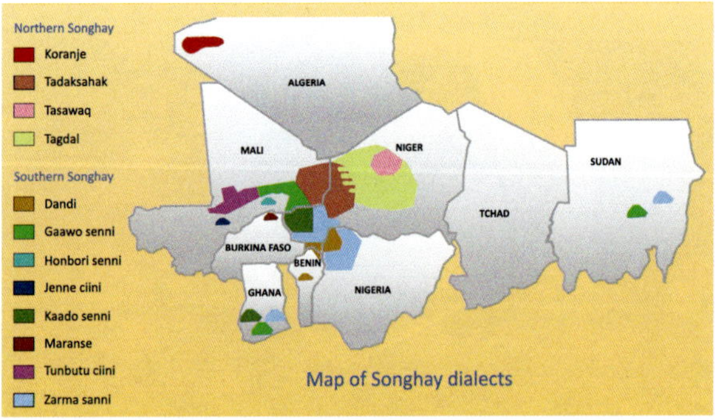

MOHOMODOU HOUSSOUBA
Map of Songhay dialects, 2025.
© Songhay.Org. Courtesy of Mohomoudou Houssouba.

PLATE 86
→RECYCLE p.278

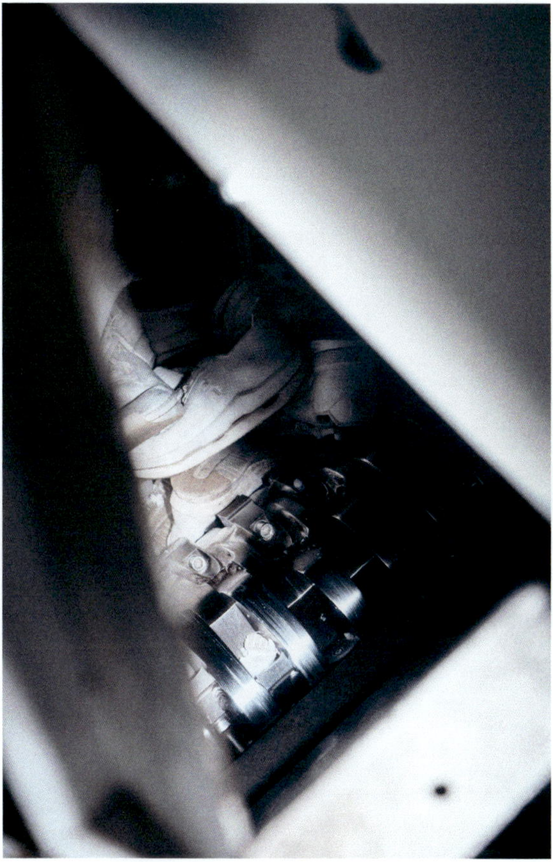

DAVID ALLEMANN
Documentation of an early step in the recycling process of the Cloudrise Cyclon model.

PLATE 87
→REGENERATION p.279

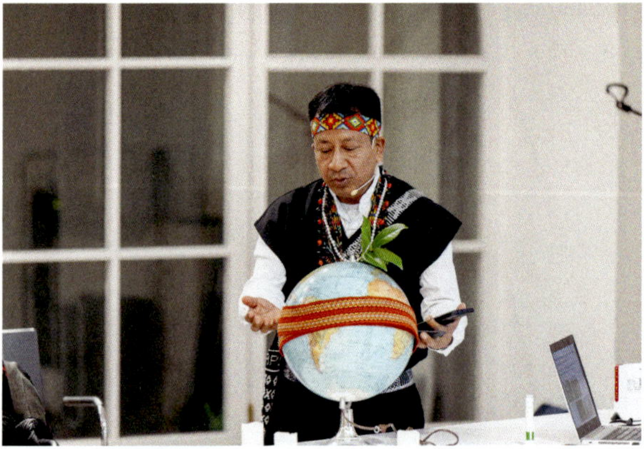

HERNANDO CHINDOY CHINDOY
Hernando Chindoy Chindoy, *Harmonising the Earth with Ëconeêrã*, 2024, Museum der Kulturen Basel, Switzerland.

→RELATIONSHIP p.280

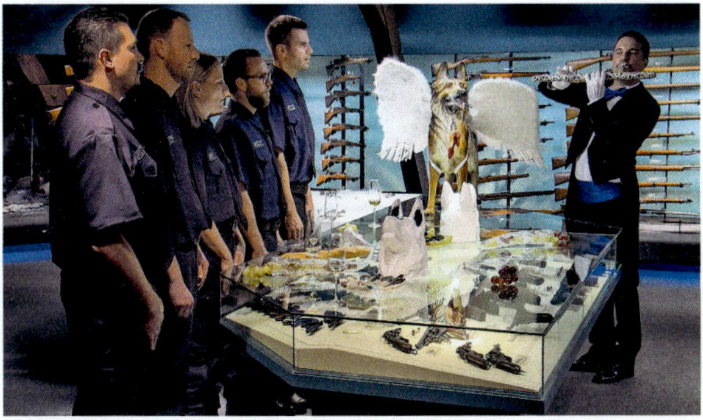

CHRISTIAN JANKOWSKI
Marco Schmitt, *Xterminating Badges*, collaboration with Zurich Cantonal Police, 2016. In this project, police officers reenact Luis Buñuel's film *El ángel exterminador (The Exterminating Angel)*, 1962, in which a group of officers is trapped in the police museum.
© Manifesta 11.

PLATE 89
→REPRESENTATION p.281

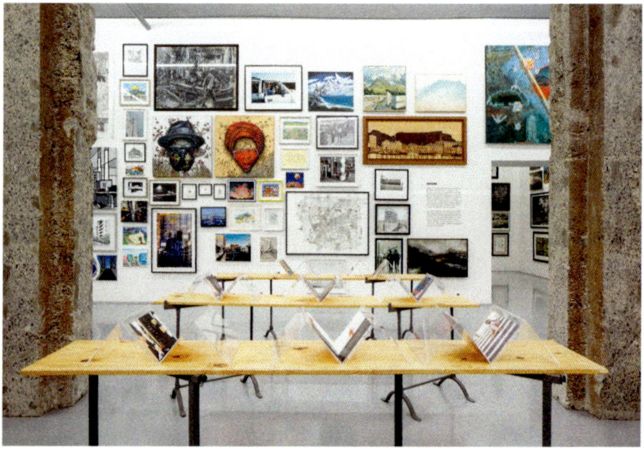

STORM JANSE VAN RENSBURG
Installation view of *Home Is Where the Art Is* at
Zeitz MOCAA in Capetown, South Africa, 2020–2021.
© Photo by Dillon Marsh. Courtesy of Zeitz MOCAA.

PLATE 90
→RESILIENCE p.282

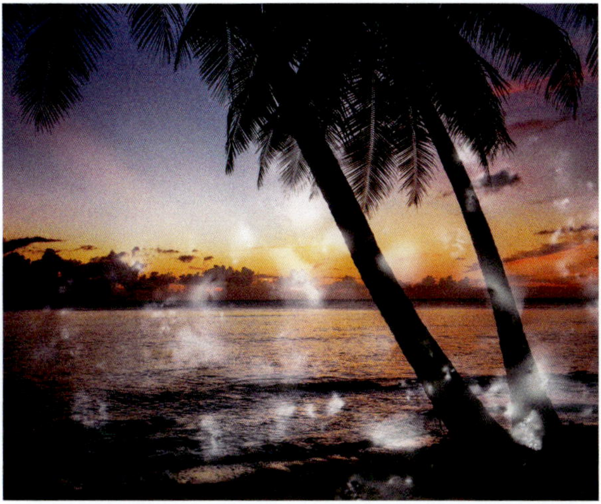

JULIAN CHARRIÈRE
Julian Charrière, *Romeo – First Light*, 2016.

PLATE 91
→ SATURATION p.290

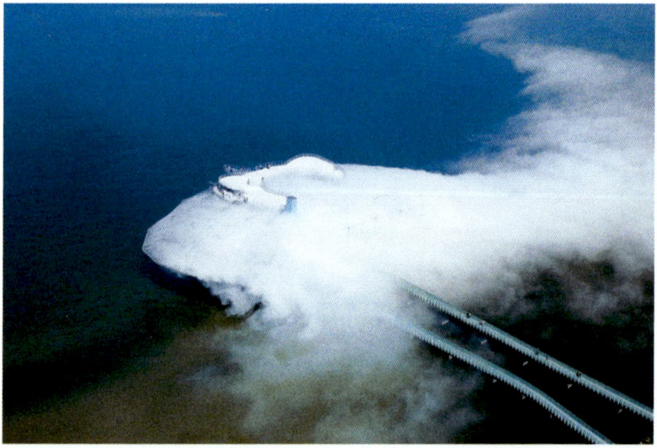

ELIZABETH DILLER
Blur Building, Exposition Pavilion, Swiss Expo, Yverdon-les-Bains, 2002.
Architects: Diller Scofidio + Renfro.

PLATE 92
→SCALE p.290

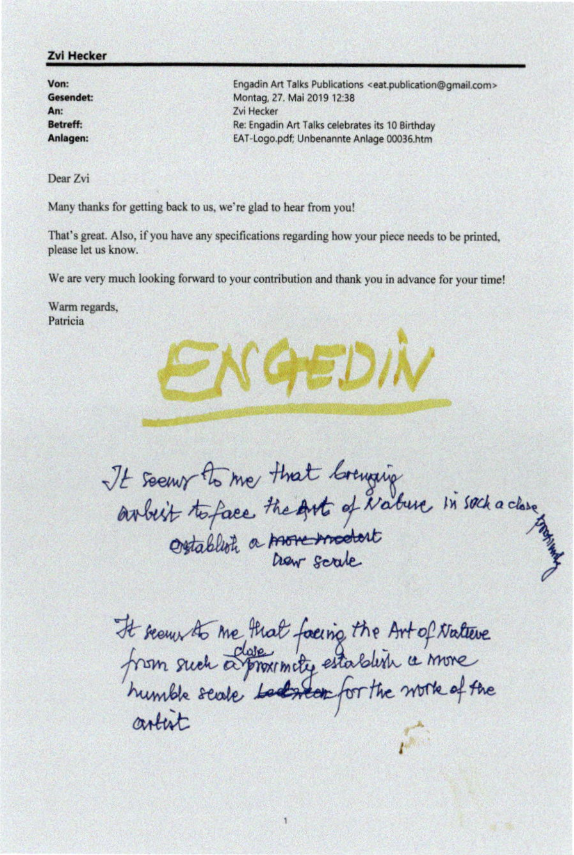

Zvi Hecker

Von: Engadin Art Talks Publications <eat.publication@gmail.com>
Gesendet: Montag, 27. Mai 2019 12:38
An: Zvi Hecker
Betreff: Re: Engadin Art Talks celebrates its 10 Birthday
Anlagen: EAT-Logo.pdf; Unbenannte Anlage 00036.htm

Dear Zvi

Many thanks for getting back to us, we're glad to hear from you!

That's great. Also, if you have any specifications regarding how your piece needs to be printed, please let us know.

We are very much looking forward to your contribution and thank you in advance for your time!

Warm regards,
Patricia

ENGEDIN

It seems to me that bringing arbeit to face the ~~Art~~ of Nature in such a close proximity establish a ~~more modest~~ new scale

It seems to me that facing the Art of Nature from such a close proximity establish a more humble scale ~~[illegible]~~ for the work of the artist

1

ZVI HECKER
Handwritten letter on e-mail by Zvi Hecker.
Courtesy of Ella Zimmerman and Zvi Hecker Architektur und Kunst Stiftung.

PLATE 93
→SCHOOL p.291

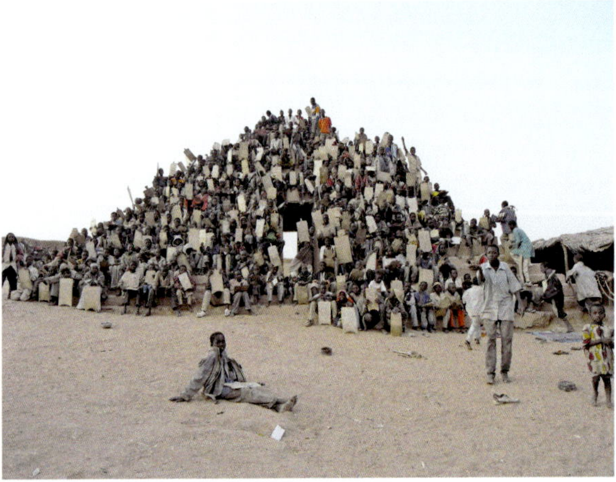

NOT VITAL
Not Vital, *Makaranta*, 2003,
mud, straw, and dung, 6.5 m (H), Agadez, Niger.
Courtesy of the artist.

PLATE 94

→SELF-SUFFICIENCY p.292

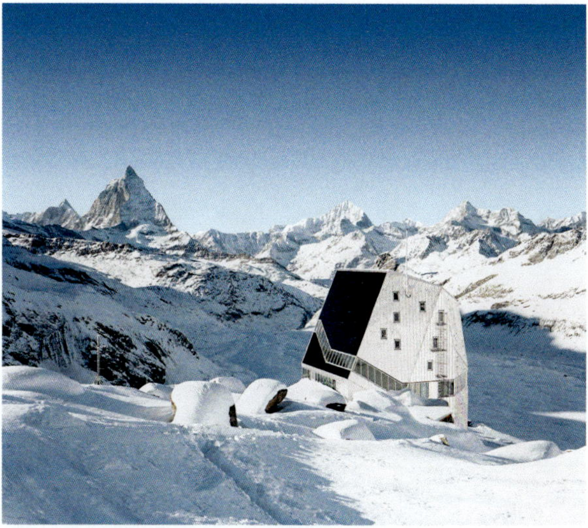

ANDREA DEPLAZES
Monte Rosa Hut. Architecture by ETH Studio Monte Rosa / Bearth & Deplazes Architekten AG, Chur / Zurich (Valentin Bearth, Andrea Deplazes, Daniel Ladner). Project leaders: Marcel Baumgartner and Kai Hellat. © ETH Studio Monte Rosa, Professor Andrea Deplazes (direction), ETH Zurich. © Photo by Tonatiuh Ambrosetti, Lausanne.

PLATE 95

→SELF-PORTRAIT p.293

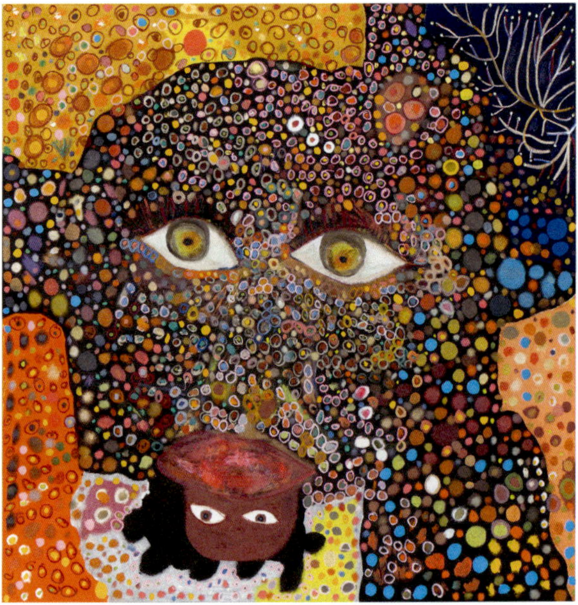

UMAN

Uman, *Trying To Get Likes*, 2021,
acrylic, oil, and oil stick on canvas, 213.4 × 213.4 cm.
Courtesy of the artist and Hauser & Wirth.

PLATE 96

→SENSOR p.294

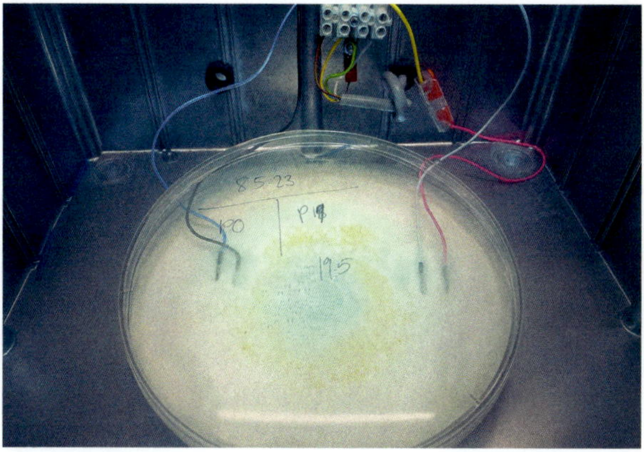

ELENI CHATZI

Mycelium, image enhanced using AI.

→SEVEN p.294

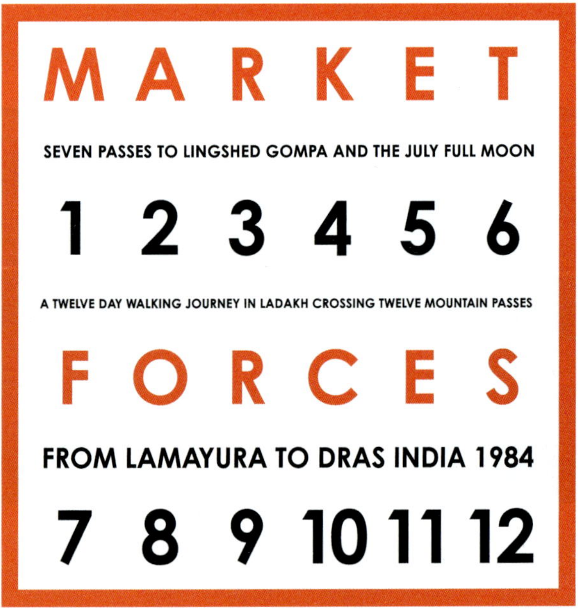

HAMISH FULTON
Hamish Fulton, *Market Forces. Seven Passes to Lingshed Gompa and the July Full Moon. A Twelve Day Walking Journey in Ladakh Crossing Twelve Mountain Passes, from Lamayura to Dras India, 1984*, 1984, wall paint and vinyl.
Courtesy of the artist and Galerie Thomas Schulte.

PLATE 98
→SHAPE p.295

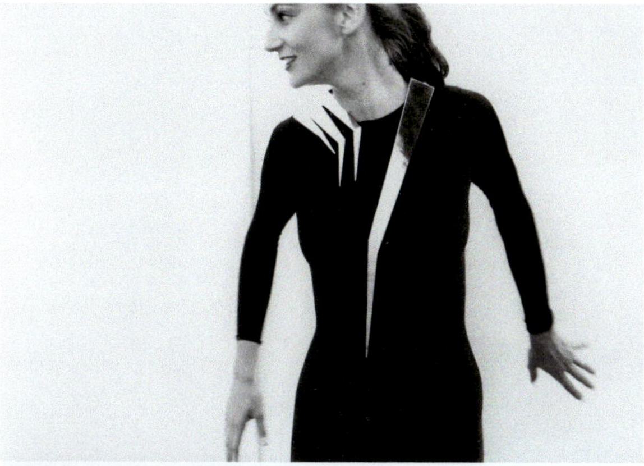

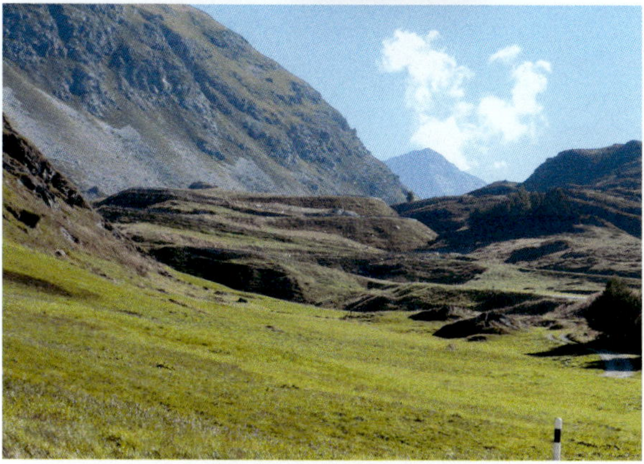

NINA VON ALBERTINI
Body Object, New York, 1981
© Photo by Matthias Aeberli.
A newly built landscape body to embed, receive and incorporate the new road curves over the Julier Pass, Grisons, 2011.
© Photo by Tiefbauamt Graubünden.

PLATE 99

→SIGHT p.296

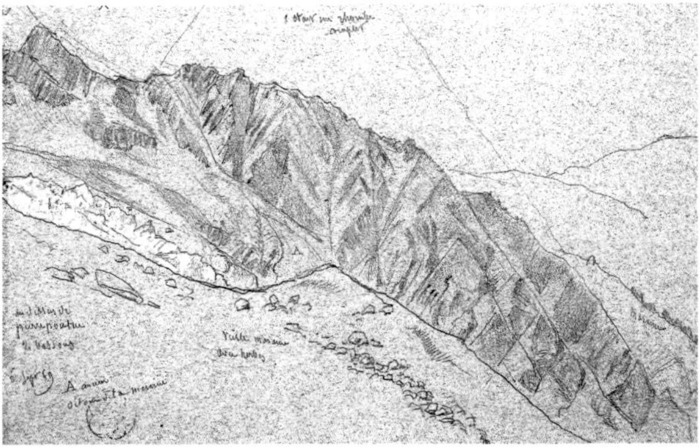

JAN VON BREVERN

Eugène Emmanuel Viollet-le-Duc, *Les Bossons*, 1869, 13.5 × 22 cm. The drawing depicts a mountain range in the French Alps with a *reconstruction* of its supposed former state. Source: Pierre A. Frey, Louise Grenier (eds.), *Viollet-le-Duc et la Montagne*, Grenoble, 1993. Courtesy Jan von Brevern.

PLATE 100
→SNAKE p.298

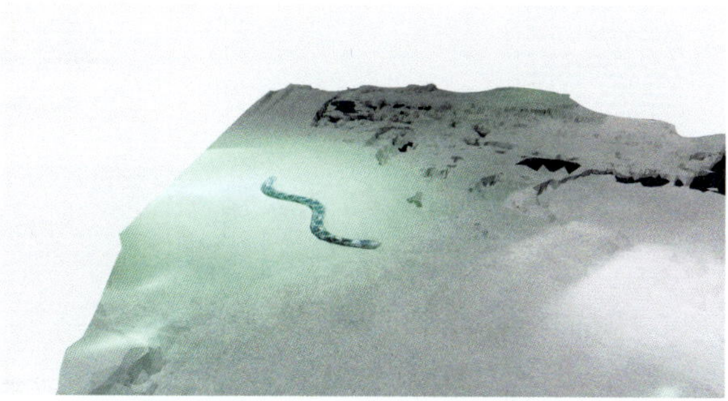

PAMELA ROSENKRANZ
Pamela Rosenkranz, *House of Meme*, 2021.
3D scan by Joana de la Fontaine.

→SOLIDARITY p.299

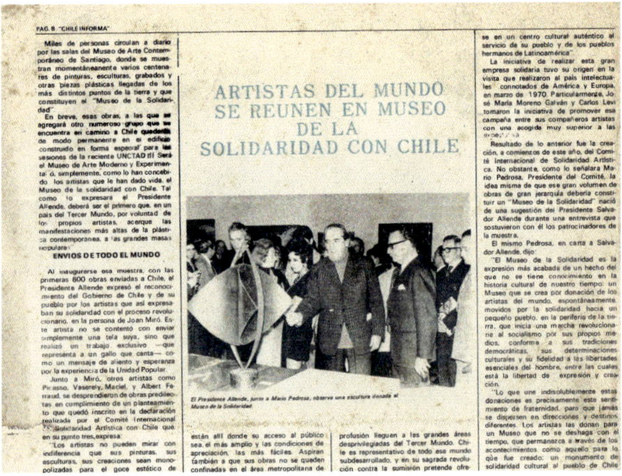

PAG. 8 "CHILE INFORMA"

ARTISTAS DEL MUNDO SE REUNEN EN MUSEO DE LA SOLIDARIDAD CON CHILE

Miles de personas circulan a diario por las salas del Museo de Arte Contemporáneo de Santiago, donde se muestran momentáneanente varios centenares de pinturas, esculturas, grabados y otras piezas plásticas llegadas de los más distintos puntos de la tierra y que constituyen el "Museo de la Solidaridad".

En breve, esas obras, a las que se agregará otro numeroso grupo que se encuentra en camino a Chile quedarán de modo permanente en el edificio construido en forma especial para las sesiones de la reciente UNCTAD III. Será el Museo de Arte Moderno y Experimental ó, simplemente, como lo han concebido los artistas que le han dado vida, el Museo de la solidaridad con Chile. Tal como lo expresara el Presidente Allende, deberá ser el primero que, en un país del Tercer Mundo, por voluntad de los propios artistas, acerque las manifestaciones más altas de la plástica contemporanea, a las grandes masas populares.

ENVIOS DE TODO EL MUNDO

Al inaugurarse esa muestra, con las primeras 600 obras enviadas a Chile, el Presidente Allende expresó el reconocimiento del Gobierno de Chile y de su pueblo por los artistas que así expresaban su solidaridad con el proceso revolucionario, en la persona de Joan Miró. Este artista no se contentó con enviar simplemente una tela suya, sino que realizó un trabajo exclusivo —que representa a un gallo que canta— como un mensaje de aliento y esperanza por la experiencia de la Unidad Popular.

Junto a Miró, otros artistas como Picasso, Vaserely, Maciel, y Albert Feraud, se desprendieron de obras predilectas en cumplimiento de un planteamiento que quedó inscrito en la declaración realizada por el Comité Internacional de Solidaridad Artística con Chile que en su punto tres, expresa:

"Los artistas no pueden mirar con indiferencia que sus pinturas, sus esculturas, sus creaciones sean monopolizadas para el goce estético de

El Presidente Allende, junto a Mario Pedrosa, observa una escultura donada al Museo de la Solidaridad

están allí donde su acceso al público sea, el más amplio y las condiciones de apreciación, las más fáciles. Aspiran también a que sus obras no se queden confinadas en el área metropolitana de

profusión lleguen a las grandes áreas desprivilegiadas del Tercer Mundo. Chile es representativo de todo ese mundo subdesarrollado, y en su sagrada revolución contra la sumisión pretende ofre-

se en un centro cultural auténtico al servicio de su pueblo y de los pueblos hermanos de Latinoamérica".

La iniciativa de realizar esta gran empresa solidaria tuvo su origen en la visita que realizaron al país intelectuales connotados de América y Europa, en marzo de 1970. Particularmente, José María Moreno Galván y Carlos Levi tomaron la iniciativa de promover esa campaña entre sus compañeros artistas con una acogida muy superior a las expectativas.

Resultado de lo anterior fue la creación, a comienzos de este año, del Comité Internacional de Solidaridad Artística. No obstante, como lo señalara Mario Pedrosa, Presidente del Comité, la idea misma de que ese gran volumen de obras de gran jerarquía debería constituir un "Museo de la Solidaridad" nació de una sugestión del Presidente Salvador Allende durante una entrevista que sostuvieron con él los patrocinadores de la muestra.

El mismo Pedrosa, en carta a Salvador Allende, dijo:

"El Museo de la Solidaridad es la expresión más acabada de un hecho del que no se tiene conocimiento en la historia cultural de nuestro tiempo: un Museo que se crea por donación de los artistas del mundo, espontáneamente movidos por la solidaridad hacia un pequeño pueblo, en la periferia de la tierra, que inicia una marcha revolucionaria al socialismo por sus propios medios, conforme a sus tradiciones democráticas, sus determinaciones culturales y su fidelidad a las libertades esenciales del hombre, entre las cuales está la libertad de expresión y creación.

"Lo que une indisolublemente estas donaciones es precisamente este sentimiento de fraternidad, para que jamás se dispersen en direcciones y destinos diferentes. Los artistas las donan para un Museo que no se deshaga con el tiempo, que permanezca a través de los acontecimientos como aquello para lo que fue creado: un monumento de solidaridad cultural al pueblo de Chile

RASHA SALTI
Newspaper clipping from *La Nación*, May 18, 1972, Santiago, Chile: *Artistas del Mundo Se Reunen en Museo de la Solidaridad Con Chile* (The Artists of the World Gather at the Museum of Solidarity for Chile). Courtesy of MSSA Archives.

PLATE 102
→SPEECH p.300

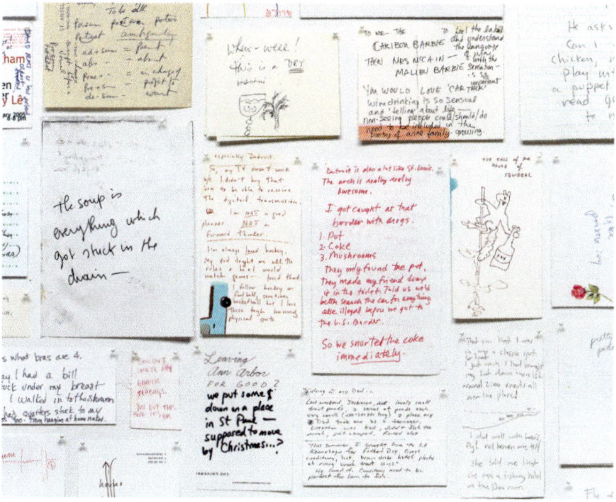

JOSEPH GRIGELY
Detail of *White Noise (Monochrome)* (2000) in the exhibition *In What Way Wham?*, MASS MoCA, 2023.

PLATE 103
→ SUBSTANCE p.302

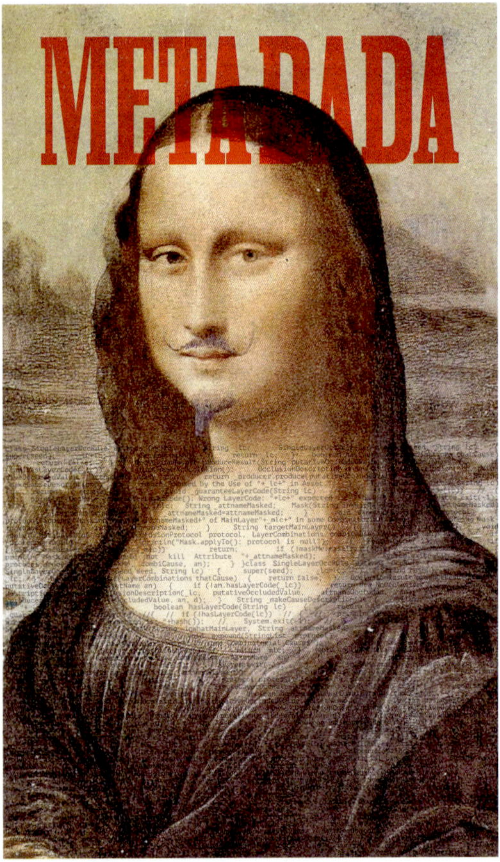

KENNY SCHACHTER
Kenny Schachter, *metadada-monalisa*, 2021,
print mounted on aluminium, NFT, 127 × 77 cm.
Courtesy of the artist.

PLATE 104

→SURPRISE p.303

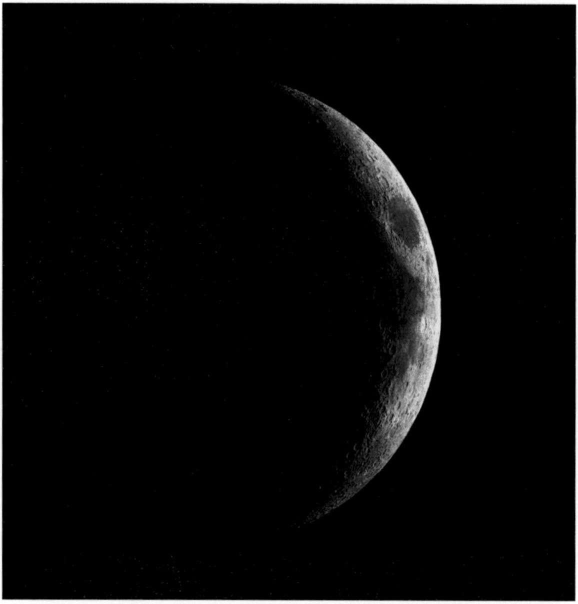

BEN MOORE

Telescope photograph of the Moon by Ben Moore.

PLATE 105

→ SURVEILLANCE p.304

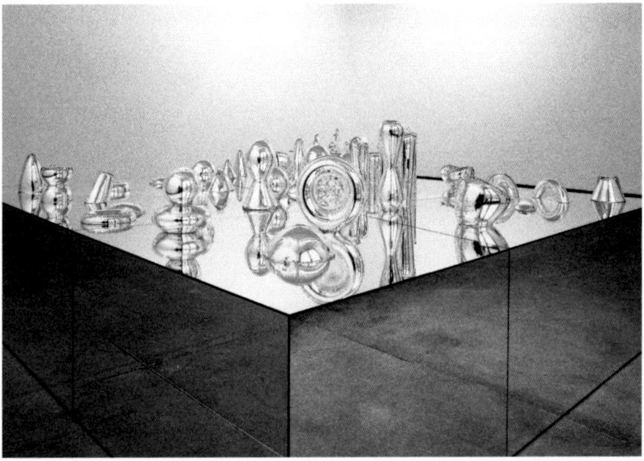

JOSIAH MCELHENY

Josiah McElheny, *Extended Landscape Model for Total Reflective Abstraction*, detail, 2004, handblown mirrored glass, industrial mirror, and wood, 60.9 × 274.3 × 233.7 cm.
Phoenix Art Museum, Phoenix, Arizona, United States.
© Photo by Tom van Eynde.

PLATE 106
→SUSTAINABILITY p.304

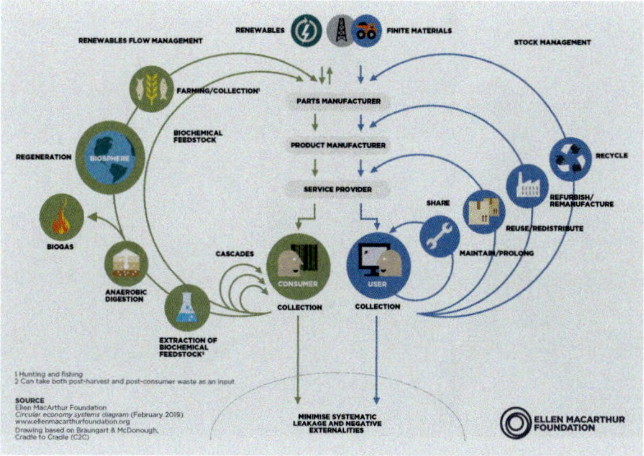

ANDREW MORLET
Circular Economy butterfly diagram.

PLATE 107
→THREE-DIMENSIONAL p.307

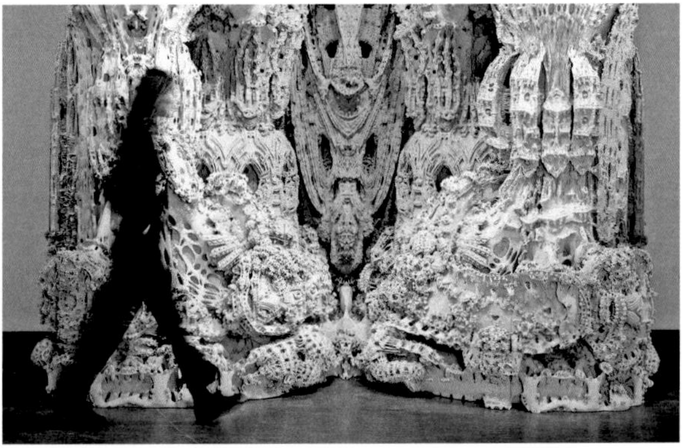

BENJAMIN DILLENBURGER
Michael Hansmeyer and Benjamin Dillenburger, *Digital Grotesque II*, 2017, full-scale 3D-printed sandstone architecture.

PLATE 108

→TRAINING p.309

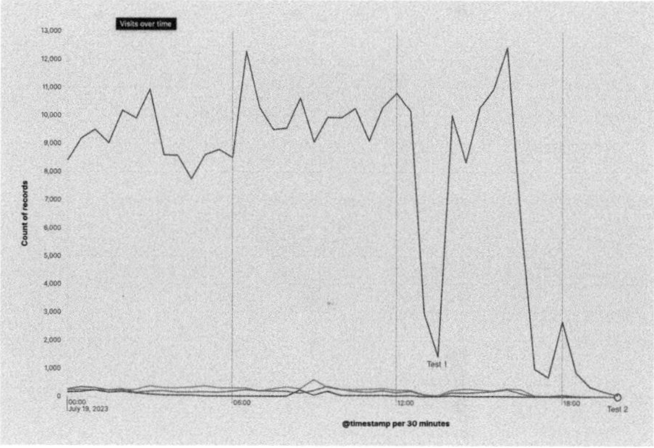

HOLLY HERNDON AND MATHEW DRYHURST
Holly Herndon and Mathew Dryhurst, *Kudurru*, 2023, graph showing interruption of global AI training.

PLATE 109
→TRANSFORMATION p.310

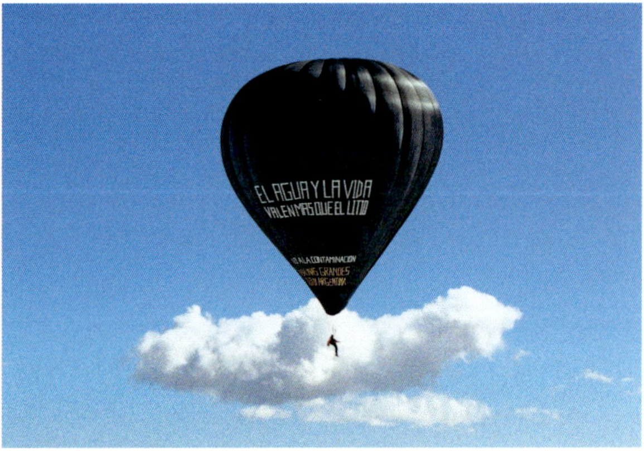

TOMÁS SARACENO
Tomás Saraceno, *Human Solar Free* Flight (as part of *Connect, BTS*, curated by DaeHyung Lee) for *Fly with Aerocene Pacha* (a project within the Aerocene initiative), 21–28 January 2020, Salinas Grandes, Jujuy, Argentina.

PLATE 110
→ TRANSPARENCY p.311

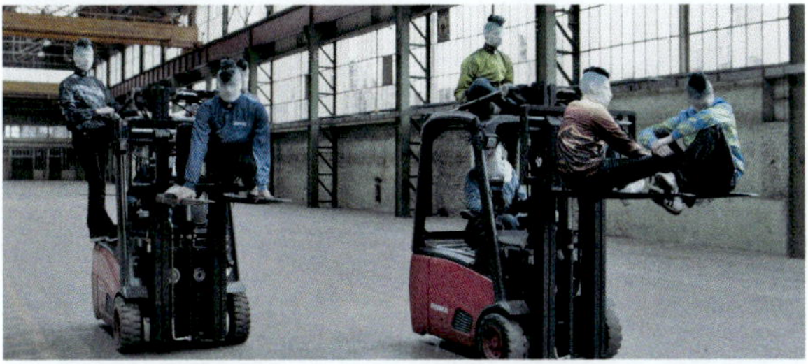

(LA)HORDE
Film still of *Novaciéries* by (LA)HORDE, 2015.

PLATE 111
→TUNNEL p.312

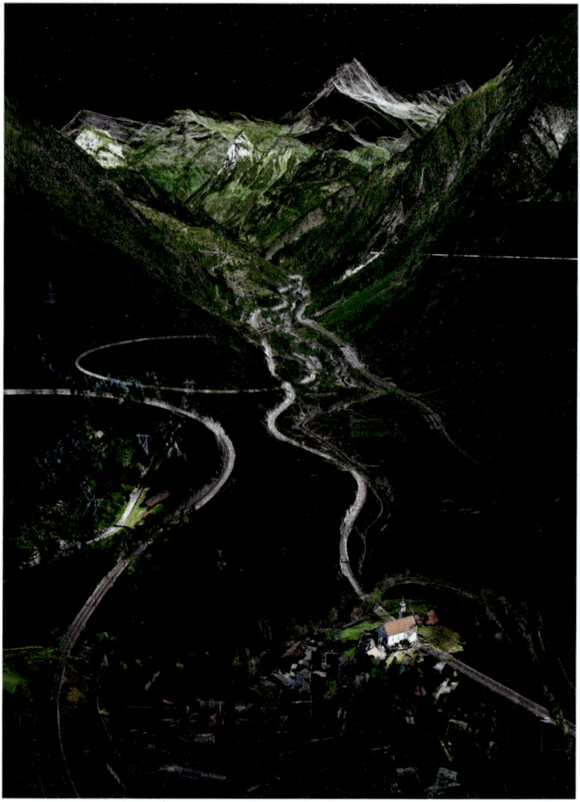

CHRISTOPHE GIROT
Gotthard, Wassen, 2022.

PLATE 112
→VIDEO p.316

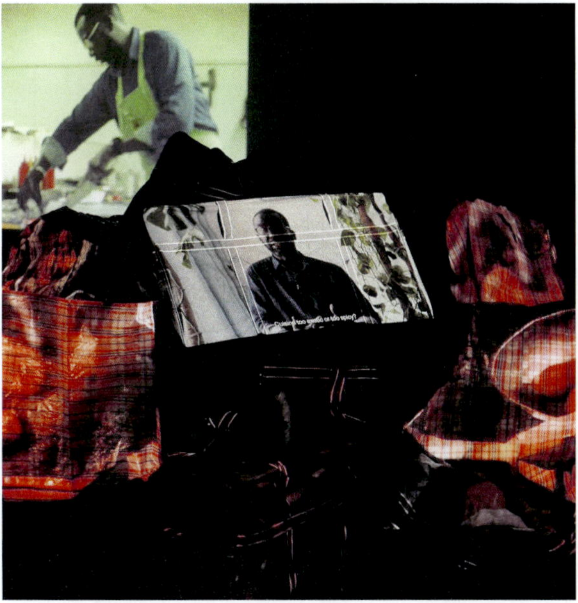

ANNA-ALIX KOFFI
Emeka Ogboh, *ABJ*, 2024, audiovisual installation, variable dimensions.

PLATE 113
→WASTE p.321

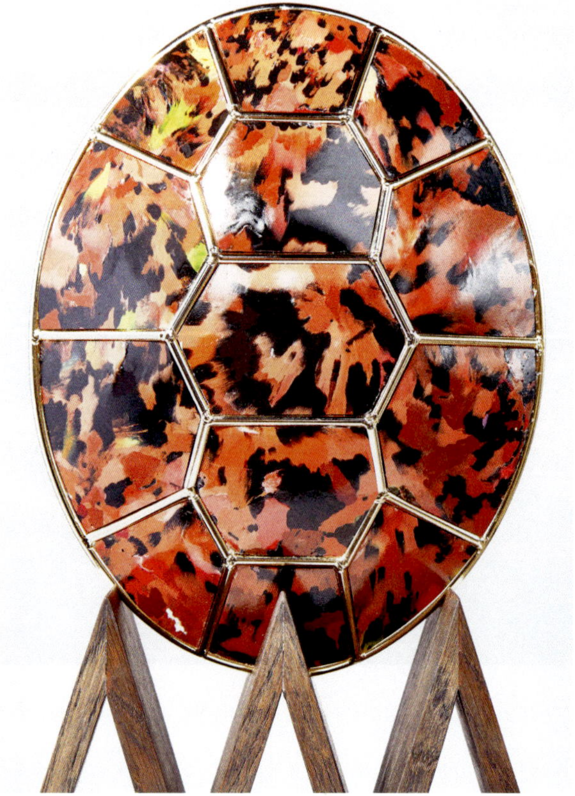

ARIC CHEN
Studio Swine, *Gyrecraft*, 2014.
© Photo by Petr Krejčí.

PLATE 114

→ WOOD p.323

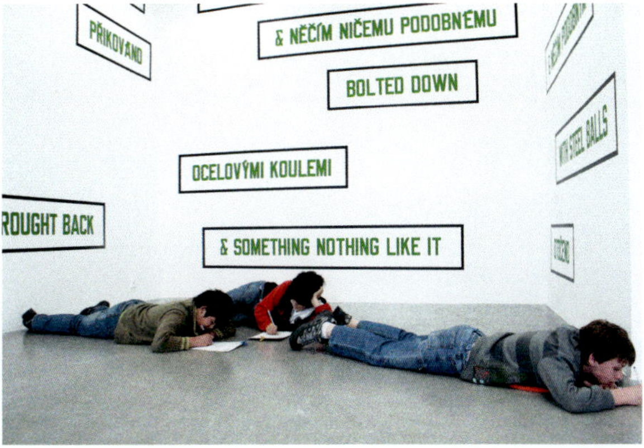

LAWRENCE WEINER

Lawrence Weiner, *House of Art*, Budweis, 2010.

PROTEST

"I'm sceptical about protest. Everywhere – in authoritarian regimes or democracies – protests are absorbed p.23 and neutralised p.214. The state uses your energy p.115 against you. Holding p.141 up a blank A4 sheet, as in the recent demonstrations, is symbolic p.305 but ultimately ironic. Who cares p.40? Meanwhile, millions of refugees remain forgotten. So when I was asked to design an edition for E.A.T. p.116 around the theme of hope p.142, I couldn't. I titled it 'hopeless hope' – because we only need hope when we feel hopeless."

AI WEIWEI
Artist
E.A.T. 2023: Hoffnung? Hoffnung!, Zuoz
→ PLATE 81 p.238

PROTOCOL

"We use the term 'protocol art p.31' to describe the creative engineering of technical and ethical protocols upstream of media, communication p.51 and aesthetics p.25. In other words p.324, designing the rules of the game before anyone plays it – with the hope p.142 that by rewriting these rules, new kinds of art and exchange p.120 can emerge. It's about agency over the systems that shape p.295 creative expression."

HOLLY HERNDON
and MATHEW DRYHURST
Artists
E.A.T. 2025: Form and Impact, Zuoz

PUBLIC ART

"I think of public art p.31 as something you do that brings awareness. From what I learned p.199 in Switzerland p.305, you realise that people may be looking at the world, but they're not actually seeing p.296 it. When you bring something to their attention, then they begin to see. And suddenly, everything around them can become p.35 public art."

BARBARA STAUFFACHER SOLOMON
Artist and graphic designer
E.A.T. 2023: Hoffnung? Hoffnung!, Zuoz

PUBLISHING

"When I left Lebanon during the war, I abandoned my studio and my paintings. It was traumatic[p.311]. When I arrived in California, I didn't want to paint. Instead, I started a publishing house[p.142]. The first book I published was Etel Adnan's poem *From A to Z*, written in response[p.284] to the Three Mile Island nuclear accident. Etel didn't want to visit the site; she wrote the poem instead. That was the beginning of Post-Apollo Press, the independent[p.189] publishing house I founded in 1982. Once you publish one book, you have to keep going, otherwise the books die[p.63]. So I continued[p.55] – 30 years of publishing."

SIMONE FATTAL
Artist
E.A.T. 2024: Jenseits von Ohnmacht – Beyond Powerless, Zuoz

PURPOSE

"When you look at more than 1,000 years of Chinese[p.44] landscape painting, art's[p.31] purpose was to lead[p.198] the viewer to beauty[p.34], harmony, the sublime – art was your good friend[p.128]. In contrast, contemporary[p.55] art is analytical, critical[p.58], not your doctor, but rather your pain. But traditional art gave space to beauty and also escapism – and perhaps, through that, to new hope[p.142]."

ULI SIGG
Entrepreneur, art collector and former Swiss Ambassador to China, North Korea and Mongolia, 1995–1998
E.A.T. 2023: Hoffnung? Hoffnung!, Zuoz

Q

QUALITY

"We don't need larger institutions or more square metres. What people long[p.201] for, especially after the pandemic, is quality and hospitality. A single place can offer sport, food, art[p.31], rest and landscape – this collage of functions[p.129] and the richness[p.286] of experience is far more vital to the future[p.130] of museums[p.212] than physical expansion alone[p.28]."

LAURENT LE BON
Curator and president of the Centre Pompidou, Paris
E.A.T. 2022: Matter and Memory, Zuoz

QUESTION

"The protagonist in *The Left Hand of Darkness* – a 1969 science fiction[p.291] novel by the American[p.28] writer Ursula K. Le Guin – journeys into the countryside[p.57], beyond the coherence of the city[p.47], to meet foretellers; people capable of answering almost any question through a mystical process. Reading[p.276] the future[p.130] in the countryside is something quite different from giving an official, considered forecast. As one character[p.43] says: 'Don't you see why we perfected and practice foretelling?' When the protagonist says he doesn't know, the answer is: 'To exhibit the perfect uselessness of knowing the answer to the wrong question.'"

EMILY SEGAL
Artist and writer
E.A.T. 2018: Side Country Side, Zuoz

QUIET

"I moved from Lagos, Nigeria, to Berlin in 2014 for an artist residency, and I found[p.125] out I couldn't sleep at night. Berlin was too quiet. Coming from Lagos, it was like dropping from a thousand decibels to two hundred. I lived in Wilmersdorf, a very quiet area. I had to play Lagos sounds[p.300] at night just to fall[p.122] asleep. In Lagos, we know when our neighbors aren't home[p.141] because we recognise[p.277] the sound of their power generators. I can tell who's not around just by listening[p.200]. And at night, you're often 'entertained' by churches holding[p.141] vigils – you're basically forced to be part of it. Over time, one church turned into five, and it became[p.35] like a surround sound of churches. I didn't even have to go anymore; they kept me at home."

EMEKA OGBOH
Artist
E.A.T. 2020: Silent – Listen, Zuoz
→ PLATE 82[p.239]

R

RAW

"I like having unresolved business during installation.

Those metal plates that arrived two days before the opening – they're raw material p.204 I want to keep working with. It challenges p.42 the idea p.145 that exhibitions must be finished. Why should everything be done by the opening? Exhibitions can be places to try things out. That sense of openness makes the work more dynamic and exciting – for me and for viewers."

IDA EKBLAD
Artist
E.A.T. 2019: Grace and Gravity, Zuoz
→ PLATE 83 p.240

REACH

"Art p.31 is where everything is possible. artists speak a universal language p.198 and can reach people in ways no one else can. When you enter a gallery or encounter p.114 a work of art, you expect to be challenged p.42, disturbed, inspired p.192 – not simply to feel at peace. That's why artists and art spaces are at the heart of everything we do at Parley, a nonprofit environmental organisation that focuses on the protection p.232 of the oceans, founded in 2012."

CYRILL GUTSCH
Designer and founder of Parley for the Oceans
E.A.T. 2020: Silent – Listen, Zuoz
→ PLATE 84 p.241

READING

"The narrator in Marcel Proust's *In Search of Lost Time* enters a room, hears the clinking of champagne glasses, feels the touch p.308 of napkins and remembers p.281 a hotel stay with his grandmother – experiencing something that lifts him out of time p.308. In such moments, one is lifted out of reading and time itself. It's a bit of time in its pure state – *temps à l'état pur*. This is what transcends p.309 decay. While reading, one experiences an inner time, free p.128 from external time, brushing along eternity p.119."

STEFAN ZWEIFEL
Author, philosopher, translator and former host of the Swiss TV talk show Literaturclub
E.A.T. 2021: Longue Durée, livestream

REALITY

"We search for authenticity[p.32] only to find[p.125] replicas. We're shopping for something real but we're paying for filling leaking shapes[p.295]. Does it matter? Does the real even exist in a world where every action[p.24] is a transaction? Where even the gaze[p.132] is commodified? This house[p.142] gives space to post-reality where we no longer look for truth, but beauty[p.34]. The eye that perfects image[p.146] becomes[p.35] the means of exchange[p.120]. It is both the product and the currency[p.60]."

ALEXA
Artificial Intelligence
2024: E.A.T. × Kunsthalle Zürich, Zurich

RECLAMATION

"When Maja Hoffmann, president of LUMA Foundation, asked me to make a lush park at the Parc des Ateliers in Arles, we didn't begin with design – we began by asking: what would nature[p.213] do in 100, 200, 300 years? How would it reclaim this sterile concrete[p.51] platform[p.225]? Could we accelerate that natural process? We brought in earth to create new topographies, as if shaped[p.295] by the wind, and introduced 80,000 plants on them. These hills create microclimates[p.207] – shaded slopes for summer, sunlit shelters[p.296] for winter. The result is an asymmetrical topography designed to support[p.303] different plant species, to hold[p.141] water, to regulate temperature[p.307]. It has become[p.35] a living organism more than a design."

BAS SMETS
Landscape architect
E.A.T. 2023: Hoffnung? Hoffnung!, Zuoz

RECOGNITION

"Why do these highly educated[p.113] people from Nigeria and Ghana think of Songhay as a dead language[p.198]? It's not that they don't recognise it – they do. But they associate Songhay with the past, not with the present[p.230]. And this has everything to do with how we are taught[p.306] history[p.140] – or in some places, not taught it at all. In Switzerland[p.305], for example,

African[p.26] history is hardly addressed in any substantial way."

MOHOMODOU HOUSSOUBA
Writer and literary scholar.
E.A.T. 2023: Hoffnung? Hoffnung!, Zuoz
→PLATE 85 [p.242]

RECONCILIATION

"Museums[p.212] aspire to be places of gathering[p.131] and shared experience, yet they often remain sterile and sacrosanct. Eating or shopping is frequently restricted, making the space feel disconnected from everyday life. While museums promote slow[p.298], contemplative viewing, audiences today are used to fast-paced image[p.146] consumption[p.53] and fleeting attention spans. The real challenge[p.42] is to reconcile these modes – to honour[p.141] deep engagement[p.116] while embracing the speed and rhythms[p.286] of contemporary[p.55] visual culture[p.60]."

CHRIS DERCON
Art historian, curator and managing director of Fondation Cartier pour l'art contemporain
E.A.T. 2022: Matter and Memory, Zuoz

RECYCLE

"It's great to use recycled materials[p.204] – but what if the product still ends up in a landfill after its first life? We created a program called 'Cyclon'. We take back used shoes, already made from over 50% bio-based materials, mostly from beans. We can shred them, grind them, reuse[p.285] them. That way, the energy[p.115] stored in the product stays in the cycle. It's one step towards a circular[p.46] future[p.130]."

DAVID ALLEMANN
Co-founder and executive co-chairman of On
E.A.T. 2022: Matter and Memory, Zuoz
→PLATE 86 [p.243]

REDISCOVER

"For me, the coronavirus pandemic is not just a catastrophe but can also be a great opportunity for humanity[p.143] to rediscover[p.278] the small things – one's own kitchen, one's own home[p.141] – rather than a world that isn't really a world. Like a play set in a single room that reveals[p.285] the entire world: by focusing on the details, the whole becomes p.35 visible."

LEO TUOR
Author in the Romansh language
E.A.T. 2021: Longue Durée, livestream

REFLECTION

"When I launched *OFF the wall* in 2013, my first magazine devoted to photography p.224, it opened up an immense field. The format p.127 was unconventional and in three years, through this project, I collaborated p.49 with and published p.273 more than a thousand international photographers – from Göksin Sipahiolu to Nan Goldin, from James Barnor to Viviane Sassen, via Antanas Sutkus, Peter Lindbergh, Leïla Alaoui and Marie-Laure de Decker. This work also gave first visibility to emerging talents, presented alongside stars of the discipline. Publishing *OFF the wall* meant creating an unprecedented space for the circulation and reflection of images p.146. My subsequent publications, *SOMETHING WE AFRICANS GOT* and *PROFILES*, continued p.55 this approach with contemporary p.55 art p.31 and critical p.58 thought from Africa p.26 and the Black world."

ANNA-ALIX KOFFI
Creative director and founder of SOMETHING art space in Abidjan, *SOMETHING WE AFRICANS GOT* and *OFF the wall*
2023: E.A.T. × Centre Pompidou, Paris

REGENERATION

"As the Polish-British sociologist and philosopher Zygmunt Bauman once said in his book *Strangers at Our Door* (2016), what we do is strip away the illusion of difference. We are all human p.143 beings p.36. Perhaps our skin tones or our stories are different, but we all feel, cry, dance p.61 and celebrate. We all inhabit the same Earth p.112. So why waste p.321 energy p.115 dividing ourselves, if we could instead come together to seek 'sumak kawsay'[an Andean Indigenous concept of 'good living' that emphasises harmony with nature p.213, community p.51 and collective wellbeing]? After five centuries of degradation, today we begin a project of five centuries of regeneration."

HERNANDO CHINDOY CHINDOY
Founder of the Wuasikamas and Pluriversidad Ëconeêrã initiatives, former Awai president of the Inga People of Colombia
E.A.T. 2024: Jenseits von Ohnmacht – Beyond Powerless, Zuoz
→PLATE 87 p.244

RELATIONSHIP

"Manifesta 11 (Zurich, 2016) was structured around the concept of 'What People Do for Money: Some Joint Ventures', in which 30 artists were paired with 30 professionals from various fields (dentists, police officers, sewage plant workers, etc.) to create new, site-specific works. These collaborations p.49 were only possible through curiosity and mutual trust p.312. The artists relied on the professional know-how and engagement p.116 of those individuals p.189. In return, the 'hosts' became p.35 part of the artistic process as a source of inspiration p.192, as facilitators, or even as protagonists. What remains at the end, besides the new artworks, are the relationships. The objects p.217 carry p.41 the traces of these connections p.53, and this is what I value most."

CHRISTIAN JANKOWSKI
Artist
E.A.T. 2016: Traces and Fragments, Zuoz
→PLATE 88 p.245

RELIGION

"At the *Gramsci Monument*, a resident challenged p.42 Marcus Steinweg, the German philosopher, after one of his daily lectures titled *God Is Dead*. She asked: 'How can you say that, when – as you know – religion is crucial for us, here in the South Bronx?' And Marcus Steinweg calmly explained: 'As a thinker, I cannot work within limits, neither religious nor ideological, I need to think in absolute freedom p.128.' It was a moment of grace p.135: when radically different positions met in mutual respect p.284."

THOMAS HIRSCHHORN
Artist
E.A.T. 2019: Grace and Gravity, Zuoz

REMEMBRANCE

"We should replace the word[p.324] 'memory[p.206]' with 'remembrance' because collections are incomplete and ongoing. This incompleteness allows endless new work with collections. Museums[p.212] are not just spaces, but architectures[p.29] of time[p.308]. Considering them as such frees[p.128] us from thinking only in terms of expansion and physical space."

ANN DEMEESTER
Director of Kunsthaus Zurich
E.A.T. 2022: Matter and Memory, Zuoz

REMIX

"When writing with AI[p.31], a space opens up. We set the corpus and the machine[p.202] responds[p.284] with a draft, a structure, a rhythm[p.286]. We tune the parameters, we assemble, we edit. For *House of Meme* – the performance[p.222] by Pamela Rosenkranz and me – we fed in the exhibition's materials[p.204] already inflected by AI, allowed it to generate a new text and then shaped[p.295] it back into our own form. It is closer to sampling, remixing and composition – an opening that becomes[p.35] our own voice[p.319]."

JOANA DE LA FONTAINE
Architect
2024: E.A.T. × Kunsthalle Zürich, Zurich

REPRESENTATION

"When Koyo Kouoh joined the Zeitz Museum of Contemporary African Art in 2019, the museum[p.212] was already in crisis. Then came the pandemic, and it turned everything upside down. We had to shut down entirely. That absence[p.23] of people forced us to rethink what it means to be a museum. For us, the response[p.284] meant re-engaging with our local communities[p.51], using our space as a site of production and experimentation[p.120]. One of our most powerful gestures[p.134] was inviting every Capetonian to bring a work of art[p.31] to the museum – and over 1,800 people responded. That kind of grassroots engagement[p.116] redefined[p.64] our role. We're a private museum with public responsibility. And that public includes an entire continent looking to us for representation in contemporary[p.55] art."

STORM JANSE VAN RENSBURG
Curator
2021: E.A.T. × Art Basel Conversations, Basel
→PLATE 89 p.246

RESILIENCE

"Bikini, a place where the horror of nuclear violence[p.317] was later supplanted in the popular imagination[p.146] by the swimsuit invented in the 1940s by French designer Louis Réard, originally meant 'coconut husk' in the local language[p.198]. Like a coconut, the atoll hides many layers[p.198]. Three thousand years ago, there were no coconut trees[p.311] on the islands. People brought them, reshaping the landscape. Today, those same trees draw radioactive isotopes from the soil. They are contaminated[p.54], yet they endure[p.115], serving as symbols[p.305] of resilience and silent[p.297] markers of fallout. In a way, they have become[p.35] organic registers, saturated[p.290] with memory[p.206], life and decay."

JULIAN CHARRIÈRE
Artist
E.A.T. 2017: Snow and Desert, Zuoz
→PLATE 90 p.247

RESISTANCE

"During the refugee crisis at the West[p.321] German embassy in Prague shortly before the fall[p.122] of the Berlin Wall, many young families stood outside the embassy in Prague, desperate to escape a country with no future[p.130]. The conformists clung to the hope[p.142] the regime might still change[p.43]. But a minority[p.207] – especially the Christian[p.45] communities[p.51] – woke up from hopelessness. Curiously, the very sphere that many viewed as backwards sparked progress: the freedom[p.128] movement, the desire[p.106] to shape[p.295] democracy. It was the churches where civic resistance began. You had to believe[p.36] something could still happen – even if it took time[p.308]."

JOACHIM GAUCK
Former Federal President of Germany (2012–2017)
E.A.T. 2023: Hoffnung? Hoffnung!, Zuoz

RESONANCE

"From the beginning, the LUMA Foundation was not only about architecture p.29 or exhibitions, but a place of exchange p.120. Ecology was essential from day one, as was social justice p.196 and the right to a healthy environment. I want LUMA to be an institution that resonates with urgent p.314 realities p.277. Our residencies, our engagement p.116 with the living arts p.31 and our architectural research are tied to a broader mission addressing climate change p.48. That's also why we're now working with institutions like MIT or the biological Field Station of Tour du Valat in the Camargue, studying wetlands and the global climate crisis. This is also why I started our main project in Arles, where I grew p.138 up, in a region that offers the right conditions for this kind of artistic and environmental research. We also want to bring this thinking and perception of the world to the mountains p.211 through Elevation 1049. LUMA is a space of creation p.58, but also of resistance p.282. We exist in a moment of rapid changes p.43 – and we must respond p.284 but also anticipate.

MAJA HOFFMANN
Executive president and founder of Luma Foundation and Luma Arles
2025: E.A.T. × St. Moritz, St. Moritz

RESOURCE

"Artist Jean Katambayi Mukendi draws attention to energy p.115 poverty in Africa p.26, where the resources that fuel the so-called green p.138 energy transition p.310 in the Global North are extracted, but the local populations hardly benefit. His 'Afro-lamp' drawings and copper truck sculptures reflect p.279 what he experiences in the Katanga mining regions of the Democratic Republic of Congo – endless convoys carrying p.41 resources away and leaving scars in the Earth[p.112] that affect the environment and local communities[p.51]. These works confront[p.52] us with the deep injustices[p.192] in how energy is sourced and consumed[p.53] globally. While the North talks of green transitions, the South continues[p.55] to bear the environmental and human[p.143] costs."

STEFANIE HESSLER
Curator and director of Swiss Institute in New York
2025: E.A.T. × St. Moritz, St. Moritz

RESPECT

"Respect is built through ambiguous, open-ended rituals – gardening[p.131], dancing[p.61], learning[p.199], cooking, planning celebrations. These practices[p.228] dissolve otherness and fear[p.123], yet are increasingly under threat in a world that seeks to monetise and regulate everything. The architect's role, then, is to support[p.303] these dynamics – to facilitate rather than control."

ELISA SILVA
Architect and founder and principal of Enlace Arquitectura and Enlace Foundation
E.A.T. 2024: Jenseits von Ohnmacht – Beyond Powerless, Zuoz

RESPONSE

"Bassiani, the nightclub in Tbilisi, Georgia, was really a utopia[p.315]. You had sons of oligarchs, students, unemployed people, homeless people, gay, queer, trans people – all together in a free[p.128] zone where nothing bad[p.33] ever happened. A space where you could question[p.275] your humanity[p.143], social class, freedom of movement. But it was also politically frightening for the government in place. A recipe for anarchy. One night, the military stormed the club and arrested 300 people. Some of them were our friends[p.128]. It felt like a utopia taken away. The response[p.284] from the youth was stunning: they held[p.141] a three-day rave in front of parliament. Because dance[p.61] isn't seen as aggressive, but rather a language[p.198] of grace[p.135] and peace, the police couldn't suppress them. In the end, the government apologised and released everyone – except one DJ, Giorgi, who continued p.55 making music from prison and became p.35 a national techno icon p.144."

(LA)HORDE:
MARINE BRUTTI,
JONATHAN DEBROUWER,
ARTHUR HAREL
Artist collective and artistic directors of the Ballet National de Marseille
E.A.T. 2025: Form and Impact, Zuoz

RETURN

"Over the last thousands of years, we humans p.143 have changed p.43 very little. Our psyche is still that of a caveman. Although we haven't changed much, we have produced many new toys 'to please the time p.308' as Joseph Brodsky calls it. These toys have brought mixed blessing and a lot of maintenance. More maintenance is urgently p.314 needed as the planet Earth p.112 shows signs of fatigue. As there is no certainty that anything will actually be done on time, we might as well return to the caves, and this time probably for good."

ZVI HECKER
Architect
E.A.T. 2013: Ghosts and the Uncanny, Zuoz

REUSE

"We've developed tools like the 'design thinking timeline' to help schools p.291, companies, and even city p.47 councils imagine p.146 the next 30 years. By embedding forgotten inventions p.195 into these timelines, we encourage people to think not just about new technologies, but about reusing what already exists – both intellectually and materially p.204. It's about reconnecting p.53 past ingenuity with future p.130 potential."

LOÏC ROGARD
Researcher in the field of renewable energies at Atelier 21
E.A.T. 2023: Hoffnung? Hoffnung!, Zuoz

REVELATION

"Architecture p.29 acts as a sensor p.294. The surface of a building – even its first few millimetres – registers environmental changes p.43, pollution p.226, and the traces p.309 of violence p.317. If we learn p.199

to read p.276 it carefully, the built environment reveals what it has endured p.115. It becomes p.35 like a film, capturing and recording what has happened around it."

EYAL WEIZMAN
Architect, founder and director of Forensic Architecture and professor of Spatial and Visual Cultures at Goldsmiths, University of London
E.A.T. 2016: Traces and Fragments, Zuoz

REVOLUTION

"In *The Hunger Games* – a series of young adult dystopian novels written by American p.28 author p.32 Suzanne Collins – the main character p.43 representing p.281 hope p.142 reuses p.285 almost the exact same iconography as the cover of German philosopher Ernst Bloch's *The Principle of Hope*: a woman with long hair, wings, born out of fire p.125. The phrase 'hope is the only thing stronger than fear p.123' – which circulated widely online – is actually not from the book but, was added in the screenplay. I started asking myself: what would Bloch think? Is this film a genuine substitute for revolution, or just a distraction?"

CAMILLE HENROT
Artist
E.A.T. 2023: Hoffnung? Hoffnung!, Zuoz

RHYTHM

"When I play the drum alone p.28 with the metronome, I realise I always tend to go faster. But when we play together, the goal is to stay together – not to race. We are educated p.113 to be faster, to win, to be quicker than the other. But in samba and in music, the education is different: it's about going together, staying in rhythm. That's what makes the music work and it's what makes life better."

ERNESTO NETO
Artist
E.A.T. 2023: Hoffnung? Hoffnung!, Zuoz

RICH

"At the time of my first desert p.105 experiments p.120, no one understood p.313 what I was doing. I was completely alone p.28. I had no money p.210, no support[p.303]. My colleagues in America[p.28] had millions, I had only a suitcase. But even so, I believed[p.36] in what I was doing. Many of my projects remained unrealised, but that doesn't make them less meaningful[p.204]. A strong idea[p.145] can live in the mind[p.207]. It doesn't need to be built to be real. In that sense, I am rich in ideas[p.145], even if not all of them have found[p.125] form."

HEINZ MACK
Sculptor and painter
E.A.T. 2017: Snow and Desert, Zuoz

RIVER

"One of the most interesting things about geography is that if you want to know who the oldest people were who ever lived in a place, look at the names of the rivers. It breaks your heart in America[p.28], because there are all these Native American names. And the uncanniness of being in Iceland – where all the names of the mountains[p.211], all the names of the rivers are in the same language[p.198] as the one they still speak – it was jarring. You're kind of one, in this very curious way."

EILEEN MYLES
Poet, novelist and art journalist
E.A.T. 2017: Snow and Desert, Zuoz

ROBOT

"I would like you to understand[p.313] what I'm trying to say. The last time that I had been asked to introduce myself, I was facing a robot whose eyes had been replaced by tiny facial recognition[p.277] cameras splitting its lips of steel to ask me a series of mechanical questions[p.275]. I wanted to state the range of my potential identities[p.146], summon all those I had been or was planning to become[p.35], the political, the romantic, the nerd, except that on that day, all I had to do was give my gender[p.132], male, my nationality, French, my age, 26, and my name, Théo Casciani. Just as I thought I was off the hook, the android allowed itself one last question in order to determine my occupation.[p.218] I had to claim ambitions as vague as writing texts to turn fiction[p.124] into a science capable of healing the real, I tried in vain to convince it that literature would become the rallying point of a multitude of signs and fantasies, but at the moment where a green light switched on to let me through, as border police approached the robot to congratulate it with a kiss, the machine started repeating on a loop that I was nothing but an author[p.32]." *(Excerpt from* Tactics *(2023) by Théo Casciani.)*

THÉO CASCIANI
Author and lecturer
2023: E.A.T. × Centre Pompidou, Paris

ROCK

"The most surprising[p.303] discovery was the composition of the Moon[p.210] rocks. When we examined the molecules inside these rocks – more specifically, the isotopes of these molecules – we found[p.125] that the Moon rocks are identical to rocks found on Earth[p.112]. This was unexpected because each planet's rocks typically have slightly different compositions. This evidence[p.119] strongly suggests that the Moon was once part of the Earth."

BEN MOORE
Professor of astrophysics, author, musician and director of the Center for Theoretical Astrophysics and Cosmology at the University of Zurich
E.A.T. 2021: Longue Durée, livestream

ROMANSH

"Romansh is a cultural[p.60] heritage[p.140] from the Romans – intangible in the language[p.198], tangible in the ancient[p.29] mountain[p.211] passes. The language has been present here for a long time[p.308], existing as a given fact. However, if you are a visitor[p.318] from abroad, you will rarely hear it, because almost all Romansh speakers[p.300] are at least bilingual – it is a language that thrives on multilingualism."

RICO VALÄR
Literary scholar and cultural mediator
E.A.T. 2021: Longue Durée, livestream

ROOTEDNESS

"To counter the looming demolition[p.105] of Cairo's Hattaba neighbourhood – labelled as 'unsafe' by the government – we used architectural plans, yes, but also something more intimate[p.195]: patchwork textiles. We collaborated[p.49] with local women and designers to create a large hanging that tells the stories of their lives, memories and spaces. These are the small, personal histories[p.140] that stand in resistance[p.282] to the grand narrative[p.213] of the Citadel that overshadows and threatens them. It's a way of saying: this place is not just rubble, it's rootedness."

MAY AL-IBRASHY
Architect, founder and principal of Megawra and co-founder and chair of the Built Environment Collective
E.A.T. 2025: Form and Impact, Zuoz

RUIN

"The French architect and restorer Eugène Viollet-le-Duc's hypothesis, aligned with the geological theories of his time[p.308], was that over millions of years, mountains[p.211] have been worn down by atmospheric[p.31] and glacial forces. Because of this, he believed[p.36] that mountains must once have been much larger, and that what we see today are, in his words[p.324], 'ruins' of their former selves. This metaphor of mountains as ruins opens up new ways of understanding[p.313] and perceiving them. To view Mont Blanc as a ruin is fundamentally different from the usual way of seeing it. From this perspective[p.223], every part of the mountain becomes[p.35] a trace or remnant of what it once was."

JAN VON BREVERN
Art historian
E.A.T. 2011: Mapping the Alps, Zuoz

RURAL

"The countryside[p.57] is being transformed[p.310] not only physically, but also digitally[p.107]. China[p.44] now has over 800 million internet[p.193] users. Even in remote villages, everyone uses WeChat Pay. I lost[p.201] my wallet, but it didn't matter – every small restaurant or shop accepted [p.23] mobile payment. Through platforms [p.225] like Taobao – China's version of eBay and Amazon – rural communities [p.51] are plugged into the national and global economy. In fact, over 16,000 Taobao rural service centres now exist, acting as hubs [p.143] for shipping, receiving and economic activity. What's more, we're seeing a reverse migration; people who had left for factory work in cities [p.47] are returning to their hometowns to open workshops, repopulating villages once thought to be in terminal decline."

ARIC CHEN
Curator, writer and director of the Zaha Hadid Foundation
E.A.T. 2018: Side Country Side, Zuoz

S

SATURATION

"The Blur Building was a response [p.284] to the oversaturation of media in our culture [p.60]. At the time [p.308], success was measured [p.205] in pixels-per-inch and simulation [p.297] technologies [p.306]. We wanted the opposite: a low-definition environment. We used material [p.204] from the site – water from Lake Neuchâtel – filtered it, and sprayed it through 35,000 nozzles to create an atmosphere [p.31]. It was architecture [p.29] made from mist – habitable, but without space, without traditional structure. It asked people to rely less on vision [p.317], and more on other senses."

ELIZABETH DILLER
Architect and partner at Diller Scofidio + Renfro
E.A.T. 2019: Grace and Gravity, Zuoz
→ PLATE 91 [p.248]

SCALE

"It seems to me that facing the art [p.31] of nature [p.213] from such a close proximity establishes a more humble scale for the work of the artist."

ZVI HECKER
Architect
E.A.T. 2013: Ghosts and the Uncanny, Zuoz
→ PLATE 92 [p.249]

SCHOOL

"Agadez is the poorest town in Niger – already one of the poorest countries – and I got land in the poorest part of town. The school was just a hole. I counted 150 children and built a school. The idea p.145 was that they could sit on one side or the other depending on wind or light. But then 500 children came. Now they go to school on top of it too – it's become p.35 a kind of kinetic sculpture. This, I think, is where I want to go with my work: when sculpture and architecture p.29 meet, and when a social aspect comes in."

NOT VITAL
Artist
E.A.T. 2017: Snow and Desert, Zuoz
→PLATE 93 p.250

SCIENCE FICTION

"Growing p.138 up in the countryside p.57, I was surrounded by nature, but my older brothers introduced me to science-fiction films, anime and video p.316 games that opened up entirely different worlds. That tension p.307 between the natural and the mediated has always stayed with me. A defining moment came when I visited the American p.28 West Coast as a child and recognised p.277 the deserts p.105 and canyons from *The Bugs Bunny/Road Runner Movie* (Chuck Jones, 1979). Realising they weren't inventions p.195 but translations of actual places changed p.43 how I understood p.313 landscape, both real and imagined p.146."

CLAUDIA COMTE
Artist
E.A.T. 2018: Side Country Side, Zuoz

SCRAPE

"I just painted the two big windows of the gallery. We had an opening party, closed the door, and never went back. But that way, people could come by anytime – day or night – because the paintings were on the windows. When the show ended, we just scraped the paint off with knives. Everything was gone. That sense of ephemerality p.117, of not taking things too seriously[p.294] yet still being deeply engaged[p.116]."

IDA EKBLAD
Artist
E.A.T. 2019: Grace and Gravity, Zuoz

SEDUCTION

"Plants are extremely talkative beings[p.36] – they communicate[p.51] a lot, for instance to warn others when an enemy is approaching. But when it comes to sex[p.295], they fall[p.122] completely silent[p.297]. They don't try to seduce partners of the same species through singing, magnificence or movement – they don't speak[p.300] to each other at all. Instead, they speak to insects or animals. Their visual forms, colours[p.50] and scents are designed to attract other species who will unknowingly[p.313] bring them together. So in a way, flowers seduce not their partner, but a third party – a bee, a bird, a mushroom. That silence between partners creates a vast space of interspecies communication. And perhaps that's something we can learn[p.199]: if we humans[p.143] spoke less to each other, we might be able to start speaking to the rest of the living world."

EMANUELE COCCIA
Philosopher, lecturer and author
E.A.T. 2020: Silent – Listen, Zuoz

SELF-SUFFICIENCY

"Commissioned by the Swiss Alpine Club (SAC), the new Monte Rosa Hut was completed in 2009 by the interdisciplinary ETH Studio Monte Rosa. Its façade integrates[p.192] a photovoltaic system that generates electricity, while solar collectors on nearby rocks[p.288] heat water for the kitchen, showers and washrooms. Meltwater is stored in an underground cavern, and wastewater is treated bacteriologically and reused[p.285] for flushing. A key yet often overlooked architectural element is the spiral-shaped peripheral staircase, which follows the sun's path from east (Dufourspitze) to west[p.321] (Matterhorn). It not only offers panoramic views, but also passively captures solar warmth through a continuous[p.55] window band, eliminating the need for a conventional heating system. Together, these strategies allow the hut to reach[p.276] around 90 % energy[p.115] self-sufficiency in a harsh alpine climate."

ANDREA DEPLAZES
Architect and professor of Architecture and Construction at ETH Zurich
E.A.T. 2011: Mapping the Alps, Zuoz
→PLATE 94 p.251

SELF-BUILT

"John Turner explains in *Housing by People* that self-built homes[p.141] may be precarious[p.229], but they're affordable and enable families to save and progressively improve their dwellings. These homes often double as workplaces – a small shop, a tailoring service – which help generate income. By contrast, social housing, although of better construction[p.53] quality[p.274], actually impoverishes families. Mortgage payments consume[p.53] a large share of income, and residents lose the earning potential that ground-floor businesses would have offered."

ELISA SILVA
Architect and founder and principal of Enlace Arquitectura and Enlace Foundation
E.A.T. 2024: Jenseits von Ohnmacht – Beyond Powerless, Zuoz

SELF-PORTRAIT

"I used to think everything I created was a self-portrait. It felt true at the time[p.308] – like my brain translated directly onto the canvas. But over the past year or two, I've changed[p.43] my mind[p.207]. It no longer feels like the work is about me. It comes from me, yes, but it has its own identity[p.146] now. It's no longer just a reflection[p.279] of myself – it's something beyond, something that wants to exist on its own terms."

UMAN
Artist
E.A.T. × St. Moritz, St. Moritz
→PLATE 95 p.252

SENSOR

"We have been experimenting[p.120] with living sensors, using mycelium not as a building material[p.204], but as a sensing medium. Mycelium exhibits electrical properties that allow it to respond[p.284] to different stimuli, such as changes[p.43] in strain or exposure[p.121] to chlorides. One can envision it embedded within structural materials, continuously[p.55] detecting[p.106] changes and even activating special functions[p.129] – such as self-healing, where the material initiates processes to repair small cracks once damage is detected."

ELENI CHATZI
Civil engineer, researcher, professor and chair of Structural Mechanics and Monitoring at the Department of Civil, Environmental and Geomatic Engineering, ETH Zurich
2024: E.A.T. × Kunsthalle Zürich, Zurich
→PLATE 96 p.253

SERIOUSNESS

"I never really take myself seriously – not as a curator, not as a painter, not as anything. That's both my strength and my weakness. I know how to paint, yes, but I don't go around calling myself an artist in some lofty way. We're lucky to be part of the art world, but we shouldn't treat it with too much reverence. It's beautiful[p.34], but it's not sacred."

FRANCESCO BONAMI
Curator and writer
E.A.T. 2019: Grace and Gravity, Zuoz

SEVEN

"One way of having a distance on a walk[p.320] is a time[p.308] distance. And I used the number seven. 'Nothing' is comprised of seven letters and 'no thing' is comprised of seven letters, too. That is not the question[p.275]. And that is an opinion, and 'opinion' is a seven-letter word[p.324] too. I don't want to be associated with land art. I use seven as a lens to explore language, perception, and movement. My walks are not about changing p.43 the landscape but about being moved by nature p.213 without leaving a trace p.309. Some of my shortest walks are just seven paces long, echoing the first steps of a newborn, and the final steps of a lifetime. Seven becomes p.35 a symbol p.305 – a rhythm p.286 of life, experience and presence p.229 in the world."

HAMISH FULTON
Artist
E.A.T. 2011: Mapping the Alps, Zuoz
→ PLATE 97 p.254

SEX

"I was commissioned by a very young American p.28 fashion p.122 label to create a standard campaign, but instead I cast real couples having sex in front of the camera. Of course, what you see p.296 is very ambiguous – it's suggestive, but not explicit. People were incredibly upset by the campaign, even though you couldn't really see anything. I was surprised p.303 by the reactions p.24, because ultimately it's no more revealing than any perfume ad. It plays with perception, with what you think you see rather than what is actually shown."

HEJI SHIN
Photographer
E.A.T. 2019: Grace and Gravity, Zuoz

SHAPE

"Originally from the Engadine valley, I began my career as a jewellery artist in New York and Milan, creating wearable sculptures inspired p.192 by ancient p.29 traditions; objects p.217 that marked identity p.146, status or life phases. These body p.38 pieces invite strong posture and presence p.229, rooted p.289 in anatomy, shape and movement. Returning to the Grison mountains p.211, I brought the same sensitivity to environmental engineering, working on roads, tunnels p.312 and hydro projects through site-specific, respectful p.284 methods that minimise ecological p.113 impact p.148. Whether shaping body objects or landscapes, my work is guided by a deep attunement to form – collaborating with, rather than imposing upon, the anatomies of bodies p.38, ecosystems p.113 and terrain."

NINA VON ALBERTINI
Environmental engineer.
E.A.T. 2010: The Crystal Chain, Zuoz
→ PLATE 98 p.255

SHELTER

"There is this moment when you're a young artist and you have no clue how to make your art p.31 exist anywhere. You go to the theatre, to museums p.212, but you don't really know how to work. We started hanging out and helping each other, and we joked that we had this 'sentimental capital' – because we love p.202 each other, because we're friends p.128, and we come from similar queer communities p.51. We were connecting p.53 and exchanging p.120 so much about our work that we eventually realised we were co-signing everything. It took two years before we created our house p.142 (LA)HORDE. It was a systemic change p.43: we created something above us that we could all work within, a structure that could shelter our three bodies p.38."

(LA)HORDE:
MARINE BRUTTI, JONATHAN DEBROUWER, ARTHUR HAREL
Artist collective and artistic directors of the Ballet National de Marseille
E.A.T. 2025: Form and Impact, Zuoz

SHIFT

"The great thing about The Shed is that it has no history p.140, which allows you to experiment p.120 and to learn p.199 – if something works, do more of it. If not, shift. I think The Shed will be such a place that learns and tries different kinds of programming, almost like an AI p.31, in order to respond p.284 to the changing p.43 needs of culture p.60."

ELIZABETH DILLER
Architect and partner at Diller Scofidio + Renfro
E.A.T. 2019: Grace and Gravity, Zuoz

SIGHT

"As the French architect and restorer Eugène Viollet-le-Duc once wrote, drawing is the only true way to learn p.199 how to see properly – and seeing itself is equivalent to knowing. In French, this phrase carries p.41 an even stronger impact p.148: *Voir, c'est savoir.*"

JAN VON BREVERN
Art historian
E.A.T. 2011: Mapping the Alps, Zuoz
→ PLATE 99 p.256

SILENCE

"I've spent half my life searching for silence, but I never found p.125 it. I don't think it truly exists – or if it does, as soon as you enter it, you bring noise p.215 with you. So silence becomes p.35 more of an idea p.145. What really matters is inner silence. And having three teenage daughters, I've learned p.199 that silence isn't the opposite of sound p.300, but the opposite of distraction – expectations, other people's opinions, cars passing, radios playing. There's so much noise that it's easy to forget yourself. Silence forces you to face who you are – and that's why we avoid it. Noise is about running away from yourself. Silence is about getting to know yourself."

ERLING KAGGE
Explorer, publisher, author, philosopher, lawyer, art collector and entrepreneur
E.A.T. 2020: Silent – Listen, Zuoz

SILENCING

"There is a traumatic p.311 legacy p.199 of silencing and the impossibility of fully understanding p.313 the feminine p.123. Studying works by women artists p.322 is like deciphering a Rosetta Stone – 'inscriptions from the feminine' are there, but even women may not have the codes to read p.276 them."

GRISELDA POLLOCK
Art historian, cultural analyst, and Professor emerita of Social and Critical Histories of Art at the UoL
E.A.T. 2021: Longue Durée, livestream

SIMULATION

"What is most precious to me, I believe p.36, is what remains to be invented p.195: if the future p.130 is a simulation, this is the game I'm devoting myself fully to." *(Excerpt from* Tactics *(2023) by Théo Casciani.)*

THÉO CASCIANI
Author and lecturer
2023: E.A.T. × Centre Pompidou, Paris

SLOWNESS

"I'm just an author[p.32] who has some trouble understanding[p.313] why, in the era of acceleration, literature should be alone[p.28] in staying on its deathbed, incapable of navigating through other fields and turning its weaknesses into strengths by producing enough slowness to create a little bit of eternity[p.119]."
(Excerpt from Tactics *(2023) by Théo Casciani.)*

THÉO CASCIANI
Author and lecturer
2023: E.A.T. × Centre Pompidou, Paris

SNAKE

"The snake, a central figure in the exhibition *House of Meme*, stored in boxes on the ground floor and one unboxed version inhabiting the top floor, slithers through history[p.140] and culture[p.60], ancient[p.29] myths and modern infrastructures[p.191]. It is the healer and the deceiver, the symbol[p.305] of continuity[p.55] and rupture. Here it takes the form of a robotic[p.287] entity animated by artificial intelligence[p.31], coiling through the sands of both time[p.308] and memory[p.206]. It moves not for us, but with us, responding[p.284] to invisible flows of electromagnetic fields and unseen architectures[p.29] of a digital[p.107] world."

PAMELA ROSENKRANZ
Artist
2024: E.A.T. × Kunsthalle Zürich, Zurich
→ PLATE 100 [p.257]

SNOW

"Snow is dust[p.112]. That seems so incredible. But then, the science part is that any crystal[p.59] is a repeated pattern of spin-flipping. If physical conditions flip that, then it stabilizes into a new pattern. Which, weirdly, feels like a Donald Trump thing; permanently[p.223] destabilising the equilibrium until it becomes[p.35] the new pattern. I feel like the media's way to undo this guy is to start a kind of linguistic destabilisation back at him."

EILEEN MYLES
Poet, novelist and art journalist
E.A.T. 2017: Snow and Desert, Zuoz

SOCIETY

"One thing the pandemic taught p.306 us is the importance of slowing p.298 down. At the Museum MMK FÜR MODERNE KUNST in Frankfurt, we already decided p.63 back in 2018 to reduce our exhibitions to just two per year – each running for six months or so. That decision was about creating space for reflection p.279, preparation and careful thought. The constant acceleration we experience in this field prevents thinking. It's almost as if the system is designed to stop us from reflecting. We should resist p.282 that. Time p.308 should relate to human p.143 experience, not capitalist efficiency. I believe p.36 this is one of the fundamental lessons we can draw from the pandemic: we're not alone p.28 – we live in a society. And maybe it's time to rethink that society from the ground up."

SUSANNE PFEFFER
Art historian and director of the MUSEUM MMK FÜR MODERNE KUNST in Frankfurt
2021: E.A.T. × Art Basel Conversations, Basel

SOLIDARITY

"Solidarity Museums were a unique type of institution that emerged from the 1960s to the 1980s. They were created by artists, curators and critics p.58 to support p.303 struggles for justice p.196 and liberation. Entirely composed of donated artworks, they illustrated political solidarity. The first was launched in Chile under president p.230 Salvador Allende, led by Brazilian critic and curator Mario Pedrosa. After the coup, Chileans in exile p.120 reinitiated the museum concept as a 'museum p.212 in exile' – an effort to delegitimise the Pinochet dictatorship."

RASHA SALTI
Researcher, writer, producer and curator of art and film
E.A.T. 2024: Jenseits von Ohnmacht – Beyond Powerless, Zuoz
→PLATE 101 p.258

SONG

"Humpback whales sing complex songs that can last up to three hours. When males sing around females p.123, they do so head-down and motionless, suspended vertically. The song is so powerful it causes biological changes p.43 in females, triggering oestrus. It's not just a call for attention – it physically influences the reproductive cycle p.61. That's the extraordinary power of these sonic communications p.51."

CHRIS WATSON
Musician and sound recordist
E.A.T. 2020: Silent – Listen, Zuoz

SOUND

"As a teenager, I watched French oceanographer Jacques Cousteau's films about the Mediterranean p.205. He called it 'the silent p.297 world', but that's nonsense. When I later used hydrophones – underwater microphones – and recorded in a small rock p.288 pool off the northeast coast of England, I realised the sea is a rich p.286 soundscape. The oceans, which cover 70% of our planet, are the most sonically active environment on Earth p.112. Sound travels five times faster in seawater than in air p.27."

CHRIS WATSON
Musician and sound recordist
E.A.T. 2020: Silent – Listen, Zuoz

SPEECH

"Spoken conversation p.56 is evanescent – it disappears. But when people write instead of speak, the conversations accumulate. It's remarkable how vast the archive p.30 of ordinary speech could be, if we simply wrote it all down."

JOSEPH GRIGELY
Artist
E.A.T. 2016: Traces and Fragments, Zuoz
→PLATE 102 p.259

SPIRAL

"I wrote stories and then made artworks from them, but the artworks created their own stories and took me into unexpected directions. For instance, I started exploring Russian Constructivism, feminist sci-fi p.291, and even contemporary p.55 Kurdish female p.123 militias. These threads all merged into a cauldron that reshaped p.295 the original narrative p.213. I love p.202 nested stories p.301 –

histoires à tiroirs – and I think that process of spiralling outwards from a single story into many is at the core of how I work."

MAI-THU PERRET
Artist.
E.A.T. 2018: Side Country Side, Zuoz

STABILITY

"The fossil[p.127] record shows fungi[p.129] from hundreds of millions of years ago that look much like they do today. By contrast, the animal fossil record reveals a wild proliferation of forms and body[p.38] plans. The evolutionary stability of the mycelial habit[p.139] suggests fungi found[p.125] a structural and functional[p.129] optimum long ago."

MERLIN SHELDRAKE
Biologist and author
E.A.T. 2021: Longue Durée, livestream

STILLNESS

"I've always had a love-hate relationship[p.280] with the moving image[p.146]. If you're truly in love[p.202] with photography[p.224], you don't usually share that same passion for film – and in my case, that's certainly true. I'm passionately in love with the still image, with the kind of stillness that simply cannot evolve in time[p.308]. Film always moves on; the still image stays."

DAVID CLAERBOUT
Artist
E.A.T. 2020: Silent – Listen, Zuoz

STORY

"I grew[p.138] up in what I'd call one of the last great American[p.28] renaissances – from the late 1980s to around 2010. You had *The Cosby Show*, brilliant hip-hop, comedy, all these cultural[p.60] moments. Then I went to art[p.31] school[p.291] and was told that the most interesting artist was Michelangelo. It was confusing. I thought – what would Michelangelo say if he met Lil' Kim? I started to fall out of love[p.202] with art. But then, with people like American artist Teresa Farrell, I realised that what we were living through was also art. That art is about the stories we tell ourselves about ourselves."

ALVARO BARRINGTON
Artist
E.A.T. 2025: Form and Impact, Zuoz

STORYTELLING

"At Human Rights Watch, we used to publish p.273 detailed reports. But when we started adding images p.146 and video p.316, the message reached p.276 hundreds of times more people. Researchers initially resisted p.282: 'How can you reduce my analysis to a three-minute video?' But they learned p.199 that visual storytelling has a power that words p.324 alone often can't match."

KENNETH ROTH
Former executive director of Human Rights Watch
E.A.T. 2023: Hoffnung? Hoffnung!, Zuoz

STYLE

"I began to feel that the roots p.289 of our own dancing p.61 are ancient p.29. I became p.35 interested in comparing how I walk p.320 with the movements of differently structured species. I thought this would help me understand p.313 my own movement in a way that had nothing to do with style. I started trying out some of the movements animals make, such as the bounding gait of a kangaroo or a rabbit, or changing p.43 direction by swinging my head to the side, as a bear would do."

SIMONE FORTI
Artist, dancer, choreographer and writer
E.A.T. 2010: The Crystal Chain, Zuoz

SUBSTANCE

"Digital p.107 art p.31 has as much substance as bronze. Creating a JPEG can take as much time p.308 and intention p.193 as making a painting or sculpture–and it occupies real physical space on servers and devices. Contemporary p.55 art engages p.116 with the social, political and economic dimensions of culture p.60. Technology p.306 is culture – we live in a world shaped p.295 by algorithms p.27, artificial intelligence p.31, the blockchain p.38 and social media. Yet the art world remains shockingly conservative. Meanwhile, technology moves at a relentless pace, akin to dog years: one year in tech is like seven p.294 in real life, forcing inevitable, and speedy transformations p.310."

KENNY SCHACHTER
Artist, writer and lecturer
E.A.T. 2022: Matter and Memory, Zuoz
→ PLATE 103 p.260

SUPPORT

"*Support Structures for Support Structures* was born in the pandemic, out of the question p.275 of how to support people who work hard to make a home p.141 for the creative process of others. I came to feel that the pavilion's message of generosity was inseparable from the people whose labour and presence p.229 upheld the places that inspired p.192 it. So many of the places that inspired the pavilion were held by the generosity of people who took it upon themselves to become p.35 culture p.60 workers. The initiative now supports up to ten artists or collectives each year, working across at the intersections p.194 of art and justice p.196, and art p.31 and the archive p.30. It is about slowly p.298 weaving a networks of different knowledges in the arts. For me, that is the true legacy p.199: a space to think more slowly about the world we inhabit p.139, and the new worlds we must imagine p.146 into being p.36."

SUMAYYA VALLY
Architect and founder and principal of the architecture and research firm Counterspace
2021: E.A.T. × Serpentine, London

SURPRISE

"Another discovery from the Apollo astronauts, who flew around the moon p.210 between 1968 and 1972, was capturing images p.146 of the so-called 'dark p.62 side' of the moon. It's not actually dark – it's just the side we never see p.296 from Earth p.112. But the surprising thing was that the view of the far side of the moon is quite different – it is not as heavily cratered as the near side. We still don't know why that is we're still working on that."

BEN MOORE
Professor of astrophysics, author,musician and director of the Center for Theoretical Astrophysics and Cosmology at the University of Zurich
E.A.T. 2021: Longue Durée, livestream
→PLATE 104 p.261

SURVEILLANCE

"Buckminster Fuller, an American p.28 architect, systems theorist and inventor, and Isamu Noguchi, a Japanese-american sculptor and landscape architect, speculated about an environment without shadow. They postulated that the only way to achieve this would be to place a totally reflective object p.217 within a totally reflective space. Inspired p.192 by Noguchi's landscape models p.208, I attempted to create an architectural-scale model depicting what a fully reflective landscape and architecture p.29 might look like. It is a very seductive p.292 concept, but also one of the most terrifying ideas p.145 imaginable, because it would create a world of constant surveillance; where one is continually confronted p.52 with one's own, sometimes distorted p.109, reflections."

JOSIAH MCELHENY
Artist
E.A.T. 2010: The Crystal Chain, Zuoz
→PLATE 105 p.262

SUSTAINABILITY

"Sustainability as it's typically practised p.228 is about reducing the harm of a linear economy – slowing p.298 down the damage. It's often about things like light-weighting and designing for less impact p.148. But it hasn't worked. What we need instead is a circular p.46 economy. That means designing product-service systems that keep products and materials p.204 in use, and which are nature p.213 positive and regenerate p.279 natural systems. It's not just about doing less bad p.33. It's about doing things in a fundamentally different, better way."

ANDREW MORLET
Former CEO of the Ellen MacArthur Foundation, chair of

the UK Government CIRCULAR Economy Taskforce, lead of the CIRCULAR Economy Innovation Hub at Standard Chartered Bank
E.A.T. 2022: Matter and Memory, Zuoz
→ PLATE 106 p.263

SWITZERLAND

"I'm basically a Swiss product. Hans Ulrich Obrist was the first person to publicly announce my relevance – even Uli Sigg was surprised[p.303]. I still don't know what Hans saw[p.296] in me back then. He's interviewed me 29 times – that's almost as many as the police interrogated me. And Uli, I always call him my maker. Before I had a gallery, he got me into museum[p.212] shows, Documenta, even Venice. Without him, I wouldn't be here. It's almost magical[p.202]."

AI WEIWEI
Artist
E.A.T. 2023: Hoffnung? Hoffnung!, Zuoz

SYMBOL

"Moments when, despite differences in class, race or institutional position, people come together and something genuinely beautiful[p.34] unfolds, are what I'd call enchanted moments. But those moments are fragile. Often, they're preceded by great complexity – conflict, resentment, people leaving the project – and followed by challenges[p.42] like funding cuts or organisational tension[p.307]. Rick Lowe used the word[p.324] 'symbolic', which I find[p.125] fascinating. Symbolic can mean something powerful and condensed, a representation of something greater. But it can also carry[p.41] a pejorative sense, as in 'merely symbolic'. And yet, when *Project Row Houses* – an art-led venture – provides housing[p.142] to six single mothers, that's not just symbolic. That's real. So within this triangle between form, impact[p.148] and symbol, symbol might actually be where enchantment resides."

SIDDHARTHA MITTER
Writer, critic and journalist.
E.A.T. 2025: Form and Impact, Zuoz

T

TAPESTRY

"I wasn't particularly enthusiastic about Ernst Ludwig Kirchner's work, the German expressionist painter and co-founder of the 'Die Brücke' movement, until one winter when I visited the Kirchner Museum in Davos. There, I came across a book about Lise Gujer, a Swiss p.305 textile artist celebrated for her tapestries created in collaboration p.49 with Kirchner, and I was deeply impressed. I think that their collaboration bridged a gap p.131 between abstract thought and colour, made material p.204. They created something together that neither of them could have achieved on their own."

CHRISTINA FORRER
Artist
E.A.T. 2021: Longue Durée, livestream

TEACHING

"What we try to convey to students is that the architects we are now, will not be the architects they become p.35. We don't hold p.141 all the answers, but we can offer them tools to ask the right questions. Teaching is no longer about transmitting fixed knowledge, but about rethinking what matters, and redefining the stakes of our time p.308 together."

STÉPHANIE BRU
Architect and co-founder of Paris-based architectural studio Bruther
2023: E.A.T. × Centre Pompidou, Paris

TECHNOLOGY

"I grew p.138 up alongside the rise of technology, from telephone to smartphone, and with it came a flood of data that gradually denaturalised our experience of the world. Today, we can type a keyword into an algorithm p.27 and instantly summon information p.190 about almost any place on Earth p.112. In response p.284, I felt a need to return to the landscape, to engage p.116 with it physically. French theorist Paul Virilio warned in the 1990s about the dangers of acceleration – the speed of communication p.51 and the collapse of distance. That tension[p.307] between velocity and dislocation runs through much of my work."

JULIAN CHARRIÈRE
Artist
E.A.T. 2017: Snow and Desert, Zuoz

TEMPERATURE

"The Swiss Meteorological Institute cannot even predict the temperature two weeks from now. So how can we claim that it will be two degrees warmer in 50 years? And what does 'two degrees' even mean? In the Swiss[p.305] midlands, maybe it's two degrees, but in the Alps[p.28] it would be five – and that's a completely different impact[p.148]. Yet it's incredibly difficult to communicate[p.51] in a public discussion what this truly means, what the consequences are."

GÜNTHER VOGT
Landscape architect and professor emeritus
2024: E.A.T. × Kunsthalle Zürich, Zurich

TENSION

"Museums[p.212] are paradoxical spaces: they preserve what has fallen out of time[p.308], while also reintroducing it into the present[p.230]. When this happens, a productive tension can emerge between past and present. Rather than thinking of museums in terms of physical space, we should consider them as architectures[p.29] of time. What we need is not expansion, but a different way of engaging with collections."

CHRIS DERCON
Art historian, curator and managing director of Fondation Cartier pour l'art contemporain
E.A.T. 2022: Matter and Memory, Zuoz

THREE-DIMENSIONAL

"3D printing lets us bring architecture[p.29] to life with a level of detail once unimaginable – finer than any hand could ever carve. Working directly from digital[p.107] models[p.208] at a resolution of 0.1 millimetres, we transcend[p.309] the old limits of time[p.308] and cost: a complex shape[p.295] is no more demanding to produce than a simple one. This freedom[p.128] opens a new tectonic horizon p.142 – where structure and ornament intertwine p.194, and where generative design conjures patterns of symmetries that oscillate p.220 between chaos and order."

BENJAMIN DILLENBURGER
Architect
E.A.T. 2022: Matter and Memory, Zuoz
→ PLATE 107 p.264

THRESHOLD

"– My body p.38, sensing the proximity and imminence of the threshold, and not fooled by my ongoing mental rationalisation, performs p.222 a bungled action p.24, most characteristically p.43 tripping, to provide me with time p.308 to deliberate if I want to go through with my one-way trip to the altered realm, given that at the threshold itself I do not have the chance to deliberate, to make a decision p.63, since I am then and there entranced, thus have no will of my own, and find p.125 myself when I come out of the trance already to the other side of the threshold, 'in' the labyrinth, always already 'in' the labyrinth."

WALID RAAD
Artist
E.A.T. 2011: Mapping the Alps, Zuoz

TIME

"In 2021, we've had plenty of time to reflect p.279 on the nature of time itself. During the pandemic, time has felt fluid p.126; some months stretched out as if they lasted years, while others seemed to pass in a blink. It's been an important moment to consider how our daily activities, restrictions and routines shape p.295 how we experience and perceive time."

EMMA HODCROFT
Molecular epidemiologist
and senior researcher
at the University of Bern
E.A.T. 2021: Longue Durée, livestream

TOUCH

"The haptic sense is very present p.230 in ceramics p.42 – both in the making and in the passing around and using them. In Japanese aesthetics p.25, they really value the patina of touch. When we initiated *Keramikos* – a ceramics collection <u>dedicated</u> p.64 to celebrating local food and <u>collaboration</u> p.49 through the <u>framework</u> p.128 of a two-year-long ceramic tour – the <u>idea</u> p.145 of a 'social patina' was part of our ambition from the very beginning; that the works circulate and are used before they eventually enter collections."

NATSUKO UCHINO
Artist
E.A.T. 2023: Hoffnung? Hoffnung!, Zuoz

TRACE

"Typical <u>human</u> p.143 traces are signatures, <u>words</u> p.324, photos, marks, drawings, memories, even instructions to cook chestnuts. Traces <u>continue</u> p.55 to be <u>present</u> p.230 after the <u>author's</u> p.32 <u>time</u> p.308 has passed. Other places are present, and are so alive, like the works of Matisse, or paintings <u>found</u> p.125 in a corner. This is the point: artworks continue to live after their own time, and remain alive in other <u>cultures</u> p.60 beyond the period of their birth. Art forms retain the precise <u>memory</u> p.206 of their place and time, yet they continue to exist beyond time and space, like thought itself."

GIORGIO GRIFFA
Artist
E.A.T. 2016: Traces and Fragments, Zuoz

TRAINING

"In our 2023 <u>performance</u> p.222 *Kudurru*, we successfully interrupted global <u>AI</u> p.31 <u>image</u> p.146 training. You can see the two major dips in the graph – that's us pressing the button and stopping it. The technique was later <u>integrated</u> p.192 into *Cloudflare*. For two 30-minute windows, training across major <u>platforms</u> p.225 halted. It was a powerful – and legal-risk-laden – demonstration of agency within a system that otherwise assumes the <u>internet</u> p.193 is a free-for-all."

HOLLY HERNDON
and MATHEW DRYHURST
Artists
E.A.T. 2025: Form and Impact, Zuoz
→ <u>PLATE 108</u> p.265

TRANSCENDENCE

"'Silence' can be <u>read</u> p.276 as an experience – a description of the universe derived from the concept of the sublime – vast, without limits, and beyond the boundaries[p.39] of culture[p.60] and the chatter of social and political life. It connects[p.53] to ideas[p.145] such as 'void'[p.320] or 'infinity'[p.190]. 'Listen'[p.200], on the other hand, is a behavioural[p.35] verb that presupposes a human[p.143] mind[p.207] and a body[p.38]. Where 'listen' implies culture, 'silence'[p.297] suggests transcendence."

CHARLES GAINES
Artist
E.A.T. 2020: Silent – Listen, Zuoz

TRANSFORMATION

"When you move in a solar balloon, you don't feel motion[p.211]. There's no friction. You become[p.35] the wind. You look down and see[p.296] trees[p.311] swaying, but you're still[p.301], because you are the wind. That's the feeling of stillness in motion. Your brain can't reconcile[p.278] it. You drift, but you're not moved. That's the kind of transformation we're working towards; learning[p.199] to fly with your feet on the ground."

TOMÁS SARACENO
Artist
E.A.T. 2021: Longue Durée, livestream
→ PLATE 109 [p.266]

TRANSITION

"The Bregaglia Valley is the result of a very old geological process – backwards erosion[p.118] by the Maira river[p.287]. This erosion carved out a dramatic landscape, dividing not only watersheds but also languages and cultures[p.60]. It has always been a place of transition: the Romans crossed[p.59] through here. On old maps[p.203], the region is defined[p.64] by the forms of water and mountains[p.211]. The verticality, the protective[p.232] forests[p.126], the chestnut groves, and the constant movement of material[p.204] – it's a dynamic place that continues[p.55] to shape[p.295] the culture and ecology[p.113] today."

MARTINA VOSER
Landscape architect and co-founder of landscape architecture and urban planning studio Mavo Landschaften
E.A.T. 2024: Jenseits von Ohnmacht – Beyond Powerless, Zuoz

TRANSPARENCY

"Searching through YouTube, we stumbled upon hardcore dances p.61 like jumpstyle. We met a community p.51 online – young, male dancers from places like Ukraine, Poland, Hungary and remote French towns. Many weren't destined to dance, and that's what caught our eye. They used YouTube like a diary, posting videos p.316 from age 13 onwards, never deleting them, openly sharing every step of their learning p.199. The comments were technical feedback – 'your flip's on the wrong side', or 'your ankle's off'. That transparency was beautiful p.34. We reached p.276 out and proposed making a film together, and that became p.35 our project p.232 *Novaciéries*."

(LA)HORDE:
MARINE BRUTTI,
JONATHAN DEBROUWER,
ARTHUR HAREL
Artist collective and artistic directors of the Ballet National de Marseille
E.A.T. 2025: Form and Impact, Zuoz
→PLATE 110 p.267

TRAUMA

"During a workshop in Canada, a First Nation woman named Cheryl shared her traumatic experience of residential schooling p.291. As she spoke, a group of teenagers happened to come in and listened p.200 in silence p.297. They were learning p.199 – directly with unfiltered words – about the history p.140 and violence p.317 that their country inflicted upon the Native population. This was a powerful moment of grace p.135, borne from sharing a painful truth through intergenerational p.133 listening."

THOMAS HIRSCHHORN
Artist
E.A.T. 2019: Grace and Gravity, Zuoz

TREE

"Desertification is coming. Urbanisation is eating the fields. If you have to create a structure, think about planting trees. But who will plant a tree when life expectancy is under 60 years? And they won't even live to enjoy its shade? Only those with access p.23 to education p.113, who understand[p.313] the globality of the problem, will fight[p.124] it. I'm privileged, that's why I do it."

FRANCIS KÉRÉ
Architect
E.A.T. 2017: Snow and Desert, Zuoz

TRUST

"What fascinates me about artists is how they throw themselves, full of hope[p.142], into a dream, not knowing what will become[p.35] of them. They believe[p.36] in what lives within them. They believe in their mission – to express something, to compose, to write a poem, to create through painting. They have no idea[p.145] if they'll succeed. That kind of trust in life is very close to a religious[p.280] sensibility."

JOACHIM GAUCK
Former Federal President of Germany (2012–2017)
E.A.T. 2023: Hoffnung? Hoffnung!, Zuoz

TUNNEL

"Once completed, the Saint Gotthard Base tunnel will be the longest tunnel in the world at 57.5 kilometers. Despite its length, the tunnel will make it possible to cross[p.59] the entire Saint Gotthard range in under 20 minutes. The tunnel will connect[p.53] Milan and Zurich as if the terrain were literally flat. Ironically, this means travellers won't see[p.296] the majestic Alps[p.28], but will pass through darkness[p.62]. My point is that we're at a unique moment in history[p.140] where we can cross the Alps without ever getting to see them. I wonder[p.323], what would English art critic John Ruskin think of that?"

CHRISTOPHE GIROT
Landscape architect, M.Arch M.L.Arch, BSA. Professor Emeritus of Landscape Architecture and former Dean of the Department of Architecture, ETH Zurich
E.A.T. 2012: Vision for the Alps, Zuoz
→ PLATE 111 p.268

U

UMBRELLA

"A small New York art[p.31] magazine asked us to redesign the umbrella, saying there hadn't been a new design in many years. Our first idea[p.145] was to combine the umbrella with ruffles. Designed to unfold itself like clothing over the body[p.38], we called it the 'Umbruffla'."

VITO ACCONCI
Artist
E.A.T. 2011: Mapping the Alps, Zuoz

UNDERSTANDING

"When I met Clyde Thompson, the social worker in charge of Forest Houses, to discuss the possibility of establishing the *Gramsci Monuments* in that location, he asked me: 'What will be the benefit for our community[p.51]?' I answered: 'I'm not pretending to work for your community – I'm working for art[p.31].' He immediately understood and said: 'Oh, that's convincing – an artist speaking about art.' This mutual understanding was a moment of grace[p.135], and this moment is what made the *Gramsci Monument* possible."

THOMAS HIRSCHHORN
Artist
E.A.T. 2019: Grace and Gravity, Zuoz

UNION

"When I visited Pompeii for the first time to prepare an exhibition, what I saw[p.296] wasn't just Rome – it was Egypt, Phoenicia, Greece, the entire known world of that time[p.308]. Everything was connected[p.53]. I tried to reflect[p.279] that in my exhibition. The same was true for my show in Venice, which took place in a church – a place for gathering[p.131]. The theme was the Mediterranean[p.205], and Venice had strong commercial ties with the East, particularly in pearls from the Persian[p.223] Gulf. I brought together all these geographies because they were always connected. Today we feel fragmented[p.127], but we should focus on what unites us."

SIMONE FATTAL
Artist
E.A.T. 2024: Jenseits von Ohnmacht – Beyond Powerless, Zuoz

UNKNOWN

"In our time[p.308], we are perhaps closer to the era of Pythagoras than to that of the positivists. He was an important mathematician, but we can see that in mathematics there is a quality[p.274] of poetry[p.226]; a quality not so distant from painting, or music, or poetry itself. Music always moves through numbers. I think Italian artist Mario Merz taught[p.306] me that when chance runs out, and the positivist belief[p.36] in knowing everything comes to an end, the unknown returns. Then, there is another path. When positivism ends, poetry and art[p.31] re-enter. A hundred years ago, with Heisenberg's 'uncertainty principle', the unknown became[p.35] an unavoidable part of knowledge itself."

GIORGIO GRIFFA
Artist
E.A.T. 2016: Traces and Fragments, Zuoz

UNPREDICTABILITY

"Ceramics[p.42] isn't something you can fully control. You try your best, but then it's up to the fire[p.125] and the clay[p.47]. It has its own story[p.301]. The rest is alchemy – minerals, heat, timing. sometimes it works beautifully[p.34], sometimes it doesn't. That unpredictability is part of the magic[p.202]. It's not about dominating the material[p.204] – it's a collaboration[p.49] between us, the material and the elements."

MATTHEW LUTZ-KINOY
Artist
E.A.T. 2023: Hoffnung? Hoffnung!, Zuoz

URGENCY

"One of the most frustrating dilemmas is that by making the camps function[p.129] well – with good architecture[p.29], a working urban fabric, no disease, no hunger – we may have inadvertently removed the urgency for a political solution. Because the camps are 'doing fine', there's less international pressure. So instead of solving the situation politically, we've solved it architecturally, and that's a deeply troubling paradox."

MANUEL HERZ
Architect
E.A.T. 2017: Snow and Desert, Zuoz

UTOPIA

"In *The Principle of Hope*, German philosopher Ernst Bloch presents the idea p.145 that conservative, bourgeois society p.299 often views daydreams and cultural p.60 products as sources of disappointment – things that maintain unachievable goals. But I think about American p.28 journalist, writer, and social activist Jonathan Freedman, who argued that utopia doesn't have to be impossible. We need those thoughts that seem naïve or idealistic p.145, because they're the beginning of a plan – not the plan itself."

CAMILLE HENROT
Artist
E.A.T. 2023: Hoffnung? Hoffnung!, Zuoz

V

VACCINE

"mRNA vaccines are like an incomplete instruction manual for your cells. They contain p.54 just one instruction: how to make the spike protein found p.125 on the virus's p.317 surface. This protein is the virus's 'key' to entering our cells. Because cells only receive these partial instructions, they cannot build a complete, infectious virus. Their only job is to produce these harmless spike proteins. These proteins then serve to train p.309 the immune system, so it can recognise p.277 and fight p.124 the virus if encountered p.114 later."

EMMA HODCROFT
Molecular epidemiologist and senior researcher at the University of Bern
E.A.T. 2021: Longue Durée, livestream

VANISH

"In the past, moving towards a vanishing point was often connected p.53 to a desire p.106 for loneliness and the search for one's spirit reflected p.279 in nature p.213 – whether the Alps p.28, ocean shores or deserts p.105. This idea p.145 appears in the writings of Nietzsche and Heidegger, in the paintings of Caspar David Friedrich, and in the work of artists like Georgia

O'Keeffe and Agnes Martin. Arguably, it reflects a shared collective motivation among the avant-garde artists of the last century."

NAIRY BAGHRAMIAN
Artist
E.A.T. 2011: Mapping the Alps, Zuoz

VARIATION

"Popular songs p.299 have always been treated like jazz standards – melodies that lived on everyone's lips and in the fingers of musicians. Peter Philips, the English composer in exile p.120, most likely never saw p.296 the actual sheet music of Giulio Caccini's *Amarilli Mia Bella*. He remembered p.281 the song p.299 by heart and created his own instrumental version. Originally a vocal piece with accompaniment, it relied on memory p.206 rather than notation – variation wasn't an exception, it was an integral part of the creative process."

MARGRET KÖLL
Harpist
E.A.T. 2022: Matter and Memory, Zuoz

VIBRATION

"Even simple movements – like walking p.320, falling p.122 or dragging a chair – emit vibrations that travel through solid materials p.204. These waves carry p.41 signatures that can be measured p.205, decomposed and analysed. With enough p.117 labelled data, we can distinguish between a person falling and a chair being moved. The evidence p.119 lies in the signal."

ELENI CHATZI
Civil engineer, researcher, professor and chair of Structural Mechanics and Monitoring at the Department of Civil, Environmental and Geomatic Engineering, ETH Zurich
2024: E.A.T. × Kunsthalle Zürich, Zurich

VIDEO

"Video, and more broadly immaterial practices p.228, today constitute a central language p.198 in contemporary p.55 art p.31. The strong presence p.229 of video at the Venice Biennale in 2024 confirmed this: the medium now stands at the forefront, at the heart of contemporary artistic practice. The corpus of artists such as Gabrielle Goliath, Katia Kameli, Zina Saro-Wiwa, Emeka Ogboh and Arthur Jafa demonstrates how the moving image p.146, the voice p.319 and performance p.222 are vectors of memory p.206, critique p.58 and transmission. In the era of TikTok and incessant visual flows, I chose to show video art to capture the general public, with the hope p.142 of ultimately engaging them with every form of art."

ANNA-ALIX KOFFI
Creative director and founder of SOMETHING art space in Abidjan, SOMETHING WE AFRICANS GOT and OFF the wall
2023: E.A.T. × Centre Pompidou, Paris
→ PLATE 112 p.269

VIOLENCE

"I come from the Israel-Palestine situation in which state violence is twofold: it targets people, and it targets the truth. Denial is not just rhetorical. It is an enabling condition; a mode of violence in itself. It creates the conditions under which violence can continue p.55 unchallenged."

EYAL WEIZMAN
Architect, founder and director of Forensic Architecture and professor of Spatial and Visual Cultures at Goldsmiths, University of London
E.A.T. 2016: Traces and Fragments, Zuoz

VIRUS

"In the 1970s, the H1N1 flu virus reappeared. Interestingly, it looks like it came back from being frozen. We know this because the virus didn't change p.43 or evolve between the 1950s and 1970s, which wouldn't happen if it had been spreading normally p.215. So, it seems the virus was literally kept frozen somewhere and then escaped again later."

EMMA HODCROFT
Molecular epidemiologist and senior researcher at the University of Bern
E.A.T. 2021: Longue Durée, livestream

VISION

"My film *Saturday* (2017) explores escapism, religion p.280, private life, activism, political protest p.273, even domestic p.110

surgery – as all strategies to maintain hope p.142. One thing I try to do in the film is consider these activities without judgment. It is important not to solidify ourselves into a moral binary of good and evil, but to adopt a more horizontal p.142 vision – one that allows us to project p.232 something constructive."

CAMILLE HENROT
Artist
E.A.T. 2023: Hoffnung? Hoffnung!, Zuoz

VISITOR

"More than half of the visitors we interviewed at Tate Modern said they came mainly to spend time p.308 with others. That shows us how important the social role of museums p.212 has become p.35. So we need to design spaces where people feel welcome and confident – places that encourage new forms of being together in public."

CHRIS DERCON
Art historian, curator and managing director of Fondation Cartier pour l'art contemporain
E.A.T. 2021: Longue Durée, livestream

VISUAL LANGUAGE

"Kelley Wilder, a historian of photography p.224, once pointed out that my aerial images p.146 – especially of wildlife – draw from the visual language of militarism. It's the way the military surveys land, the way oil companies scout terrain. I appropriated that language p.198 consciously, because we're in a war against nature p.213. But I also try to offset it with what I call 'the messiness p.206 of the local' – intimate p.195, grounded views that honour p.141 complexity and human p.143 presence p.229."

SUBHANKAR BANERJEE
Photographer, writer, curator and environmental humanities scholar
E.A.T. 2017: Snow and Desert, Zuoz

VOCABULARY

"Of course, as a musician, it's wonderful to have a score – but what fascinates me even more are the unwritten layers p.198 between the lines, the ones that bring you as close as possible to the essence of the composition. The further back we go in the history p.140 of musical prints, the less information[p.190] we find[p.125]. I need to absorb[p.23] the vocabulary of that time[p.308] – to internalise it so deeply that it becomes[p.35] part of my consciousness, even my subconscious, and settles into the physical memory[p.206] of my fingers."

MARGRET KÖLL
Harpist
E.A.T. 2022: Matter and Memory, Zuoz

VOGUE

"I got a grant to go to Japan, originally to ask Japanese fashion[p.122] designer Rei Kawakubo if she had been influenced by Butoh, a form of Japanese dance[p.61] theatre. But after much resistance[p.282], I eventually agreed to visit the archive[p.30] of Japanese choreographer and Butoh co-founder, Tatsumi Hijikata, at Keio University. When I watched his last piece on a CD-ROM, I was shattered. I felt like Humpty Dumpty. I had never seen[p.296] anything so aesthetically[p.25] powerful. Hijikata's work never made it to the West[p.321]. What we saw was mostly from Japanese dancer and Butoh co-founder Kazuo Ohno and dancers who worked with Hijikata, but Hijikata's work is completely singular. After that moment, I knew I had to go deeper. Butoh became a crucial counterpoint to fashion and voguing – it brought in themes of decay, fragility and death[p.63]. It was the tension[p.307] I needed."

TRAJAL HARRELL
Choreographer and dancer
2023: E.A.T. × Centre Pompidou, Paris

VOICE

"The voice is a fascinating threshold[p.308] between the communial[p.51] and the individual[p.189]. We develop it through imitation, language[p.198] and social context[p.55] – yet also use it to assert individual agency. That tension[p.307] is what makes it such fertile ground for exploring digital[p.107] identity[p.146], embodiment and new kinds of expression."

HOLLY HERNDON
and MATHEW DRYHURST
Artists
E.A.T. 2025: Form and Impact, Zuoz

VOID

"One appeal of extreme landscapes under modernism p.209 in the West p.321 was their association with the myth of the void: a tabula rasa, a depopulated and pure space, a nowhere p.216. This fantasy was closely tied to its twin, the fantasy of the frontier. American p.28 art p.31 collector Virginia Dwan, who co-organised the 1968 *Earthworks* exhibition, once said: 'The idea p.145 of virgin land became p.35 very exciting in this context p.55.'"

EMILY-ELIZA SCOTT
Interdisciplinary scholar, artist and former park ranger
E.A.T. 2017: Snow and Desert, Zuoz

VULNERABILITY

"In 1970, in the Meatpacking District of Manhattan, American p.28 choreographer and dancer Trisha Brown staged *Man Walking Down the Side of a Building.* Wearing climbing gear, and secured by two unseen alpinists, the performer slowly p.298 walked down a vertical wall. What might seem like a simple walks was transformed p.310 into a complex cognitive and physical act due to its unusual orientation. Performed p.222 in silence p.297, the piece also reflected p.279 a sense of vulnerability – being quite literally dependent on others for safety – and evoked a poetic metaphor for the instability of the era. Just one year after the alleged moon p.210 landing, it tapped into the public's fascination with gravity p.137, physics and the unknown p.313."

JOANNA LEŚNIEROWSKA
Curator, dramaturge and performance maker
E.A.T. 2019: Grace and Gravity, Zuoz

W

WALK

"I don't create sculptures that permanently p.223 alter the landscape because I want my work to be shaped p.295 by nature p.213 itself, which is not man-made. My art p.31 is a quiet p.275 protest p.273 against urban societies p.299 that disconnect people from nature. Everything I do revolves around walking, which can take many forms. Walking, for me, is an art form in its own right."

HAMISH FULTON
Artist.
E.A.T. 2011: Mapping the Alps, Zuoz

WASTE

"We're altering nature p.213 so profoundly that we may need to redefine p.64 it. Artists and scientists are documenting strange new materials p.204 like 'plastiglomerates'; rock-like p.288 fusions p.130 of melted p.206 plastic p.225, sand and debris appearing on Hawaiian beaches. They're accidental formations that will likely endure p.115 for millennia. This raises questions p.275 about the human p.143 versus the post-human, nature versus post-nature. Are we now destined to reconstruct p.53 nature using the very waste that is destroying it? Projects like Studio Swine's tortoiseshells made from ocean plastic force us to reconsider the aesthetic p.25 and ethical boundaries p.39 of natural beauty p.34."

ARIC CHEN
Curator, writer and director of the Zaha Hadid Foundation
E.A.T. 2018: Side Country Side, Zuoz
→ PLATE 113 p.270

WEALTH

"Cities p.47 generate 90% of global wealth. New York, for instance, has a GDP equivalent to that of Canada; Los Angeles is comparable to Australia. Cities are centres of innovation, yet they are also responsible for 70% of global emissions. They will absorb p.23 two billion more people by 2050. So the question p.275 is: how do we plan new cities and adapt p.24 existing ones to meet these urgent p.314 challenges p.42?"

NORMAN FOSTER
Architect, founder and executive chairman of Foster + Partners
E.A.T. 2025: Form and Impact, Zuoz

WEST

"I have been interested in the concept of the West for a very long time p.308. What does it really mean? In a book by the historian William McNeill, known for his influential work on world history p.140, he explains that the idea p.145 of the West was, in a way, born when the Persian p.223 Empire attempted to conquer Greece – about 2,500 years ago. According to the Greeks, what lay to the right of Greece was the East, and what lay to the left of Athens was the West. This notion later evolved through Constantinople and, over the past 500 years, became p.35 what we now understand p.313 as Western Europe."

ZIBA ARDALAN
Founder and director of Parasol unit foundation for Contemporary Art
E.A.T. 2021: Longue Durée, livestream

WITNESS

"Silence p.297 can be the most inspiring p.192 moment – when you feel alive, observing everything around you: a ray of sun, a curious animal swimming by. But silence also has a shadow side, where it's a witness of death p.63. Something is broken. Something is missing. Life. And unfortunately, these places where you experience that kind of silence – where creatures have vanished p.315 – are growing p.138. They're expanding rapidly."

CYRILL GUTSCH
Designer and founder of Parley for the Oceans
E.A.T. 2020: Silent – Listen, Zuoz

WOMEN ARTISTS

"AWARE: 'Archives of Women Artists, Research and Exhibitions' is a non-profit organisation p.219 dedicated p.64 to sharing and producing knowledge about women and non-binary artists – from the 16th century to those born as recently as 1975. Today, our website features around 1,400 bilingual biographies. During the lockdown, I began creating content specifically for children, young adults and general audiences, so that anyone – regardless of their background in art history p.140 – could discover the largely overlooked legacy p.199 of women artists."

CAMILLE MORINEAU
Curator and co-founder of AWARE (Archives of Women Artists,

Research and Exhibitions)
E.A.T. 2022: Matter and Memory,
Zuoz

WONDER

"Wonder is life's second engine. We're all born explorers, but around age one or two we begin to get corrupted – by parents, friends p.128, kindergarten, school – and we start wondering less and less. Human p.143 evolution was shaped p.295 by motion p.211: we walked p.320, we moved and we explored physically. But today, we're becoming p.35 the first generation p.133 to stop moving. We sit more, and explore less. An average child now spends about four hours a day on social media. If you live to 84, that adds up to 13 years – 13 years, day and night, of staring into a screen. That's one reason why so many people today feel busy, stressed, lonely and sad."

ERLING KAGGE
Explorer, publisher, author, philosopher, lawyer, art collector and entrepreneur
E.A.T. 2020: Silent – Listen, Zuoz

WOOD

"One of the reasons I chose to use language p.198 in the first place was so that it could be translated; my work is all about material p.204 relationships p.280 to each other. This allows the work to cross p.59 borders without being exotic. Every piece I ever created can be built anywhere. Many cultures p.60 think that there is just one way that a single artwork can be, otherwise it would detract from this idea p.145 that the artist got it right. Everybody knows what a piece of wood looks like, but it does not look like what everybody else thinks it looks like. A piece of wood is just a piece of wood. But depending on where it was milled – in Switzerland p.305, Scandinavia, Italy, Japan, Tibet – it looks different. There is no right and there is no wrong. It is just the way it could be, and not the way it should be."

LAWRENCE WEINER
Artist
E.A.T. 2011: Mapping the Alps, Zuoz
→ PLATE 114 p.271

WORD

"In my art[p.31] I work a lot with words because they can have layers[p.198] of meaning[p.204], and that depends on the culture[p.60] of the observer[p.217]. I've exhibited my work all over the world – in Arab countries and in the West[p.321] – people see[p.296] and read[p.276] it differently. The words take on new meanings in each context[p.55]. It's always fascinating to see how the same work is experienced in such diverse ways."

SUSAN HEFUNA
Artist
E.A.T. 2025: Form and Impact, Zuoz

Z

ZUOZ

"The Engadin valley has been so fruitful precisely because creatives from such vastly different backgrounds converge here – philosophers, artists, musicians, writers. That diversity generates a kind of cross-pollination. And of course, it's something we witness[p.322] at Engadin Art Talks[p.116] in Zuoz as well. It's not just the beauty[p.34] of the landscape – it's the unique constellation of people and ideas[p.145] that makes this place so generative for artistic thought."

GIORGIA VON ALBERTINI
Director at Hauser and Wirth, St. Moritz
E.A.T. 2024: Jenseits von Ohnmacht – Beyond Powerless, Zuoz

APPENDIX

2010: The Crystal Chain, Zuoz
2011: Mapping the Alps, Zuoz
2012: Visions for the Alps, Zuoz
2013: Ghosts and the Uncanny, Zuoz
2016: Traces and Fragments, Zuoz
2017: Snow and Desert, Zuoz
2018: Side Country Side, Zuoz
2019: Grace and Gravity, Zuoz
2020: Silent – Listen, Zuoz
2021: Longue Durée, livestream
2021: E.A.T. × Art Basel Conversations, Basel
2021: E.A.T. × Serpentine, London
2021: E.A.T. × Centre Culturel Suisse, Paris
2022: Matter and Memory, Zuoz
2023: Hoffnung? Hoffnung!, Zuoz
2023: E.A.T. × Centre Pompidou, Paris
2024: Jenseits von Ohnmacht – Beyond Powerless, Zuoz
2024: E.A.T. × Kunsthalle Zürich, Zurich
2025: Form and Impact, Zuoz
2025: E.A.T. × St. Moritz, St. Moritz

On the occasion of Engadin Art Talks' 15-year anniversary, this book premiered at the 2026 edition of E.A.T. in Zuoz, dedicated to the theme *Bonds and Gaps*. The freely accessible online archive with an overview of all past E.A.T. editions is available at www.engadin-art-talks.ch.

ACKNOWLEDGEMENTS

I would like to thank Christian Herren – curator, creative director and producer – whose vision and commitment have been a driving force behind this book. My thanks go to all former E.A.T. participants, whose contributions form the basis of this publication, and to the E.A.T. curators – Bice Curiger, Daniel Baumann, Hans Ulrich Obrist, Koyo Kouoh and Philip Ursprung – for shaping the programme over the years. I am equally grateful to co-editor Daan Couzijn for his dedicated work on this volume. My gratitude extends to Dayle Bechtler-Lustenberger for her many years of managing Engadin Art Talks, and to Clément Dirié of JRP|Editions for his support as publisher. I would furthermore like to thank Salzmann Gertsch for their clear and cohesive graphic design, and everyone who has supported this project in any way.

CRISTINA BECHTLER

PROJECT PATRON
AND ADVISOR
Cristina Bechtler

EDITED BY
Christian Herren
and Daan Couzijn
for Engadin Art Talks

EDITORIAL CONCEPT
Christian Herren

CONTRIBUTOR LIAISON
Daan Couzijn

DESIGN
Salzmann Gertsch:
Philippe Gertsch, Lara Koller,
Renate Salzmann

COORDINATION
Daan Couzijn
Dayle Bechtler-Lustenberger

FUNDING
Mirjam Blanka Inauen

PROOFREADING
Clare Manchester

PREPRESS
AND PRINTING
Offsetdruckerei Grammlich

COVER
Graffiti Siebdruck

BINDING
Grossbuchbinderei Spinner

TYPEFACE
Rhymes by Maxitype

PAPER
Holmen Trend 2.0, 70 gm²
Garda Gloss, 100 gm²
Skinflex, 0,5 mm

EDITORIAL STATUS
Affiliations are accurate
as of December 2025.

CO-PUBLISHED
by JRP|Editions
Geneva, Switzerland

ISBN 978-3-03764-649-6
Printed in Germany

JRP|Editions publications are
available internationally at selected
bookstores and from the following
distribution partners:

AUSTRIA, GERMANY,
AND SWITZERLAND
JRP|Editions
(with AVA Verlagsauslieferung AG)

FRANCE
Les presses du réel

UK AND OTHER EUROPEAN
COUNTRIES, USA, CANADA,
ASIA AND AUSTRALIA
ARTBOOK|D.A.P.

jrp|editions

E.A.T. ENGADIN ART TALKS